Making Meanings, Creating Family

MAKING MEANINGS, CREATING FAMILY

Intertextuality and Framing in Family Interaction

Cynthia Gordon

OXFORD
UNIVERSITY PRESS

2009

OXFORD
UNIVERSITY PRESS

Oxford University Press, Inc., publishes works that further
Oxford University's objective of excellence
in research, scholarship, and education.

Oxford   New York
Auckland   Cape Town   Dar es Salaam   Hong Kong   Karachi
Kuala Lumpur   Madrid   Melbourne   Mexico City   Nairobi
New Delhi   Shanghai   Taipei   Toronto

With offices in
Argentina   Austria   Brazil   Chile   Czech Republic   France   Greece
Guatemala   Hungary   Italy   Japan   Poland   Portugal   Singapore
South Korea   Switzerland   Thailand   Turkey   Ukraine   Vietnam

Published by Oxford University Press, Inc.
198 Madison Avenue, New York, New York 10016

www.oup.com

Oxford is a registered trademark of Oxford University Press

Library of Congress Cataloging-in-Publication Data

Gordon, Cynthia, 1975–
Making meanings, creating family : intertextuality and
framing in family interactions / Cynthia Gordon.
p.   cm.
Includes bibliographical references and index.
ISBN 978-0-19-537382-0; 978-0-19-537383-7 (pbk.)
1. Communication in the family—United States—Case studies.
2. Discourse analysis—United States.   I. Title.
HQ536.G667 2009
306.8701′4—dc22   2008042017

2 4 6 8 9 7 5 3 1

Printed in the United States of America
on acid-free paper

For my parents
Karen Gordon
and
Greg Gordon

Acknowledgments

The research project on which this book is based was funded by the Alfred P. Sloan Foundation (grant no. 99010-7 to Deborah Tannen and Shari Kendall and grant no. B2004-20 to Deborah Tannen, Shari Kendall, and Cynthia Gordon). I thank project officer Kathleen Christensen and the Sloan Foundation for their support of this project. I also thank fellow researchers Deborah Tannen and Shari Kendall, who were such a pleasure to work with. Participating in this project has profoundly affected my development as a scholar, and I am extremely grateful to have had this opportunity. I am also grateful to the other research team members on the project: Philip LeVine, Sigrid Norris, Alla Tovares, and especially Alexandra Johnston, who helped me identify a number of key examples of intertextuality.

I owe a great debt to Deborah Tannen, whose scholarship, continual support and enthusiasm, mentorship, and teaching has deeply influenced my research, my writing, and my thinking about discourse analysis, family interaction, and the role of language in everyday life. I cannot thank her enough for the careful attention she has given my work, including my dissertation, for which she served as director at Georgetown University; the articles based on it which are published elsewhere; and now this book as well. I thank her for the guidance and reassurance she has continually provided; and for the example she sets as a scholar, teacher, and mentor. I thank Heidi Hamilton and Deborah

Schiffrin for the support, guidance, and advice they provided me as a graduate student and beyond, and for insightful comments they provided on portions of individual chapters. I am especially thankful to Heidi Hamilton for her comments regarding my conceptualization of intertextuality. I am also indebted to Najma Al Zidjaly, Sylvia Chou, Elisa Everts, Andy Jocuns, Miriam Locher, Karen Murph, and Alla Tovares for providing me with feedback during the early stages of my analyses. My indebtedness to Deborah Keller-Cohen goes further back; I am thankful for her continued support since my time as an undergraduate at the University of Michigan, where I was first introduced to discourse analysis.

I owe thanks to the Sloan Foundation for supporting the Center for Myth and Ritual in American Life (the MARIAL Center) at Emory University; much of this book was completed while I was a postdoctoral fellow there. I thank the center's director, Bradd Shore, who also served as my mentor, as well as the staff, faculty, and fellows who made it such a wonderful place to work. I especially thank Robyn Fivush for deepening my contemplation of family narratives; Bradd Shore for helping me think about family ritual and the complex nature of play in family talk; and Kristin Celello and Drew Whitelegg for providing valuable feedback on individual chapters and data extracts. Through my work at Georgetown and Emory, I was able to connect with researchers at the Center for the Everyday Life of Families (CELF) at the University of California, Los Angeles, also funded by the Sloan Foundation. I am very appreciative of the scholarship of this group, as well as the conversations I have had with individual members, particularly Charles Goodwin, Marjorie Harness Goodwin, Elinor Ochs, Karen Sirota, and Leah Wingard.

Members of various audiences made helpful comments regarding specific analyses I presented on different occasions; these audiences include faculty and fellows of the MARIAL Center, members of the Emory University Program in Linguistics, the University of Michigan's Sociodiscourse group, and Wayne State University's Department of English, as well as audiences at various professional conferences. I am grateful to have had the opportunity to present my work to such diverse groups and for the feedback I received. I especially benefited from conversations with Philipp Angermeyer, Benjamin Bailey, Richard Buttny, Donal Carbaugh, Kristine Fitch, Barbara Johnstone, Debra Spitulnik, Inge Stockburger, Susan Tamasi, Anna Marie Trester, and Donald Tuten. I am also grateful for comments on individual chapters provided by Carl Bon Tempo and Stanton Wortham, and for those I received from two anonymous reviewers on the entire manuscript. In addition, Najma Al Zidjaly and Alla Tovares carefully read my manuscript and provided not only many helpful suggestions but also moral support; for this I am very thankful.

I am grateful for the families who participated in this study; their generosity, courage, and good humor in allowing recorders and a team of sociolinguists into their lives made this study possible. I also thank the staff at Oxford University Press for their help and support in the production of this book.

Studying family discourse has made me all the more aware of how much my own family means to me, and all the more appreciative of the various intersecting circles of individuals that constitute it. I thank Dan Beckett, my partner in life, for his love, support, and wit; for his comments on this manuscript; and for putting up with the "shenanigans" that being married to an academic entails. I am thankful for Frances, who brings Dan and me much joy on a daily basis. I am thankful for my sisters and symbolic sisters—Sarah Gordon, Whitney Gordon, Najma Al Zidjaly, Alla Tovares, Lydia Springer, Isha Youhas, Sarah Foley, and Heather Whitten—with whom I have shared much coffee, chocolate, and conversation over the years. I am also thankful for the Becketts, who have always treated me like a member of their family, and for my stepmother, Dina Giurini-Gordon, whose good humor fits right in. Finally, most of all, I am grateful to my parents, Karen Gordon and Greg Gordon, for each creating a family I love, for helping me develop an open mind and an appreciation of language, and for teaching me how to laugh.

Contents

Making Meanings,
Creating Family

ONE

Introduction

Intertextuality and Framing in Family Discourse

"YOU JUST POP THEM IN": A FIELDWORK NARRATIVE

On the morning of March 8, 2000, I arrived at Janet and Steve Neeley-Mason's suburban townhouse around 11 A.M.[1] It was my second day of observing Janet going about her daily life as if she were not being observed by a sociolinguist. After accompanying Janet to pick up the couple's nearly three-year-old daughter, Natalie, from her Montessori preschool, I went back home with them to eat lunch and observe them eating lunch. Natalie, a very verbal child not used to being observed, repeatedly tried to engage me in conversation. At one point during lunchtime, I was eating grapes I had brought with me when Natalie commented, "You just pop them in." I agreed, though I was not entirely sure what this was supposed to mean, or why she had said it to me (other than to talk). Nevertheless (or perhaps because of this), I later scribbled the sentence into my field notebook, following it with a question mark.

This family had participated in a study focusing on everyday family discourse. As part of their participation in this sociolinguistic study, Janet and Steve had carried digital audiotape recorders with them for one week (February 23–29, 2000), recording nearly continuously throughout each day at home and at work. The purpose of my visit that Wednesday in March was so that I could see where the family lived, where Janet worked, and what this family's daily life "looked like," which would help me make sense of Janet's tapes when I listened to them and logged their contents.

Later that same week, I began listening to Janet's audiotapes, finding out what her daily family life sounded like. I was listening to a lunchtime conversation between Janet and Natalie that was recorded on Thursday, February 24 when I heard a familiar string of words (transcription conventions appear in the appendix; underlining is used to highlight repeated words that are analytically in focus):

Natalie:	Um,
	can I share those grapes?
Janet:	Sure!
Natalie:	First of all they have to be peeled.
Janet:	<laughs>
	I'm not peeling grapes!
Natalie:	They're good—
Janet:	They're good when <u>you just pop them in</u>.
	Remember how we did the other day?
	Mm.
Natalie:	They're good with skin,
	see?
Janet:	Mhm.
Natalie:	They're good with skin.
Janet:	Yeah.
Natalie:	Yeah.
	And you don't even have to peel.
Janet:	That's right,
	<u>you just pop them in</u>.
Natalie:	<u>You just pop them in!</u>
	Like that.
	[Yeah.]
Janet:	[Delicious.]
Natalie:	(Yeah).
Janet:	<laughs>

The moment I heard this interaction, Natalie's comment to me as I ate grapes the day of my visit, "You just pop them in," took on a new meaning. Natalie was not simply observing that I was eating grapes. She was drawing on "prior text" (Becker 1995) and using her memory to recall a shared interaction (and likely interactions) with her mother on the topic of how to eat grapes. Natalie was recycling her mother's words in a conversation with me, commenting on the fact that I was eating grapes the way her mother did, and the way her mother thought was best (without peeling them), using her mother's exact words to do so. Natalie's comment suddenly made sense in a new way.

PURPOSE OF THIS BOOK

In what follows, I examine linked family interactions such as these everyday, mundane conversations about grapes—as well as others with greater symbolic significance—to explore how repeating words, phrases, paralinguistic features, and speech acts across interactions serves as a means of creating meanings, and, indeed, of creating family itself. In other words, I investigate how what has been called "intertextuality" (Kristeva 1980 [1967]) is vitally important to meaning- and family-making, specifically, how intertextuality serves as a resource for both making meanings in interaction and binding members of a family together into a distinctive social group. The notion of intertextuality has received increasing attention in discourse analysis and sociolinguistics, linguistic anthropology, communication, and related fields. I contribute to the dialogue on this topic by analyzing intertextuality as it manifests in interaction and by showing how it relates to framing, an interdisciplinary theory of meaning-making. The analyses I present in the chapters that comprise this book have two primary aims: (1) to elucidate the vital role of intertextuality in family conversations, specifically pertaining to how family members use intertextual repetition to construct themselves as a social group and to create meanings in interaction; and (2) to demonstrate how intertextuality and framing, two powerful notions that have been applied widely (and largely independently) across disciplines, are best understood as fundamentally interconnected.

This study is thus about families. I examine family conversations primarily from an interactional sociolinguistic perspective to investigate how individuals use language in everyday family life to actually *construct* their families—to create shared meanings and craft the group's culture.

More specifically, I analyze the talk of three families that recorded their own conversations for seven to fourteen days as part of their participation in a family discourse study undertaken at Georgetown University, the Work and Family Project.[2] This project, funded by the Alfred P. Sloan Foundation, was designed to examine the role of verbal interaction in the everyday lives of middle-class dual-income American families. In particular, it was designed to investigate how parents linguistically manage the multiple demands of family and work and constitute their parental and professional identities through talk; a variety of family and workplace conversations was captured as a means of exploring these issues.

This book is also a study of the repetition and intertextuality that characterize family conversations. It is about why family members repeat words and phrases that they and other family members have said before—in some cases tens or scores (or possibly hundreds, even thousands) of times before—instead of saying something "new," and in what ways and situations they do so. As Deborah Tannen (2007 [1989]:47) writes—deliberately illustrating repetition while also pondering it—"Why is there repetition in conversation? Why do we waste our breath saying the same thing over and over?" In exploring these questions in the family context, I highlight the role of repetition in two fundamental human processes—meaning-making and social group construction—by analyzing naturally occurring conversations.

The three families whose conversations I examine are alike in some notable ways—all are dual-income, American-born, roughly middle-class, white, and live in the metropolitan Washington, DC, area; the parents are highly educated, having at least a bachelor's degree; all families have one child under age five.[3] They are also distinctive from one another; in listening to the recordings, I, like the other researchers, was struck by how each family seemed to be its own world, with its own ways in which family members use language. This informal observation, as it turns out, is consonant with prior research (not focusing on language) suggesting that every American family constitutes its own "little world" (Luckmann 1970) or "universe" (Gillis 1996).

However, regardless of the perceived variation among these families, their discourse is (of course) not intended to represent that of all families, or even the talk of all families that are demographically similar. I present a qualitative case-study analysis of three families' conversations, with particular attention paid to one family that serves as the book's focal point—the family whose interactions in many ways inspired my thinking about intertextuality: the Neeley-Mason family, consisting of Janet, her husband, Steve, and their daughter, Natalie.

I focus on this family for several reasons. First, I wanted to explore one family's discourse in depth, giving a "thick description" (Geertz 1973) while using the others as points of comparison, rather than give a broad overview of all three families' discourse. Second, methodological considerations played a role. This family recorded the most, and the most consistently, thus providing what I view as the richest data set for a study of intertextuality; the Neeley-Masons even hooked up a recorder to their home phone. Third, I was particularly drawn to this family's remarkable good humor and playfulness as well as the ways they symbolically invited non-family members into their family. I wanted to learn more about how members of this family used language in making meanings, in creating themselves as a social group, and in extending their "familyness"—including their family language or "familylect" (Søndergaard 1991)—to other people in their lives. In presenting an in-depth examination of the discourse of one family, and using the talk of two others for comparative purposes, I identify, describe, and offer interpretations of intertextual repetition by integrating theoretical perspectives of intertextuality and framing. In so doing, I also contribute to the ongoing exploration in linguistics, communication, and related fields of how social groups and meanings are created through talk.

INTERTEXTUALITY AND FRAMING AS THEORY

Intertextuality

Natalie repeating her mother's words by saying "You just pop them in" in conversation with me, the linguistic fieldworker observing her, is not unique; the conversations that make up our social worlds are filled with repetition. Indeed, research in discourse analysis has illustrated that repetition—of words, phrases, syntactic structures, ideas, and so on— is prevalent in conversations across a variety of contexts, in literary discourse, and in the media.[4] Such repetition serves to generate links not only within but also between various written and conversational texts; it creates what Julia Kristeva (1980 [1967]) calls *intertextuality* in her presentation and interpretation of literary theorist M. M. Bakhtin's work on *dialogicality* (1981, 1984, 1986). Kristeva (1980 [1967]:66) describes intertextuality in metaphorical terms: "any text is constructed as a mosaic of quotations; any text is the absorption and transformation of another." As constructing a mosaic is a creative process in which bits and pieces from here and there are selected, adjusted, and fitted together to create something "new," so too is repeating. In A. L. Becker's (1995) words, "prior text" is continually "reshaped" in interaction in various ways; moreover, this is what comprises language use or what he calls "languaging." Thus, repetition and intertextuality are fundamental parts of communicating in general. Importantly, the theory of intertextuality captures the idea that the meaning-making process extends beyond individual conversations or texts. In what can be viewed as an early discourse analytic study of intertextuality, Tannen (2007 [1989]) analyzes repetition, both within and across interactions, as a fundamental meaning-making strategy in conversational discourse. As Bakhtin (1986:69) explains, any speaker "is not, after all, the first speaker, the one who disturbs the eternal silence of the universe." Current uses of language always hearken back to those prior, giving all discourse an intertextual (or, in Bakhtin's words, dialogic) dimension, whether or not speakers intend to do so.

The dialogic dimension of language is highlighted when a speaker uses the words of another person intentionally to create what Bakhtin (1986) refers to as "double-voiced words." These are words that both refer to a referential object or event in the current interaction and are directed toward the other person's prior discourse. The speaker shapes the words so they are (intended to be) heard with metaphorical "quotation marks" (Morson & Emerson 1990), enabling him or her to comment on them in some way, such as to show agreement or disagreement, admiration or contempt. In other words, the speaker takes an evaluative stance toward the words he or she is reshaping.[5] It is possible that Natalie's utterance about grapes fits into this category: Natalie perhaps voiced her mother's words so that she could show her mother—who could have overheard our conversation, as she was in the same room—that she now endorsed those words and agreed that grapes are best eaten unpeeled. Even more compelling examples of double-voicing in family interaction occur when an adult speaker repeats a spouse's words as a means of teasing or gentle mocking, as analyzed in chapter 4.

Whether intended or not, all words that are repeated necessarily have, to some extent, this "twofold direction" (Bakhtin 1986:185). This is so because in repeating the words of others—even verbatim, as in direct quotation—speakers fundamentally alter them as they use them for their own purposes in new contexts. Tannen's (2007 [1989]) introduction of the term "constructed dialogue" as an alternative for the term "reported speech" highlights the creative, poetic, and evaluative nature of creating dialogue through doing what many think of as rote "repeating" or "reporting" (hence her introduction of the new term). Scholars such as M. H. Goodwin (1990), Buttny (1997, 1998), and Holt (2000) have also demonstrated how speakers use a range of features—such as prosody, voice quality, volume, and gesture—to evaluate and thereby take stances toward so-called reported dialogues.[6] In one sense, as Becker (1994:26) explains, repeating can be described as "speaking the past"; however, "there is always something of the present, some variable of the communicative act that is free to express the now." In a similar spirit, Tannen (2007 [1989]) emphasizes that all words have a history; indeed, she cites the works of both Bakhtin and Becker in stating that words are "given to us by previous speakers, traces of whose voices and contexts cling inevitably to them" (100).

In repeating (and "reporting"), interlocutors reshape and recontextualize both within texts (intratextual repetition) and across texts (intertextual repetition) to perform a variety of functions and create a range of meanings, a number of which are present in the family discourse data set I examine. For instance, studies in linguistics and discourse analysis suggest that repetition can serve to emphasize, joke, play, mock, create rapport, clarify, and confirm.[7] Furthermore, repetition can even serve a means of orchestrating action, as M. H. Goodwin (1990) finds in her analysis of "instigating" practices among girls. What function(s) repetition accomplishes in interaction depends on a number of factors, including (but not limited to) the situational context, whether the repetition is of the self or the other, the amount of temporal displacement between the repetition and its "original," what linguistic feature is repeated (e.g., words versus syntactic structures), and uses of prosodic and other paralinguistic features. According to Johnstone et al. (1994:11) in an introduction to the edited volumes *Repetition in Discourse*, "The functions of repetition probably will be almost infinite."

In family talk, repetition seems to have an "almost infinite" number of functions, too. For instance, it plays a key role in "negative" or conflict-based family interactions, like family arguments (C. Goodwin 2006; M. H. Goodwin 2006; Tannen 2006) and in the speech event known as "nagging" (Boxer 2002); it also structures "positive" exchanges, like sociable talk between parents and small children (Ervin-Tripp & Strage 1985), the construction of intergenerational alliances in talk (de Léon 2007), and the creation of "parenting teams" (Gordon 2003). In other words, repetition is a linguistic strategy that is potentially *ambiguous* (has unclear meanings) and *polysemous* (has multiple meanings at once).[8] Therefore, there is no one "true" meaning of a linguistic strategy such as repetition. As a number of interactional sociolinguists have shown (e.g., Gumperz 1982; Tannen 1994, 2005 [1984]), a speaker's intent in using a linguistic strategy and the listener's interpretation of that strategy in a given context do not always match. Thus, the analysis and interpretation of repetition in discourse is necessarily a context-bound process.

However, I suggest that on an underlying level, repetition, especially intertextual repetition, functions as a means of binding people together, and this function is the primary focus of this book. Repetition serves this binding function because it is a metalinguistic strategy; it directs a hearer or reader back into their memory as if to say, "Pay attention to this again" (Johnstone et al. 1994:13). It thus affirms interlocutors' shared history, mutual access to a set of prior texts, and membership to the same group. In doing so, it aids in the creation of what Tannen (2007 [1989]:12) calls *involvement*, which refers to "an internal, even emotional connection individuals feel which binds them to other people as well as to places, things, activities, ideas, memories, and words." Through repetition, conversations are co-constructed and co-interlocutors experience a sense of coherence and connectedness (Tannen 2007 [1989]:13). In Becker's (1994:165) words, "social groups seem to be bound primarily by a shared repertoire of prior texts." These prior texts include those that are "public," for instance media texts (see Spitulnik 1997; Tovares 2006). They can also include prior texts that are intensely private—interactions among family members and even internal conversations (or thoughts). In a similar spirit to Becker, Bakhtin theorizes "culture" by conceptualizing it as "discourses retained by the collective memory" (Todorov 1984 [1981]:x). Thus, repetition and intertextuality are essential not only to meaning-making and the structuring of individual interactions but also in the creation of social groups like families.

Framing

Framing, which is also referred to as frame(s) theory, is the theory I use and develop to uncover how family members create meanings in interaction. The notion of *frame* (Bateson 1972; Goffman 1974) captures "what people think they are *doing* when they talk to each other" (Tannen 1993b:6). In other words, a frame (or an "interactive frame") can be understood as "a definition of what is going on in interaction" (Tannen & Wallat 1993:59).[9] Interlocutors must have a shared sense of this definition to create mutual understanding of individual utterances as well as activities in general. Because meaning-making entails looking beyond the boundaries of a single text or conversation, framing is, I suggest, best understood as inextricably intertwined with intertextuality. This builds on Tannen's (2005 [1984]) extensive discussion of how the construction of shared frames and meanings relates to the backgrounds and nature of the relationships between interlocutors, including both their cultural and language experiences. Likewise, it extends anthropological linguist John Gumperz's (1982:162) proposal that previous interactive experience is a central part of conversational inference, or what he describes as the "context-bound process" by which participants interpret others' utterances (Gumperz 1982:153).

The idea of framing as it has been widely drawn on in discourse analysis and sociolinguistics traces back to work in anthropology by Gregory Bateson (1972). Bateson introduced his notion of frame while writing about the rich insights into communication he gained observing monkeys at play at the zoo; he suggests that something in behavior can establish a *play frame*. For instance, he remarks that if one monkey bites another during a "play" interaction (in other words, one monkey "nips" another), it means something different than what a bite would mean outside of play (it would be considered a serious act of aggression). As Bateson (1972:180) explains, "The playful nip denotes the bite, but it does not denote what would be denoted by the bite." Frames such as play frames are viewed by Bateson as psychological constructs defined by *metamessages* (1972:188); metamessages instruct receivers how to interpret messages (e.g., "this is play"). This is what helps a monkey determine whether a bite from another monkey is play or combat and what helps an anthropologist observing them identify playing versus fighting.

Humans, like our primate cousins, send metamessages about how our actions are intended; in addition, we send metamessages pertaining to how we mean what we say. In *Frame Analysis*, Goffman (1974) uses the notion of frame as a means of exploring how human beings make sense of—and create—everyday situations. Goffman (1981:52) suggests that as participants create frames, they also construct particular *footings*, which can be conceptualized as alignments between participants as well as between participants and topics of talk. Another way of thinking about this is by viewing footing as "the way in which framing is accomplished in verbal interaction" (Hoyle 1993:115): Interlocutors create certain alignments vis-è-vis one another (e.g., playful, combative), and in so doing, define the nature of social situations or frames (e.g., "this is play," "this is combat"). Sociolinguists have demonstrated how what Gumperz (1982, 1992) calls *contextualization cues*—including pitch, rhythm, loudness, timing, intonation contours, and nonverbal cues (like gaze, gestures, facial expressions, and so forth)—are used to construct footings and frames. For instance, the notions of footing, alignment, and framing have been drawn on by research that explores how framing occurs moment by moment in interaction as well as how interlocutors discursively construct identities.[10] For example, in Gordon (2004) I demonstrate how members of one family (the Shepherd-Sylvan family, whose discourse is also touched on in this book) use referring terms, repetition, laughter, storytelling, and constructed dialogue in their talk to create recurrent alignments vis-è-vis one another and topics of talk that together construct their shared family identity as Democrats and supporters of Democratic Party candidate Al Gore in the 2000 presidential election.

An important aspect of framing in everyday interaction between humans, and one that is central to this book, is that frames are frequently not as straightforward as "this is play"; individuals *laminate* both frames and footings (Goffman 1974, 1981). Research exploring this idea from an interactive perspective demonstrates how interlocutors use a variety of linguistic features to switch quickly between various footings and frames (Hoyle 1993; Ribeiro 1993, 1994; Tannen & Wallat 1993; Kendall 1999, 2006; Gordon 2002, 2008), how co-conversationalists embed frames and footings within one another (Hoyle 1993; Gordon 2002; Campbell 2003), and how frames can be in conflict and accidentally "leak" into one another (Tannen & Wallat 1993). This conceptualization of framing—and everyday discourse—as layered is important for investigating family talk. Further, I suggest that to capture the complexity of family interaction, framing and intertextuality should be viewed as inextricably intertwined: Intertextual repetition is a fundamental means of constructing and laminating frames; it not only creates shared meanings but also actually contributes to constructing the family as a social group.

INTERTEXTUALITY AND FAMILY DISCOURSE STUDY METHODOLOGY

Exploring Family Talk across Contexts

Naturalistic and ethnographic studies of family discourse in the 1980s and 1990s were in large part studies of family dinner table discourse, as "family dinner" is both a convenient site for recording data and a widely recognized speech event in many families across a number of cultural groups.[11] This body of work has yielded important insights into how family members tell stories, create meanings, and reinforce family beliefs and the family power structure in this context. However, recently, a growing number of family communication studies look beyond the dinner table. For example, the Work and Family Project (of which this study is a part) examines family interaction across a range of contexts, as does research being undertaken at the University of California, Los Angeles, Center on Everyday Lives of Families (CELF).[12] Such studies are important to more fully consider the phenomenon of intertextuality in everyday conversational discourse and gain a deeper understanding of family talk more generally. This is particularly true as everyday family life changes: as the family car becomes part of "home" (M. Jackson 2002), as family members engage in "family discourse" while at work through the telephone (Gordon, Tannen, & Sacknovitz 2007), as family talk occurs in front of the television (Tovares 2007), and as concerns grow that family dinner is a rapidly declining ritual (Mestdag & Vandeweyer 2005).

Explorations of the creation of meanings and the construction of a family culture across speech events are especially important in the context of contemporary American middle-class families such as those whose discourse I consider. Such families, according to anthropologist Bradd Shore (2003:11), have been built to "self-destruct"—they are formed, children are born, children grow up and move out and begin their own families. This means each new family faces the challenge of "creating a new miniature society with a distinctive set of traditions and coordinating practices" (Shore 2003:6). According to Shore, one way families rise to this challenge is by crafting for themselves new rituals, including not only "canonical" rituals (like wedding and holiday celebrations) but also noncanonical ones, such as what Goffman (1967) calls "interaction ritual," or day-to-day patterns of interaction. Researchers in psychology and psychiatry investigating families also conceptualize daily patterns of interaction as routines or rituals and have likewise investigated their importance (e.g., Wolin & Bennett 1984; Fiese 2006). Indeed, scholars from a range of fields have suggested that everyday rituals can be viewed as "the glue that holds families, groups, and communities together" (K. Jackson 2005:ix).

Collecting and Analyzing Data: Intertextual Chains and Webs

Though it has been observed that everyday language use commonly features repetition across interactions, the relationship between intertextual repetition and how meanings and identities and are negotiated in verbal discourse has only begun to be examined. For instance, Wortham (2005, 2006), investigating the process of identity socialization and construction in classroom discourse, considers recorded interactions drawn from one academic year's worth of ethnographic fieldwork. He analyzes words, topics, and themes that are repeated intertextually. Hamilton (1996:64) takes a similar approach in proposing a "linguistic definition" of intertextuality as "the ways in which speakers/writers use language to establish and maintain ties between the current linguistic interaction (i.e., conversation) and prior ones involving the same participants, as well as the ways in which listeners/readers identify and use these ties to help them (re)construct a (the speaker's/ writer's?) meaning." Using this definition and drawing on long-term ethnographic fieldwork and recording, Hamilton considers how one Alzheimer's patient and her interlocutor (Hamilton) co-construct the patient's identity across two conversations occurring months apart. Long-term studies such as these facilitate the analysis of what have been called "intertextual chains" (also called "interdiscursive chains") (Fairclough 1992, 2000; Solin 2001, 2004; Agha 2005; Wilce 2005; Wortham 2005, 2006), or discourses or texts linked across chronological sequences, as well as the consideration of more complex "webs" of interrelated texts (Solin 2004:277).

In the case of many sociolinguistic studies, an intertextual approach—by which I mean looking across conversations that involve the same participants—is not feasible due to data-collection methodology that consists of recording isolated individual conversations. Though interactions are analyzed within their broader cultural and social context (and sometimes analyzed using insights from ethnographic research), they are extracted from the everyday lives of interlocutors and essentially treated as stand-alone units for analysis. This is often done for ease and practicality of data collection. Indeed, in the introduction to the edited volume *Repetition in Discourse*, Johnstone et al. (1994:5) note, in offering possible answers to the question "What counts as repetition," "it might be useful to imagine an intratextual/intertextual continuum and then focus on the intratextual end of the spectrum for methodological convenience."

The instances of repetition I analyze are drawn from a family discourse study that involved recording over a relatively lengthy period of time (at least one week), as well as the collection of supplementary data (e.g., informal interview data, email messages). These data provide a rich site in which to investigate intertextual phenomena, such as the repetition of key words and phrases, familylect features, and ritualized family interactions, as well as to consider how these relate to everyday meaning-making, although this was not the original focus of the Work and Family Project. I examine the discourse of three participating families, each with one young child: Janet and Steve Neeley-Mason and their daughter, Natalie (age two years, eleven months), Kathy Patterson and Sam Foley and their daughter Kira (age two years, one month), and Clara Shepherd and Neil Sylvan and their son Jason (age four years, ten months). (The fourth family had older children, ages seventeen, twenty, and twenty-two.)

Each parent in these families was provided with a small digital tape recorder, as well as with a simplified set of instructions for using it.[13] While recording, participants wore the recorders on their belts, carried them in their purses, or set them down on a table or desktop while they were stationary. Lavaliere microphones were used at the participants' discretion. The small size of the recorders and the fact that tapes were able to hold four continuous hours of recording allowed participants to keep the recorder running nearly nonstop and carry it with them throughout the day. Audio rather than video recording provided for easy recording and helped minimize the "observer's paradox" (Labov 1972b), however there was a trade-off in that gestures, facial expressions, and other visual cues were not captured.

After recording was complete, each spouse was shadowed at home and at work by a research team member for at least one day.[14] During this time, we were able to talk informally with participants, meet co-workers whose voices we heard in the recordings, see the participants' homes and places of work, and observe them going about their everyday lives. Once the tapes were collected and after the family visit, research team members logged the contents of the tapes recorded by each couple and divided the contents into segments for transcribing. Approximately 460 hours of recording occurred in the four families, amounting to over a million words of transcription. (Three hundred eighty-eight of these hours occurred in the three families whose interactions I examine; transcription conventions developed for the project and used in this book appear in the appendix.) Janet and Steve recorded 165 hours over the course of seven consecutive days beginning February 23, 2000. Kathy and Sam recorded 134 hours over the course of fourteen consecutive days beginning February 18, 2000. One reason they recorded more than seven days was due to some technical difficulties experienced with one of their recorders early on; Sam wanted to "complete the cycle" by recording another full week. Clara and Neil recorded eighty-nine hours over seven days beginning November 6, 2000 (although for one day they taped only two hours). (The fourth family recorded the least—seventy-five hours—over nine days beginning June 19, 2000.)

In considering the phenomenon of intertextuality in the context of these data, the issue of what counts as intertextuality necessarily emerges. The primary way of linking interactions together—in other words, of examining intertextuality or intertextual chains—that I focus on in this book is through the repetition of preexisting fragments of language, a perspective that has been taken in prior research to examine the repetition of referring terms across texts (Schiffrin 2001a, 2001b), of bits of media texts in conversation (Schilling-Estes 2004; Tovares 2007), and of words used in prior shared conversations (Hamilton 1996; Gordon 2002, 2004; Schilling-Estes 2004; Wortham 2005, 2006). Repetition is an important means of reshaping prior text. Becker (1995) suggests that reshaping can be realized as repetition, the substitution of words, rearrangements, expansion, inflexion, and embedding. However, the category of repetition in a way subsumes the others Becker identifies, as they all constitute some type of variation on a pattern. Identifying intertextual (versus intratextual) repetition is not a straightforward endeavor by any means. As has been suggested by Johnstone et al. (1994), intertextual and intratextual repetition exist on a continuum; what is considered each type depends on the criteria used for classification. The examples I examine count as intertextual repetition in the sense that they fall toward the intertextual end of that continuum: Words are repeated across (rather than within) conversations. However, determining what actually constitutes a conversation is not a straightforward process either, particularly in the family context, in which there often seems to be what Goffman (1981:135) might identify as a "chronic conversation in progress" or an "open state of talk." However, from listening to the recorded talk of these families, I repeatedly remarked that there are discernible, relatively bounded units that can be identified as "conversations" or "stretches of talk." As Gunther Kress (2000:132) notes, "We—as language users—have a good sense when a conversation is finished or a lecture, an interview, or the news on television is completed. These are textual entities, made in a particular social environment."

The conversations I examine are displaced in time (by days or hours) and sometimes in space; I draw on Hamilton's (1996) linguistic definition of intertextuality in considering interactions involving the same interlocutors through time. In addition, I conceptualize inter-actions occurring only minutes apart but involving a change in parti-cipants as two "different" conversations. My understanding of what might be thought of as "intertextual conversations" is in some ways similar to Schiffrin's (2000) discussion of "intertextual narratives." Like Schiffrin, I segment a larger discourse into smaller, relatively bounded units. In other words, the perspective taken in this book is that family discourse is not comprised of a single text but is a web of texts—face-to-face and phone conversations, conversations with only family members and with outsiders, and so on.

The Families

The families whose discourse I examine here live in the greater Washington, DC, area. As mentioned, in keeping with the research interests of the Sloan Foundation, all are dual-income and can be described as middle class (by study design); all families are also white. Parents in the participating families are highly educated, holding at least a bachelor's degree. In addition, all three mothers were pursuing master's level degrees, one mother already had a master's degree in public administration, one father had a master's in business administration and was also certified in accounting, and one father was pursuing a doctorate. Although all names are pseudonyms, they reflect the parents' use of the same, different, or hyphenated last names.

Janet, Steve, and Natalie Neeley-Mason

At the time of recording, Janet, Steve, and Natalie Neeley-Mason lived in a suburban townhouse on the outskirts of the Washington, DC, metro area. The parents volunteered to participate in the project when Janet saw a flyer posted at one of her places of employment. Janet and Steve's married last name, Neeley-Mason, is a combination of their given last names (Neeley and Mason, respectively).

Janet and Steve both grew up in northern Virginia. Both are trained as actors, and they met while performing in theater. At the time of recording, Janet and Steve performed together in a professional children's theater troupe on weekends. Both parents were thirty-three years old; they had been married for six years. Natalie was two years, eleven months old. Janet was approximately seven months pregnant with the couple's second child and was working as a therapist part-time in two locations (typically eight to nine hours per week) as part of a master's degree program in psychotherapy. Steve was working full-time for a video production company and part-time as a waiter at two different restaurants. Janet typically watched Natalie during the day; Natalie also attended Montessori preschool three days a week (from 8:30 A.M. until noon). When needed, Natalie's maternal grandmother, who lived in the area, provided child care, although at the time of taping she was not always able to do so because she was battling an ongoing illness. Natalie was very verbal for her age; she also frequently threw temper tantrums and was in the process of being toilet trained during the recording week.

As in all of the families, the recorders captured family members engaged in various everyday tasks like doing housework, arguing about various issues, watching television, joking around, and interacting with people outside the nuclear family, although this family did the latter to the greatest degree. The Neeley-Masons also used language to symbolically include others—in particular, two family friends—in their family. Members of this family additionally talked about Natalie's soon-to-be-born baby brother, career and financial issues, popular culture, and Janet's mother's illness. A great number of this family's recorded interactions, however, revolved around Natalie: managing her (mis)behavior, getting her ready in the morning, reading to her, and, very often, playing with her and keeping her entertained through language.

Kathy Patterson, Sam Foley, and Kira Foley

Kathy, Sam, and their daughter, Kira, live in a house in a suburb just outside the border of Washington, DC. Kathy and Sam volunteered for the project after a professor for a course Kathy was taking mentioned a call for volunteers Tannen had made during a radio interview.

Kathy grew up in Baltimore, Maryland. Sam grew up in the suburb in which the couple was living at the time of recording. Kathy and Sam were both thirty-seven years old; they had been married five and a half years. Kira (frequently called Ki-Ki) was two years, one month old. Kathy was about eight months pregnant with the couple's second child.

Kathy worked as an advertising sales agent for a nonprofit organization; she was also taking classes one day a week toward a master's degree in psychology. Sam was working full-time as a physicist for a government organization; he was also taking advanced coursework toward a Ph.D. in a branch of physics. Both parents worked four days a week so each could spend one weekday at home with Kira. (The federal government makes the full-time, four-day schedule an option for most of its employees; Kathy worked thirty hours a week.) For the three weekdays that neither parent was home during the day, Kira was in day care at Kathy's workplace. At just over two years old, Kira was not yet very verbal; much of the talk she produced consisted of reduplicated words and sounds and one-word utterances; nonetheless, many of the family's interactions revolved around her. Kathy and Sam were in the process of toilet training their daughter, and this fueled much conversation. In addition, Kathy practiced extended breastfeeding; feeding Kira and managing her behavior were also frequent topics of talk. Like the Neeley-Mason parents, Kathy and Sam also cleaned the house, argued (about money, for the most part), joked and teased, watched television, and talked about the upcoming birth of their second child.

Clara Shepherd, Neil Sylvan, and Jason Sylvan

Clara Shepherd, Neil Sylvan, and their son, Jason, live in a house on a quiet suburban street at the outer edge of the Washington, DC, metro area. They had two small dogs that were also considered members of their family.[15] This couple volunteered following a lecture Tannen gave at the organization where Clara worked.

Both parents were forty-three years old. Clara and Neil met at a YMCA in a city in Virginia. They never married, but they had been together for sixteen years—much longer than the other two families with a young child.

Clara was assistant director in a government organization; she had a master's degree in public administration and was taking courses toward a master's degree in marriage and family therapy. Neil was vice president for a nonprofit organization; he had an MBA, and he is a Certified Public Accountant. Their son, Jason, age four years, ten months, attended junior kindergarten at a private school full-time.

This family recorded during the week of the 2000 U.S. presidential election; this affected many of their interactions, especially because Clara's immediate boss was a presidential (Clinton) appointee and both parents were very interested in politics.[16] Although these parents were less child-focused than the others (perhaps in part because the child was older), Jason was a central component of many interactions. As in the other families, the parents watched television (especially election-related news), argued (about chores; see Tannen 2006), joked around, and engaged their child in conversation across various contexts.

Managing and Enriching Recorded Data: Making Other Intertextual Connections

Research team members who shadowed participants also listened to their recordings in their entirety, logged the contents of the tapes, and participated in transcription. Through these activities I became familiar with the different families, especially the Neeley-Masons, whose discourse is the focus of this book (I shadowed Janet Neeley-Mason as well as Clara Shepherd). In addition, weekly (or biweekly) meetings were held during which each researcher reported on what she or he had listened to and transcribed that week, which also helped me familiarize myself with all families participating in the project, even the two for which I did not shadow a parent.[17]

Most of the examples I discuss in this book I discovered myself, either from logging the contents of the tapes or transcribing the recorded interactions. Because the transcripts were stored in searchable documents, I was able to locate linked interactions. For instance, I recalled the phrase "rocks and rubs"—a phrase that refers to Natalie's bedtime ritual in which a parent rocks her in a rocking chair and then rubs her back as she lies in bed—being used multiple times in the Neeley-Mason's recorded interactions, so I did a search for those words. Other research team members also helped identify examples once I outlined my interests in repetition.

The tapes and transcripts were enriched by observations of the families at home and observations of the parents at their workplaces; we also informally interviewed the families after recording as a means of gathering more information as well as to learn about how family members felt about recording. These observations and conversations resulted in detailed field notes that included information about how the parents met, their beliefs about child-rearing, the layout of their homes, and so on. Follow-up visits with the families and email contacts with them after the recording period supplemented the primary database. I have remained in email contact with the Neeley-Masons, whose discourse is the focus of my analysis. This enabled me to email them questions I encountered while listening to the tapes and to do a kind of "playback" with them.[18] For instance, for chapter 5, in which I examine the repetition of bits of language from children's storybooks in an extended conversation between Janet and Natalie, I emailed the family to ask about a particular children's book they indirectly referenced in conversation, which I then purchased and read. In addition, I have been able to learn about how the families have changed over the years and how they reflect back on some of their prior interactions.

PREVIEW OF THE CHAPTERS

Chapters 2 and 3 demonstrate that viewing intertextuality and framing as fundamentally intertwined reveals important insights into the discursive construction of families as small group cultures. These chapters are inspired by the initial impression that I and the other researchers taking part in the Work and Family Project had that each family in essence constituted its own social—and linguistic—"world." They are shaped by Bakhtin's broadest understanding of dialogicality as an omnipresent feature of utterances and words and bring this understanding together with frames theory as a way of illuminating the linguistic creation of culture and identity.

In chapter 2, I focus on how linguistic family worlds are constructed, drawing on the concept of familylect. My understanding of familylect demonstrates how intertextuality and framing are interconnected, and what this means for viewing the family as a social group: I propose that the familylect is best understood as a kind of extreme intertextuality, as repeated, ritualized ways of speaking that recreate family-specific frames. This understanding builds on Bakhtin's theorizing about culture as consisting of "discourses retained by the collective memory" (Todorov 1984 [1981]:x) and Becker's suggestion that prior text in a sense means "cultural memory" by integrating these ideas with the proposal that culture can be conceptualized as a system of frames (Agar 1994; see also Goffman 1963, 1974; Frake 1977). I examine the discourse of the Neeley-Mason and Patterson/ Foley families, using the discourse of the Shepherd/Sylvan family as a point of comparison in my discussion of familylect lexical items. I demonstrate how repeated patterns of language use—including not only uses of specialized family words but also pitch, accent, intonation, and address terms—(re)create family-specific frames that contribute to the construction of each of family's culture and identity. One primary type of frame that emerges in the culture of the two families whose discourse I focus on is those that are child-centered, however, these frames are constructed through different linguistic means in each family. This reinforces research by Varenne (1992) and Blum-Kulka (1997) suggesting that American families tend to revolve around children, while also highlighting the role of language in differentiating the families.

Chapter 3 further demonstrates how intertextuality and framing are best understood as intertwined by investigating, from this new perspective, two phenomena that have been widely examined in family discourse research: parent–child behavior regulation and evaluation, and family storytelling. Viewing the family as discursively constructed,

I explore these phenomena as they occur in conversations involving the Neeley-Masons and two family friends, Jill ("Auntie Jill") and Tim ("Uncle Noodles"). I show how the adults use intratextual and intertextual repetition of words and speech acts to construct co-parenting frames (in which the child's behavior is directed and evaluated) and narrative frames (in which stories are elicited and told); these frames are used as contexts for extending family boundaries to encompass Jill and Tim. I identify repetition as a key element in the (re)construction of co-parent footings within these frames. I thus illustrate how an intertextual analysis of frames gives a new impression of what exactly constitutes family. I suggest that the analysis is particularly relevant for our understanding of contemporary American families, as they are often not limited to two legally married parents and their biological or adopted child(ren) but extend to include others, whether it be extended family members, friends, ex-spouses, step-parents, pets, and so on. In this way, this chapter engages with Holstein and Gubrium's (1995) idea that the family is not a "monolithic" construct, and instead there exists a diversity of families created in local interactions.

Chapters 4 and 5 illustrate the fundamental role of intertextuality in creating (and identifying) meanings in interaction. These chapters engage in particular with Bakhtin's notion of double-voiced discourse, as family members in the examples I analyze use the words of another person and seemingly intend for the voice of the original speaker to be heard. I focus on how interlocutors use repetition to manipulate frames, that is, to create and make sense of everyday activities. I demonstrate how the meaning-making process entails looking beyond individual conversations, presenting a moment-by-moment, intertextual analysis that develops Goffman's (1974, 1981) idea that frames are often laminated in social interaction.

In chapter 4, I examine how family members repeat words previously uttered by another member in a specific prior interaction to create and layer meanings. Building on Goffman's theorizing, I identify and describe two different kinds of frames lamination—*embedded* and *overlapping*—created through the repetition of shared prior text. Thus, drawing on and extending frames theory as developed in anthropology, sociology, and linguistics, I illustrate how meaning-making fundamentally depends on access to shared prior text and how family members use intertextual repetition as a means of conveying layered meanings, or multiple meanings at once. I do so by examining interactions drawn from the tapes of the Neeley-Masons and the Patterson/Foleys. The analyses I present aim to contribute to our understanding of how frames are laminated in discourse moment by moment and how framing can be viewed as interrelated to intertextuality by demonstrating how family members use intertextual repetition of words to convey a complexity of meanings based on their shared past experiences.

Chapter 5 explores the process of *reframing* and identifies and describes a different type of laminated frame: *blended* frames. In doing so, it illustrates how language from children's storybooks—gleaned from books read as part of a child's bedtime and naptime rituals—is repeated and reshaped in the discourse of one mother (Janet) and her daughter (Natalie). My analysis shows how this mother and child draw on material from children's storybooks to manipulate frames and create various meanings in everyday talk. I demonstrate how these interlocutors reshape prior text to (re)define what is going on in a given interaction and to undertake different activities: to play in various ways, display knowledge, and parent (and thereby blend frames). I compare blended frames with overlapping and embedded frames and discuss how these laminations—blended frames especially—relate to work in cognitive linguistics on *conceptual blending* (e.g., Coulson & Fauconnier 1999), a theory of meaning-making that is related to sociolinguistic conceptualizations of framing. In addition, I discuss how this kind of repetition works toward binding family members together in the collaborative activity of remembering and reshaping.

In chapter 6, I summarize the findings of this study and contextualize them in larger questions in the field of linguistics and in the interdisciplinary study of social interaction: how to explore intertextuality in interaction, both theoretically and methodologically, and how intertextuality is related to meaning-making and small-group culture construction. I also discuss how this study helps elucidate our understanding of the role of talk in creating and shaping what we think of as family.

ENTERING INTO DIALOGUE ON THE FAMILY

In writing this book, I enter into dialogue on "the family," an ongoing inquiry or exploratory conversation that involves politicians and policy makers, academics from a range of fields (psychology, sociology, anthropology, linguistics, communication, and so on), social workers and clinical psychologists, and the media. My analyses provide primarily linguistic—more specifically, sociolinguistic and anthropological linguistic—insights into the family. Following the theorizing of Bakhtin, Gary Saul Morson and Caryl Emerson (1990:336) describe what it means to enter into a dialogue on topics that have been discussed before, requiring the use of words that have been used many times before: "We may observe generally that each time a phrase is repeated, its 'already-spoken' quality is foregrounded. As it is incorporated into different contexts, passed through different voices, and made to figure in different projected acts of self-justification, we detect an 'influx of sense' from each hybrid to the next." My research builds on prior research on family interaction as well as on past work by Bakhtin, Kristeva, Goffman, Becker, Tannen, and others, giving concepts they discuss (e.g., dialogicality, intertextuality, framing, and prior text) a new "influx of sense" through bringing them together in an innovative way to analyze a rich data set. In integrating and building on past work, I propose a theory of intertextuality and framing in family discourse that hopes to serve as prior text for future studies considering meaning-making and intertextuality in social interaction, in particular in the very important context of everyday family talk.

My analyses recontextualize not only the voices of academic researchers but also the voices of the family members whose private, everyday talk I examine. I have done my best to treat these voices with fairness and respect throughout. It is my hope that in experiencing these voices through reading the transcripts, the reader will not only consider them from an academic perspective but also take a moment to reflect on them from a personal one. We all engage in family discourse of our own, no matter how we define family; that talk likely will have some things in common with the family discourse that is the focus of this book (and of course, many features that are completely different). Regardless, in addition to contributing to the academic understanding of intertextuality, framing, and family discourse, I hope that this study helps us gain a better understanding of the ways in which "the family" is not a monolithic construct but a phrase that stands in for an important human form with a diversity of realizations. Language is but one resource (albeit a vital one) that we draw on in everyday life to remember, reshape, ritualize, and create family.

"All Right My Love?" "All Right My Dove"

Extreme Intertextuality and "Framing Family"

One of the first things I noticed while listening to the recorded conversations of the Neeley-Mason family, the Patterson/Foley family, and the Shepherd/Sylvan family was how incredibly different the families were. Considering daily schedules, topics discussed, television programs viewed, music listened to, books read and talked about, uses of humor, and so on, each family seemed like a different world. In this chapter I delve into patterned language use in the Neeley-Mason and Patterson/Foley families, documenting prominent features of the familylect of each family and demonstrating how these features work toward constructing for each one a distinctive family culture. Although the idea that language is inextricably intertwined with culture is not new—as evidenced, for instance, by the introduction of such terms as "linguaculture" (Friedrich 1989) and "languaculture" (Agar 1994)—I examine *family* language and culture; I also incorporate and integrate the theoretical notions of intertextuality and framing by considering the familylect as a manifestation of extreme intertextuality among members of a group that (re)creates specific frames. In so doing, I demonstrate how viewing intertextuality and framing as interconnected is crucial to understanding the discursive construction of culture. My analysis explores the reshaping of a wide variety of types of prior text, including words and strings of words as well interactive routines structured by repeated uses of lexical items, address terms, pitch, accent, and intonation. In creating family-specific frames, these features metaphorically frame the family.

FAMILYLECTS, FAMILY-SPECIFIC FRAMES, AND FAMILY CULTURES

The term *familylect* was introduced by Søndergaard (1991) as a way of describing the sociolect of one multilingual family. Søndergaard's likening of a familylect to a sociolect is useful in that it implies that a familylect, like a dialect, can be thought of as a "variety of a language which is shared by a group of speakers" (Wolfram & Schilling-Estes 1998:2), in this case, by members of a single family. Thus, like a dialect, a familylect might be expected to consist of distinct uses of linguistic features, such as lexical items, syntax, and pronunciation. Other scholars, although not using the term *familylect*, have suggested that every family has a "private language" shared by its members (Tannen 2001: xxiv) or "a spoken shorthand" or "insider language" (Nydegger & Mitteness 1988:710). Specialized "family expressions" (Randall 2005) and "family words" (Dickson 2007) have also been documented, and the idea that a family may have its own unique verbal "family humor style" has been explored in a case-study discourse analysis (Everts 2003). However, to my knowledge, there has been no systematic study to date of what constitutes a familylect and how it functions in the everyday lives of family members.

My understanding of the familylect in terms of extreme intertextuality builds on Bakhtin's theorizing about culture: According to Todorov (1984 [1981]:x), Bakhtin reinterprets culture as something that "consists in the discourses retained by collective memory..., discourses in relation to which every uttering subject must situate himself or herself." In this understanding, shared culture grows out of a shared (and remembered) set of discourses, an idea similar to Becker's proposal that social groups are held together through a shared repertoire of prior language experiences, as well as his suggestion that prior text in a sense means "cultural memory." I demonstrate how prior language experiences are drawn on in the (re)construction of ritualized, family-specific frames, drawing on the idea that culture can be viewed as a system of frames (Agar 1994; see also Frake 1977 and Goffman 1963,

1974). Repeating family-specific prior text thus symbolically frames the family by sending metamessages of shared family membership, defining each family's culture and identity, and constructing family boundaries.

Underlying this analysis is a constructionist view of family that regards language as a primary means of creating not only family meanings but family itself. In fact, numerous scholars have pointed out that "the family" is not a naturally occurring or biological phenomenon, but a small culture constructed through various discursive practices (Gubrium & Holstein 1990; Varenne 1992; Langellier & Peterson 1993; Holstein & Gubrium 1995, 1999; Sillars 1995; Aronsson 2006). This may be viewed as a particularly relevant approach to American families, which are temporary and must be created anew each generation (Shore 2003). It is also a useful approach in that it enables researchers to examine a diversity of family types, including nontraditional contemporary families, such as those headed by same-sex parents (e.g., Bergen et al. 2006; Pash 2008a, 2008b), as well as other kinds of families that reach beyond traditional family boundaries.

The two families whose discourse I focus on in this chapter were both young and evolving at the time of taping: Kathy Patterson and Sam Foley had been married for five and a half years, and they were parents of one small child (Kira, age two years, one month), with a second child on the way; Janet and Steve Neeley-Mason had been married for six years; their daughter, Natalie, was two years, eleven months old; and they were also expecting a second child. I also consider the discourse of the third family (Clara Shepherd, Neil Sylvan, and Jason Sylvan [age four years, ten months]), as a point of comparison, although this family was different in that it was more established (Neil and Clara had been together for approximately sixteen years, though they were never officially married); this family also recorded less consistently.

The Neeley-Mason and Patterson/Foley families are very much alike not only in terms of their makeup but also in their creation of a family culture with a young child at its center. How these child-centered cultures are created is illustrated through my analysis. Although both families draw on the cultural options available to them for interacting with children (see Ochs & Schieffelin 1984; Schieffelin & Ochs 1986)[1]—for instance, both parents talk to their child using specialized words—they do so in different ways; thus, the impression that I and the other project researchers had that these families are very distinctive from one another is supported by the in-depth analysis their language.

I begin by highlighting lexical differences in all three families to illustrate how their familylects differ on perhaps the most apparent level—how they repeatedly use different words to talk about the same things. This is followed by a more in-depth look at the linguistic features comprising the Patterson/Foley and Neeley-Mason familylects and a discussion of how these work intertextually toward constructing two unique family cultures through the creation of family-specific frames.

COMPARISON OF THREE FAMILY LEXICONS

Each family has a unique repertoire of family words. For instance, in the Patterson/Foley family, "nu-nu" means "noodle"; for the Neeley-Masons, "shenanigans" refers to Natalie talking instead of taking a nap at naptime; in the Shepherd/Sylvan family, a "cuddle day" is a weekend day or any other day when a parent stayed home with Jason (and he did not go to prekindergarten). These are just a sampling of terms; rather than document them in their totality, in this section I compare and contrast terms used by each family for essentially the same thing. Because at the time of taping the child in each of the families still needed help or encouragement to perform everyday personal care such as using the toilet ("going potty") and teeth brushing, these such issues were frequent topics of talk; the appearance of words to talk about them provides the opportunity to examine how the family lexicons differ. These words also show how, in terms of family vocabulary, much of it was child-centered.

Adult members of both the Neeley-Mason and Patterson/Foley families talked at great length about their child's urination and defecation habits (both children were being toilet trained during the taping period); however, they used different terms to do so. (Note that Clara Shepherd and Neil Sylvan did not typically refer to the specifics of using the toilet in conversation with their son, perhaps because he was older; however, like both other families, they did use the expression "go potty.") Thus, the original impression of these families having unique languages is supported by concrete linguistic evidence as the families discuss intimate, everyday topics related to their children.

For the Neeley-Masons, when referring to Natalie's toilet functions, the word "poops" was used every day of taping (as a singular noun) to refer to excrement, as in "make (a) poops" ("poopy" was also used on several occasions), while the word "tinkles" was used to refer to urine, and urination was referred to as "make (a) tinkles." Repeated use of these unusual terms by all family members about this intimate topic reinforced family in-group membership while also indexing the uniqueness of this family.

These terms used by the Neeley-Masons were never used by members of the Patterson/Foley family during their recording period. Instead, all family members (Kira included) used the terms "poo-poo" and "pee-pee" (along with the verbs "go" or "make") when talking about Kira's bathroom habits (and sometimes Kathy's and Sam's). This fits into Kathy's, Sam's, and Kira's repeated uses of reduplicated terms for many everyday concepts and objects (e.g., "ba-ba" for "bottle," "wa-wa" for "water"). Even something as small as terms used for children's bodily functions can reflect a unique familylect.

Another personal care issue discussed in all three families was the child's need to brush his or her teeth or have his or her teeth brushed. In the Patterson/Foley family and the Shepherd/Sylvan family, only the word "teeth" is used. In contrast, all members of the Neeley-Mason family use "choppers" to refer to Natalie's teeth (though they exclusively use the term "teeth" for Janet's and Steve's teeth). Just as "tinkles" and "poops" are somewhat unusual terms, so is the word "choppers." The playfulness of the term also indexes the overall tenor of the family's interactions; the activity of brushing teeth is framed as playful. In fact, Steve reported to me via email that there was a special song about "brushing choppers" that often accompanied the activity (during the week of taping, family friend Tim—whose discourse is examined as part of the next chapter—was captured on tape singing this song with Natalie).

Typical uses of "choppers" in conversation with Natalie occurred on the first morning of recording when Janet said to Natalie, "Okay peaches, we've got to brush those choppers" and "Time to brush choppers." In addition, Janet and Steve used the term when talking about Natalie's teeth when she was not present. For instance, one day while Natalie was at preschool and Steve and Janet were waiting in the doctor's office for an obstetrician appointment, Steve describes part of his morning at home with Natalie by saying, "So I took her upstairs and brushed choppers."

Natalie also uses this bit of familylect vocabulary. Excerpt 1 shows Natalie repeating a portion of Steve's utterance about "choppers" while Steve is getting her ready in the morning as she resists his wishes. Here, although Natalie repeats a familylect phrase, she does so in contradicting her father: He wants Natalie to brush her teeth in the (upstairs) bathroom, but she wants to go downstairs. (This excerpt, like those that follow, uses underlining to highlight word repetition of particular interest; block arrows indicate other lines of analytical interest.)

(1) 1 Steve: Come in here please.
     2 Natalie: Why.
     3 Steve: Because,
     4   we brush our choppers in the BATHroom.
     5 Natalie: <*with toothbrush in mouth*> We brush →
     6   our choppers downstairs.>
     7 Steve: No,
     8   we brush our choppers right here.
     9 Natalie: <*with toothbrush in mouth*> No →
    10   we brush our choppers downstairs.>
    11 Steve: <*quietly, sarcastically*> Oh you're delightful.>

Though disagreeing with her father in this excerpt, Natalie "agrees" to use his words—the familylect words. This is similar to Tannen's (2007 [1989]:78) observation that repeating something said by another person can be used in conversation to disagree but still create rapport and ratify another participant's conversational contribution.

Excerpt 2 shows the only instance where the word "teeth" was used during the recording period to refer to Natalie's teeth. Janet apologizes to Natalie, who is crying as Janet brushes her (Natalie's) teeth.

(2) 1 Janet: Okay,
     2   well I'm sorry sweetie, ((*Natalie crying*))
     3   I'm not trying to hurt you, ((*Natalie crying*))
     4 ⇨   I'm just trying to brush your teeth. ((*Natalie crying*))

The absence of the word "choppers" in this interaction could be explained by the tone of this exchange. It is not playful, as Natalie is crying throughout, and "choppers" has playful connotations.

All three members of the Neeley-Mason family used the term "choppers" in the form of "brush (-/those/your/our) choppers." Though family members also use the word "teeth," this word was only used to refer to Janet's and Steve's teeth (with only one exception, as just shown in excerpt 2). "Choppers" was never used to refer to Janet's and Steve's teeth; it has specialized meaning in the Neeley-Mason family, referring to Natalie's teeth only.[2]

In sum, familylects can subtly differ from one another on the lexical level. This has been informally observed in prior research (e.g., Randall 2005); in addition, a wide variety of family lexical items and expressions have been documented (e.g., Dickson 2007). However, the uses of lexical items I have described point to broader interactional patterns—the Neeley-Mason family's use of inventive language not appearing in the language of the other families to create frames of play and teasing, and the Patterson/Foley family's use of reduplicated words and baby talk to create frames in which the parents' identities as "Mama" and "Dada" are highlighted. I now turn to considering features of the Patterson/Foley familylect and the frames they create.

REDUPLICATION AND VENTRILOQUIZING: CREATING CHILD-CENTERED FRAMES IN THE PATTERSON/FOLEY FAMILY

Two prominent features of the Patterson/Foley familylect emerged through analysis; together these work to linguistically create child-centered frames across the recording period that focus on Kira as not just the child but as "the baby" of the family.[3] First, this family uses a notable amount of reduplication and baby talk intonation. These uses extend beyond interactions with Kira (whose linguistic production often consists of reduplication) to private interactions between Kathy and Sam. A second, related feature of this familylect is the routine use of Kira as a means for Kathy and Sam to speak to one another, which is a form of what Tannen (2003, 2004) refers to as "ventriloquizing." Both of these features allow Kira's "voice" to be heard even if she is not talking or even present; these features also show Kira's parents' incorporation of her speaking competency into their own ways of speaking.

Reduplication and Baby Talk Intonation

All members of the Patterson/Foley repeatedly use baby talk intonation and reduplication. Excerpt 3, for instance, shows Kathy doing so as she talks to Kira. The phrase "go night-night" means "go to bed." The term "ba-ba" (bottle) also appears here, as does "no" in the reduplicated form "no-no." It is late evening and Kathy is taking care of Kira while Sam works at the family computer.

(3) 1 Kira: <u>Night-night</u>.
2 Kathy: You wanna <u>go night-night</u>?
3   ((*short pause*))
4 Kira: <u>Ba-ba</u>!
5   <u>Ba-ba</u>!
6 Kathy: <*high-pitched*> <u>Ba-ba</u>!
7   Do you wanna <u>go night-night</u>?
8   No:.
9   Don't wanna <u>go night-night</u>.
10   <u>No-no</u> <u>night-night</u>.>
11   Wanna eat?
12 Kira: Eh.
13 Kathy: Okay.

Here Kathy repeats Kira's reduplicated terms. Speaking using a high-pitched voice, which is repeatedly used in talking to Kira, Kathy tries to guess what her daughter wants.

In excerpt 4, Kathy and Kira again use reduplicated terms, this time a different set. Here they use "nu-nus" for "noodles," "wa-wa" for "water," and "more-more" for "more."

(4) 1 Kira: Eat eat eat eat.
2 Kathy: You done eating?
3   You want more?
4   <u>More-more</u>?
5   <u>Nu-nus</u>!
6 Kira: <u>Nu-nu</u>, peeze.
7 Kathy: <u>Nu-nus</u>, please.
8 Kira: <u>Nu-nu</u> peeze. ((*Kathy begins to wash up*))
9   <*urgent*> Uh uh UHHHHH>

10	Kathy:	<*laughs*> What.>
11		You got a lotta <u>nu-nus</u> in your mouth, girl.
12		LOTTA <u>nu-nus</u>.
13	Kira:	Oh <u>nu-nus</u>.
14		Oh <u>nu-nus</u>.
15	Kathy:	Lotta <u>nu-nus</u>.
16	Kira:	Oh <u>nu-nus</u>.
17		((*sound of pouring liquid into a glass*))
18	Kira:	<u>Wa-wa</u>,
19		<u>more-more wa-wa</u>.
20	Kathy:	Yeah.
21	Kira:	<u>More-more wa-wa</u>.

This interaction is created by reduplication produced by both participants. In the excerpt, Kathy, like Kira, speaks like a baby. In doing so, she aligns with and accommodates to Kira.

The reduplicated terms introduced in the previous excerpts as well as others are combined in a number of ways in conversations across the fourteen days of recording and are used by all family members. When draining the bathtub after Kira's bath, Sam says, "Bye-bye wa-wa," and when flushing the toilet after Kira went potty he says, "Bye-bye poo-poo." When Kira finds a dirty bottle, he says to Kira, "That's a yuck-yuck ba-ba, Ki-Ki." Other phrases that appear during the week of taping used by family members include "bye-bye ba-ba" (as Sam takes a bottle from Kira), "no-no ba-ba" (Kathy telling Kira it is not time to have a bottle), "bye-bye night-night" (Kathy taking Kira upstairs to go to bed), and "ba-ba night-night" and "ba-ba nap-nap" (meaning, Kira will have a bottle and go to bed or go down for a nap). All of these constructions point to a language Sam, Kathy, and Kira all share consisting of reduplicated words they are all capable of pronouncing and understanding. Their many combinations show the creativity possible within this aspect of their familylect.

Though these terms are most often used by the parents when talking to Kira, Kathy and Sam also use reduplication when talking to each other in Kira's presence; for instance, they report to each other whether Kira went "poo-poo" or "pee-pee" on the potty. Likewise, they do this when Kira is not present. For example, in one conversation, Sam described his afternoon with Kira to Kathy, who was at work, saying "And she drank her ba-ba, and then slept with Dada," and in another they talk extensively about Kira going poo-poo. In speaking in this way, Kathy and Sam frame these interactions as being built around Kira.

Perhaps most interesting are those instances in which Kathy and Sam use baby talk between the two of them in private conversations, when Kira is neither present nor the topic of talk. Though this occurred rarely, it shows how pervasive baby talk is in this family and how child-centeredness creeps into interactive frames that seemingly have nothing to do with Kira. For instance, Sam and Kathy use the baby talk expression "go bye-bye," which is used repeatedly in interactions with Kira, while talking among themselves. When used in interaction with Kira, "go bye-bye" indicates the end of an activity or marks the leaving of a location, for instance, Sam uses the expression to explain to Kira that the video she had been watching had ended, saying "That went bye-bye, it's all done"; he also uses it when they leave Kira's day care center and when something is all gone or taken away. Excerpt 5 shows Sam using "go bye-bye" while talking to Kathy about the family computer; Kira is upstairs napping. Sam is working on paying bills and doing other things on the computer when it freezes, and the following ensues:

(5) 1 Sam: Well my computer went bye-bye.
    2 Kathy: Why.
    3 Sam: I don't know.
    4   Just locked up.

Approximately fifteen minutes later, Sam again uses this phrase when his computer once more "locks up." This time Sam works on the computer while Kathy is in another room. Particularly interesting is the contrast between the baby talk "go bye-bye" and the first word Sam says when his computer locks up again ("Damn").

(6) 1 Sam: Damn.
    2   I think it locked up again.
    3 Kathy: Huh?
    4 Sam: I think it locked up again.
    5 Kathy: Hm.
    6 Sam: Yep.
    7   ((short pause))
    8   Yep,

9		computer <u>went bye-bye</u>.
10		((*short pause*))
11	Kathy:	Huh?
12	Sam:	Computer <u>went bye-bye</u>.
13	Kathy:	(?????)

Excerpts 5 and 6 demonstrate how Sam and Kathy at times communicate using baby talk even when Kira is neither present nor the topic of talk. In this instance, in using the phrase "go bye-bye," Sam speaks as if talking to Kira (or for Kira), animating what happened in a way she might understand (or possibly produce). This strategy can be viewed as a way of bringing Kira into the conversation, just as constructed dialogue might, though she is not present. By using a reduplicated word that Kira is capable of uttering and did utter during the week of taping ("bye-bye"), and using a phrase she might understand ("go bye-bye"), Sam brings Kira's perspective and voice into the conversation, as if quoting her. Using the reduplicated baby talk phrase "go bye-bye" thus can be seen as indirectly solidifying Kira's place at the center of the family (and family frames of interaction), though she is not physically present in the conversation. It also can be viewed as a strategy that works to lighten the tone of the interaction, showing that Sam is not really upset, despite his earlier uttering of a curse word.

"Ventriloquizing" and Communicating through Kira

A related phenomenon to reduplicated baby talk vocabulary and child-directed intonation occurring in the Patterson/Foley family's interactions is the use of talk much like what Tannen (2003, 2004) identifies as "ventriloquizing" in family discourse. A canonical instance of ventriloquizing for Tannen is when one family member (usually the mother) communicates to a second (either the father or child) by speaking *as* a third (typically a small child or a pet). A ventriloquizing-like conversational maneuver occurs when parents communicate to one another *through* their child (Tannen 2003). In both of these moves, a high-pitched baby talk register is often used. Kira's parents frequently exhibited both ventriloquizing and ventriloquizing-like dialogue. I suggest that these ways of speaking can be viewed as part of their familylect, specifically as strategies that repeatedly create child-centered frames.

Tannen (2003) identifies the following example of ventriloquizing-like dialogue in the discourse of the Patterson/Foley family: One day of taping, Sam was going skiing with his friends. He woke up very early that morning (also waking up Kathy and Kira), despite the fact that his typical tendency was to sleep late on workdays. Tannen (2003:58) notes that "Kathy uses this as an occasion to register not only her annoyance at being awakened earlier than necessary but also her dissatisfaction with Sam's habitual sleep schedule." Kathy does this by talking *through* Kira; she says, using a baby talk voice, "Tell Daddy to wake up this early on other days." Tannen argues that Kathy's utterance serves simultaneously as a power and connection maneuver—in other words, it is *polysemous*. Of particular interest for this chapter is the connection aspect, that is, how in repeatedly using this strategy intertextually, it creates a ritualized frame of interaction that indexes the family's shared past and ways of speaking, living in family members' collective memory. Furthermore, because this conversational move involves all three family members, it links participants together as into a triadic exchange although Kira herself does not have to speak when the strategy is used: The interaction is framed as both triadic and child-centered.

Another example of Kathy using a ventriloquizing-like maneuver to criticize Sam (not analyzed by Tannen) appears in excerpt 7. Here she does so when she catches Sam and Kira eating upstairs.

(7) 1   Kira: (Nana).
     2   Kathy: Mm, you probably should be eating downstairs.
     3   Sam: Ye:::s.
     4 ⇨ Kathy: <*baby talk*> We eat downstairs,
     5 ⇨   not [in bed.>]
     6   Sam: [Daddy] was eating in front of her,
     7   it wasn't fair.
     8 ⇨ Kathy: Why was Daddy [eating] upstairs.
     9   Kira: [(Nana!)]
    10   Sam: <*chuckles*>
    11   'Cause.→
    12   Kathy: Okay, [Daddy, take her down.]
    13   Sam: [(???) something.]
    14   Okays.
((*Sam takes Kira and the food downstairs*))

After confronting Sam directly (line 2), Kathy speaks through Kira, referring to Sam as "Daddy" and using a baby talk register. This allows her to express her disapproval to Sam and also include their daughter in the conversation (and lessen the imposition of the criticism; like the "go bye-bye" example, this strategy shows the speaker is not terribly upset). Sam co-participates in the child-centered framing by referring to himself as "Daddy" and by speaking on Kira's behalf (lines 6–7).

Excerpt 8 shows how members of this family also use ventriloquizing and ventriloquizing-like dialogue without criticizing one another and in moments of family harmony. Kathy had just arrived home from work to discover that Sam had made dinner. She was very pleased. Sam ventriloquizes Kira here, with Kathy speaking through Kira to Sam.

(8)	1	Kathy:	<*delighted voice for Kira*> He::y!>
	2	Sam:	Somebody was missing you::!
	3	Kathy:	Yeah!
	4		(Mama was missing you.)
	5	Kira:	Mama.
	6	Kathy:	I missed Daddy too-too!
	7	Sam:	[(?)]
	8	Kira:	[<*makes noises*>]
	9	Kathy:	[[<*laughs*>]]
	10	Sam:	[[<*laughs*>]]
	11 ⇨		<*baby talk voice*> I made you dinner!>
	12 ⇨	Kathy:	<*baby talk voice*> <Oo::::!>
	13 ⇨		<*gasps in an exaggerated way*>
	14 ⇨		<*baby talk voice*> Did you make Mommy dinner?>
	15 ⇨	Sam:	<*baby talk voice*> Yes.
	16 ⇨		And I got your salad ready!>
	17	Kathy:	<*gasps in an exaggerated way*>
	18		Daddy cooked!

In this excerpt, the family shares a moment of harmony as Kathy and Sam both speak using a baby talk voice associated with speaking *to* Kira or speaking *as* Kira. Though Sam made dinner without Kira's help, by speaking in the baby talk voice, he includes her as someone who did something for "Mommy" and as someone who is participating in the conversation. By responding using baby talk intonation, Kathy contributes to this framing. This conversation thus works to bind Kathy, Sam, and Kira into a family centered around Kira as "the baby."

Both Sam and Kathy talked as or through Kira during the recording period; in contrast such maneuvers occurred extremely rarely in the Neeley-Mason family's discourse. In the Shepherd/Sylvan family, ventriloquizing was a strategy typically used by Clara; she ventriloquized not human family members but the family's two dogs (see Tannen 2004). In contrast, speaking as and through Kira was a central part of the Patterson/Foley's familylect that involved both parents and child. Ventriloquizing makes dyadic exchanges between two adults triadic, allowing Kira to symbolically take part in conversations despite her limited linguistic competence. (Note then that Natalie's talkativeness may in part explain the fact that her parents do not often ventriloquize her, although they find other ways to involve her. For example, Janet often prompts Natalie to "tell Daddy" about events that happened during the day, examples of which are shown in the next chapter.)

In summary then, ventriloquizing and ventriloquizing-like conversational moves allow minimally verbal Kira to play a central role in conversations for which she is present: Utterances between her mother and father flow not around her but filter *through* her as they speak to one another by ventriloquizing. Likewise, through the recycling of prior text in the form of baby talk intonation and reduplicated words (e.g., "ba-ba," "nu-nu," "wa-wa," "more-more"), Kathy and Sam build interactive frames—and a family culture—that Kira can participate in and participate in creating, despite the fact that she cannot yet speak in fully formed utterances. Furthermore, by talking in these ways even when Kira is not present, Kathy and Sam continue to construct their talk around her as center of the family, and highlight their family roles as Mama and Dada.

LEXICON AND ROUTINES: CREATING CHILD-CENTERED FRAMES, COUPLE-CENTERED FRAMES, AND FRAMES OF PLAY AND PERFORMANCE IN THE NEELEY-MASON FAMILY

The Neeley-Mason family is also built very much around the child. However, Natalie, older than Kira Foley by ten months, is extremely verbal. Even before listening to the family's recorded interactions I was aware of this; while I was observing Janet and Natalie at home, Natalie repeatedly tried to engage me in conversation—as seen in the grapes fieldwork example presented in chapter 1. At another point, Janet left me in her car for a moment with Natalie as she stepped out to place a letter in a mail box; at that point Natalie said to me, "Let's talk." In addition to being very verbal, around the time of taping Natalie had recently started throwing temper tantrums and was generally resistant to doing what her parents wanted her to do. Natalie's talkativeness and frequent tantrums work in conjunction with the parents' styles to create an entirely different family culture from the Patterson/Foleys, despite the similar compositions of these families (two parents and one young child), and despite the child-centeredness of both families. I consider both the Neeley-Mason family's specialized set of child-focused lexical items and how they use language to repeatedly construct playful frames. These familylect features—words; manipulation of accent, intonation, volume, and pitch; and uses of reciprocal terms of endearment—reflect a playful, child-centered family culture and a style that shows appreciation for talk as an activity in itself and values linguistic inventiveness, verbal performance, and play.

Words Used for Child Misbehavior: Creating Child-Centeredness

One way child-centered framing is achieved in the Neeley-Mason family is through repeated uses of lexical items focused on the child. These familylect items are related to Natalie's misbehavior and have specialized family meaning; they emerge from and contribute to creating the family's distinctive culture.

"Shenanigans" at Naptime

On all seven days of recording, someone in the Neeley-Mason family used the word "shenanigans." It was used to refer to Natalie playing and talking to herself or to her dolls instead of quietly taking her afternoon nap. "Shenanigans" are something negative and constitute misbehavior of some kind. Janet, in particular, disliked "shenanigans"; because she was approximately seven months pregnant, she wanted to nap along with Natalie. On the other hand, the word is playful, indicating mischief, and reflects (or perhaps grows out of) a playful family culture where talk is equated with play. In excerpt 9, Janet describes Natalie's "shenanigans" to her own mother, Laura, as she and Steve sit with Laura while she waits to see a doctor at the emergency room (as mentioned in chapter 1, Laura was very ill at the time of taping; one day of taping Steve and Janet took her to the emergency room while Janet's brother Kevin babysat Natalie.) Note that Natalie is not present; she is at home with Kevin.

(9) 1 Janet: She uh . of course, you know →
     2   naptime is taking longer [(with her)] →
     3 Steve: [Oh boy.]
     4 Janet: <u>shenanigans</u>.
     5 Steve: We're at the end of that day-long CD,
     6   before she . even starts to settle.
     7 Laura: <*chuckling*> Oh no.>
     8 Janet: She's . she's a one-woman show,
     9   she's talking,
    10   [she's doing] characters,
    11 Laura: [<*chuckles*>]
    12 Janet: she's . y'know,
    13   I don't know what she's doing.

Interestingly, in this excerpt, Janet characterizes Natalie's naptime behaviors as a "one-woman show" as Natalie enacts different characters (for instance, she pretends to be a mommy to her dolls); later in the chapter it becomes apparent that the phrase "one-person show" could be used to describe both Janet's and Steve's linguistic behaviors as well.

The term "shenanigans" is also used during naptime. In excerpt 10, Janet and Steve are trying to put Natalie down for a nap on the weekend (Sunday); they plan on taking a nap with her. Natalie had agreed to rest quietly if they left the light on. However, she had not been doing so, and Steve threatens to turn off the light if shenanigans occur.

(10) 1 Steve: Natalie.
      2 Natalie: What.
      3 Steve: If you don't lay down with us quietly,

4		then we're just gonna turn the light back off.
5	Natalie:	Why.
6	Steve:	You're on your way.
7		My hand is right on the switch.
8		It's comin' right off, ((*"it"* = *the light*))
9		unless you lay right down.
10	Natalie:	No.
11		((*short pause*))
12		Why's your hand right on the switch.
13	Steve:	Just so you know that I'm ready to turn these off,
14		if there's any <u>shenanigans</u> at all.
15		((*short pause*))
16	Natalie:	<*whiney*> I don't want your hand on the switch.>
17	Steve:	Well when I'm s—
18		When I'm confident that you're laying down →
19		quietly,
20		I'll take my hand off the switch.
21	Natalie:	<*whiney*> I'm laying quietly.>
22		((*short pause*))

Notice that in talking during naptime, Natalie is not only responding to Steve's talk *about* shenanigans, she is also "doing shenanigans" by talking (e.g., in lines 10, 12, 16, 21); she is not "laying quietly" (although she says she is in line 21).

The term was also used in conversation with Natalie when it was not actually naptime but when naptime was the topic of talk (as in excerpt 9); this includes not only talk about Natalie but also conversations in which she was present. For instance, one day when Janet asks Natalie if she napped the day before with her grandmother and Natalie replies that she did, Janet subsequently asks, "Were there any shenanigans?" (Natalie says no and her mother praises her.)

Natalie also produces the familylect word "shenanigans." In fact, the first time it surfaced during the family's recording period was on the first day of taping when Janet was putting Natalie down for her afternoon nap. Janet and Natalie lay in Janet and Steve's bed. Janet has just finished reading stories to Natalie. In the excerpt, Natalie utters the word "shenanigans," prompted to do so by Janet by a fill-in-the-blank intonation to involve her. This suggests that the term was used many times before recording began and has a long history as family prior text.

(11) 1   ((*recorder turned off, then on*))
2   Janet: It is time— yes,
3   you may look at those, ((*"those"* = books))
4   QUIETLY.
5   Let's have a talk.
6   Natalie: What.
7   Janet: No . ((*waiting for Natalie to fill in the blank*))
8   Natalie: <u>Shenanigans</u>.
9   Janet: Right,
10   no <u>shenanigans</u> today,
11   and we'll have our naptime,
12   and then when we wake up →
13   do you know what we're doing?
14 Natalie: What are we doing after naptime.
   ((*Janet describes activities for the afternoon/evening*))

Here, Janet prompts Natalie to use a familylect word. Natalie's proper identification of the word indicates not only her acquaintance with the word "shenanigans" but also how naptime in the Neeley-Mason household is supposed to work.

The next day, "shenanigans" surfaces again, this time with Natalie using the word to contradict what Janet expects her to say about them. In excerpt 12, Janet and Natalie are about to take a nap, and Natalie talks about wanting to play doctor afterward. Again, Janet prompts her to say the word "shenanigans." It is first uttered excitedly by Natalie, who, undoubtedly knowing shenanigans are not allowed at naptime, proposes that they are. This could be an attempt to be humorous or to engage her mother in verbal interaction.

(12) 1 Natalie: We can play doctors when we wake up,
2   and I'll be the mommy and you be the doctor,
3   okay?
4 Janet: Okay,

5		but what's there- what do we have to do first?
6	Natalie:	What.
7		Have naptime.
8	Janet:	Right.
9		And what are you gonna do today.
10	Natalie:	Shenanigans!
11	Janet:	NO shenanigans.
12	Natalie:	YES shenanigans!
13	Janet:	Well then there won't be time for doctor.
14	Natalie:	What.
15	Janet:	Then they'll be no time to play doctor.
16		Yesterday was WA:Y too many shenanigans,
17		today we have to settle down.

This example is parallel to the earlier example (shown in excerpt 1) in which Natalie disagreed with Steve using his words, saying that "we brush our choppers downstairs" to contradict his comment that "we brush our choppers in the bathroom." Here Natalie uses the familylect term "shenanigans," but not in the way it was intended. This leads to an extended conversation between Janet and Natalie— thereby putting off naptime. Talking about shenanigans itself becomes shenanigans.

There was only one instance on the Neeley-Masons' tapes in which the word "shenanigans" was used to refer to the behavior of a family member other than Natalie. In excerpt 13, Steve and Janet talk about recording, and Janet uses the word when talking about Steve. In line 1, Steve teases Janet for not keeping track of the tapes she has recorded for the project (a response, in fact, to her teasing him first, about having said something she perceived as embarrassing on tape), and Janet uses the term to refer to the fact that Steve accidentally taped over some of his previously recorded material. In using the term "shenanigans," Janet frames Steve's behavior as child-like.

(13)	1	Steve:	So what tape are you on.
	2		Oh that's right you're not counting.
	3		Never mind.
	4	Janet:	Oh [okay brown-noser.]
	5	Steve:	[<laughs>]

6   Janet: At least I haven't tried to over-tape on . old tapes.
7   Steve: Well I'm sure they won't miss the sound of my typing.
8   Janet: Haven't been any of THOSE sorts of <u>shenanigans</u> on →
9   my end!
10   Okay.
11   Now where were we (lee-lee.) ((*to Natalie*))
((*Janet and Steve announce the date and time into their recorders*))

In this example, Janet uses "shenanigans" when talking about (and teasing) Steve. Use of this word in this new context points to the shared prior experiences where Janet and Steve had to deal with Natalie's misbehavior during naptime (e.g., excerpt 10), or discussed Natalie's naptime misbehavior (e.g., excerpt 9). Intertextual links to shared prior experiences and the humorousness of Janet's "criticism" of Steve (for taping over previously recorded data) here builds solidarity between them; the familylect word "shenanigans" plays a central role in this.[4]

Overall, the word "shenanigans" is used repeatedly to refer to Natalie's misbehavior before naptime. Interestingly, this term is used only in reference to naptime misbehavior and not in reference to other situations in which Natalie is expected to behave in a particular way (e.g., during dinner or while taking a bath). It thus has a specialized family meaning; it describes a family-specific frame—a situation in which Natalie misbehaves in a particular way (by talking and playing) at a particular time (naptime). When I asked the family (via email) where the use of the term came from, Steve replied by saying he did not recall where they picked up the word and that he thought it was "part of the greater accepted vernacular." However, as previously mentioned, there were no occurrences of this word in the recorded interactions of the Patterson/Foley or the Shepherd/Sylvan families. This terminology and its specialized meaning are a part of the Neeley-Mason familylect. "Shenanigans" are situated in the Neeley-Mason family culture and the specific context of naptime (or talk about naptime), which at their house at the time of recording always entailed the possibility of Natalie misbehaving by talking when it was time to be quiet. Intertextually, production and comprehension of the term indexes a child-centered frame and binds members together as they enact (Natalie), talk about (Natalie, Janet, and Steve), or attempt to manage (Janet, Steve) shenanigans.

Having a "Meltdown"

As with "shenanigans," the term "meltdown" was used in the Neeley-Mason family and was not used at all by members of the other families during their recording periods, though Kira and Jason did have what could be describe as "meltdowns." (The Patterson/Foleys and the Shepherd/Sylvans did not, at the time of taping, have a particular word they used for tantrums, though on two occasions Kathy used the term "melt" to refer to Kira crying and throwing a tantrum.) "Meltdown" was used by Janet and Steve to refer to Natalie having a tantrum where she whines, cries, and possibly screams. This is quite different than the misbehavior captured by the word "shenanigans." In addition, the term "meltdown" was also used to refer to times when an adult loses his or her composure. However, like "shenanigans," the term centers on Natalie, and intertextual use of it plays into the construction of a child-centered family culture.

Excerpt 14 shows a typical use of the word "meltdown" in conversation between Janet and Steve. Steve uses the term in a phone conversation with Janet, who is at home with Natalie. (This conversation has been reconstructed using Janet's and Steve's separate recordings, thus, overlapping speech between Janet and Steve is not shown.) In the beginning of the excerpt, Steve explains why he had been upset that morning at home and had left without saying goodbye to Janet (this had upset her): Natalie had thrown a tantrum, thereby delaying his leaving and ultimately making him late for work (this was a recurrent pattern in this family). Natalie talks intermittently in the background to Janet; this is shown in the excerpt as well.

(14) 1 Janet: I'm sorry you were so stressed out this morning.
      2 Steve: <*sighs*>
      3   It-it- things seemed to be →
      4   going so well,
      5   but then she just [had that <u>meltdown</u> and,]
      6 Natalie: [Who is stressed out.]
      7 Janet: I know.

8   Steve: [I just have not been able to get out] →
9   Natalie: [(Who are you on the phone with) Mommy.]
10 Steve: of the house,
11   and-and it just- and that just put me in a bad →
12 Janet: Yeah.
13 Steve: way so,
14   I-I do apologize for that,
15   I-I- I know it was out of proportion but- →
16 Janet: [Well as I say,]
17 Natalie: [Why is Daddy] stressed out.
18   [(?? ?? ???)]
19 Steve: [but just that SCREAMING,]
20   it just—
21 Janet: I know.
22 Steve: Sometimes it just cuts you to the core.

Here, Steve uses "meltdown" to talk about how Natalie screamed and cried that morning at home. I suggest that along with his apology and explanation, Steve's using the familylect word "meltdown" helps smooth over the conflict caused by Steve leaving for work without saying goodbye: Janet affirms that she understands Steve's frustration (lines 7 and 21: *I know*; line 12: *Yeah*) and peace is restored. The familylect word contributes to this by indexing Janet and Steve's shared past (and ongoing struggle) dealing with Natalie's meltdowns, a struggle that binds Janet and Steve together on a day-to-day basis as a team of parents.

Janet's brother Kevin also produces the word when talking about Natalie. This shows that familylect vocabulary can extend beyond nuclear family boundaries. In excerpt 15, Kevin begins to describe to Janet and Steve the difficult time he had babysitting Natalie while Janet and Steve were at the hospital with Natalie's grandmother Laura.

(15) 1 Janet: How was your day.
      2   ((*short pause*))
      3 Kevin: Challenging.

4   Janet: Uh oh.
5   Steve: Oh boy.
6   Janet: <*slightly laughing*> What happened.>
7   Kevin: There were a few <u>meltdowns</u>.
8   Steve: [Oh no.]
9   Janet: [Oh no,]
10   really?
11   What happened.

As the conversation continues, Kevin describes how Natalie spilled water on her dress and screamed and cried when he tried to change it and how she had a tantrum when he tried to put her to bed (see Gordon 2007a for a detailed analysis of this conversation, including the repeated uses of "oh no" and "oh boy" by Janet and Steve). Kevin uses the term "meltdown" to refer to a tantrum, just as Janet and Steve do; this member of the extended family shows access to this familylect vocabulary item.

Though "meltdown" is normally used in reference to Natalie's behavior, Janet used the term when talking about Steve's behavior on two occasions. Excerpt 16 gives one example (a second example appears in chapter 4). Janet and Steve talk while watching television (the TV show has gone to commercial) on a Wednesday night. Steve sounds tired throughout, and Janet tries to figure out what's bothering him; she refers to what is happening to him as a "meltdown."

(16) 1   Janet: You all right?
      2   Steve: Yea::h.
      3   Janet: What's the matter.
      4   Steve: <*sighs*>
      5   I'm wasting away.
      6   Janet: Tired?
      7   Steve: Yeah a little bit.
      8   Janet: What's the matter.
      9   Steve: My conscience is guilty.
     10   Janet: Why?
     11   Steve: 'Cause I'm sitting here doing nothing.
     12   Janet: Oh <*chuckling*> God.>
     13   Well what you think you should be doing.
     14   Oohff! ((*baby kicks Janet, it seems*))

15	Steve:	Whopper? ((*meaning, "big kick?"*))
16	Janet:	Come tell your son to calm down.
17		What do you think you should be doing my love.
18	Steve:	I should be productive.
19	Janet:	Oh boy.
20		<*clears throat*>
21		You can go put this on the shelf,
22		if you really want to be productive.
23	Steve:	See this is my dilemna, ((*pronounced with an "n"*))
24		[<*laughs*>]
25	Janet:	[You don't want to be productive!]
26		Why do you have to be productive dear.
27		Can't you relax?
28	Steve:	The:::—
29		((*short pause*))
30	Janet:	<*small groan of physical discomfort*>
31		((*long pause*))
32	Steve:	Hmm.
33		(It's difficult for me.)
34	Janet:	<*laughs*>
35		What's difficult dear.
36		Sitting?
37		Flipping through? ((*re: channels? magazine pages?*))
38		What's the— what's the trauma.
39	Steve:	I can't describe it.
40	Janet:	Oh boy.
41		Yep,
42		you're having a <u>meltdown</u> all right.

((*Janet leaves the room to go to the bathroom*))

In this excerpt, Janet uses "meltdown" to describe the emotional crisis Steve seems to be having. The meaning of the word here is different (though related) to how it is used in relation to Natalie. Though Steve does not cry or scream, he expresses an emotional crisis through words. In fact, the alignment between Janet and Steve constructed in this conversation shows interesting parallels with alignments between Janet and Natalie when she has a meltdown. Janet encourages Steve to verbalize his thoughts and emotions, asking him questions and trying to determine *what's the trauma* (line 38). Steve responds that he *can't describe it* (line 39). In "meltdown" interactions with Natalie, Natalie cries and screams and Janet and Steve encourage her to "use her words." Thus the word "meltdown" not only reinforces its position in the familylect but also highlights recurrent alignments in the family: When one family member is having a "meltdown," another will encourage that person to verbally share their feelings about it. Note that Sillars (1995:381) identifies operation on the principle that "putting thoughts into words" is important as a "mainstream American" phenomenon; the fact that Janet is training as a psychotherapist may contribute to the frequency of these kinds of interactions.[5]

"Meltdown," though not as ubiquitous as "shenanigans," is a recognizable part of this family's way of speaking. It describes a particular type of misbehavior nearly three-year-old Natalie was regularly manifesting at the time of recording, although the term is also used to describe how the parents might react in dealing with such a meltdown—with a meltdown of their own. Using this word across interactions not only reproduces a familylect feature intertextually, it also indexes the family's (and the familylect's) child-centeredness. The word's use binds Janet and Steve together in their everyday dealings with meltdowns of all types.

"Buppie": Signal of Discontent and Despair

Whereas "shenanigans" is fairly easily understood as occurring when Natalie talks and plays during naptime, and "meltdown" is essentially a synonym for tantrum when talking about Natalie or emotional crisis when talking about an adult, the term I consider next, "buppie," is not as easily defined. In fact, it took me some time to realize that it was a meaningful word at all. This word has three variants ("buppie," "boppy," and "buppa"), but all seem to be the same word. When I asked Steve about this word via email approximately fifteen months after they recorded, he had two explanations of what the word meant. First, he describes "boppy" as a "life-preserver shaped pillow" given to the family by a friend when Natalie was a baby, the purpose of which was to hold up the baby before she was able to sit up by herself. (There is a company named Boppy that makes such pillows.) Second, Steve noted this was a word Natalie used to soothe herself when she was upset, though the word could have also meant "anything or nothing" to her. The excerpts in this section show that Natalie indeed utters "buppie" or one of its variants when she is upset, frustrated, or on the verge of a tantrum; they also demonstrate that the parents recognize the term and at times use it as well.

Steve was actually captured on the recording describing "buppie" to his sister, Sylvia. Sylvia had come over to babysit Natalie while Janet and Steve went to their Saturday children's theater performance (recall that Janet and Steve are actors). Steve and Sylvia chatted before they left, and "buppie" came up (in the form of the variant "boppy").

(17)	1	Steve:	Whoo!
	2	Sylvia:	Who's on your underwear. ((*to Natalie*))
	3	Natalie:	(?)
	4	Sylvia:	Hunh?
	5	Natalie:	Mulan. ((*Disney's Mulan, most likely*))
	6	Sylvia:	Mulan oh.
	7	Natalie:	<*laughs*>
	8		Bah!
	9	Sylvia:	Bah.
	10	Natalie:	<u>Boppy</u>.
	11	Sylvia:	<u>Boppy</u>?
	12	Steve:	<u>Boppy</u> is the . is the word.
	13		I don't- can't explain it.
	14		But→
	15	Sylvia:	<u>Boppy</u>!
	16	Steve:	if she's in a [moment] of despair→
	17	Natalie:	[<u>Boppy</u>]
	18	Steve:	it's usually "<u>boppy boppy boppy</u>."
	19	Sylvia:	It's my friend's daughter's name for her grandfather.
	20	Steve:	Oh yeah?

((*conversation turns to talking about Steve's work*))

Here Steve explains "buppie" (here, the variant "boppy" is used) to his sister; this reveals that when this conversation was recorded, Sylvia was not familiar with the Neeley-Mason family's use of this term (for her, it has other connotations). Her nonaccess momentarily positions her as a relative outsider, though because Steve explains the meaning of the word, she will have access to it in the future. Although Natalie uses the word here and a tantrum does not seem to be immediately forthcoming, a transition (a prime time for tantrums) is in the works, as her parents will soon leave her in the care of her aunt.

Excerpt 18 shows "buppie" in action, as Natalie utters it in a whiney voice during a tantrum. Here Janet is packing Natalie's backpack for preschool when Natalie starts kicking or hitting something, producing a banging sound (line 1).

(18) 1   ((*short pause, banging sound*))
      2   Janet: Natalie,
      3   what are you doing.
      4   What are you doing.
      5   Why are you so angry this morning.
      6   Natalie: <*whiney, loud*> Buppie!>
      7   Janet: Why are you angry.
      8   Natalie: <*yelling*> Because!>
      9   Janet: Because why.
      10 Natalie: <*yelling*> Because!>
      11 Janet: Use your words.
      12 Natalie: <*whiney*> No.>
      13 Janet: Try to use your words.
      14 Natalie: <*whiney*> No,
      15   [I can't.>]
      16 Janet: [Well,]
      17   we can't- we can't help you →
      18   if we don't know what's going on.

This excerpt also shows Janet encouraging Natalie to "use [her] words" (lines 11, 13) during a meltdown, similar to how she encouraged Steve to talk about his feelings in excerpt 16.

Later that same day, while Janet is reading Natalie books at naptime, Natalie says "buppie" again, this time using it in a sentence as a noun, though still using it to signal discontent. This time, she wants

Janet to put a "scrunchie," a type of cloth ponytail holder, in her (Natalie's) hair.

(19) 1 Janet: Okay,
      2   what's next. ((*re: which book is next*))
      3 Natalie: The scrunchie [is next.]
      4 Janet: [What's—] Christmas is Coming?
      5 Natalie: I want the scrunchie.
      6 Janet: <*reading*> Wrapping presents [is such fun,>]
      7 Natalie: [Awawawawawa] →
      8   scrunchie.
      9 Janet: You can hold the scrunchie.
     10   Would you like to hold it.
     11 Natalie: No.
     12 Janet: Okay.
     13   <*reading*> Eating [cookies one by one.>]
     14 Natalie: [I want <u>buppie, buppie</u>!]
     15   <u>Buppie</u>!
     16 Janet: Natalie,
     17   <*reading*> Time to play in the snow,>
     18 Natalie: (???)
     19 Janet: All right,
     20   then I'm not reading books.
     21 Natalie: <*whiney, loud*> I want- I want <u>buppie</u>,
     22   I want to read books!>
     23 Janet: Well I don't like the way you're acting.
     24   I don't like it.
     25   Are you going to listen to the stories or not.
     26 Natalie: <*quietly*> Yes (I am.)>
     ((*Janet resumes reading*))

In this excerpt of talk, "buppie" indicates Natalie's displeasure that Janet will not put the scrunchie in her hair (although Janet does offer to let her hold it). It also signals that she does not want to take a nap but would rather read books. In the end, Janet does not put the scrunchie in Natalie's hair, though she does continue to read books to her.

The next excerpt shows Natalie using "buppie" (here as "buppa") to signal a tantrum yet to come; it also reveals how Steve feels about Natalie's recurrent tantrums. It is morning—a prime time for tantrums—and Steve had been making himself a peanut butter and jelly sandwich to take to work for lunch and has been telling Natalie that they need to brush her choppers. But Natalie wants the sandwich, and a huge tantrum erupts. (This is an interaction Steve later describes as a "meltdown" to Janet.)

(20) 1 Natalie: <u>Buppa</u>!
      2 Steve: *<quietly, perhaps to himself>* Please no <u>buppa</u>.>
      3 Natalie: AHHHH!
      4   <u>Buppie</u>!
      5 Steve: Why <u>buppie</u>.
      6 Natalie: I want some peanut butter and jelly sandwich.

Here "buppie" precedes and signals one of the biggest tantrums Natalie threw during the recording period.

Excerpts 17–20, which include "buppie" or its variants ("boppy," "buppa") show that Natalie frequently utters this word when she is frustrated, angry, or on the verge of a tantrum. What it means is known by people who are clearly part of the nuclear family (Janet, Steve, and Natalie) but is not necessarily known by extended family members. It is also notable that the parents mirror whichever form of the word Natalie produces at a given time, thus showing attentiveness to her when she is upset. This shows how the word is centered around Natalie and how she "controls" the word.

"Buppie" is a word seemingly created by Natalie to soothe herself when she is upset, and it may relate to comfort she felt as an infant sitting in the Boppy pillow. "Shenanigans," "meltdown," and "buppie" together capture Natalie's everyday misbehaviors and her parents' efforts to deal with them; their existence points toward the centrality of Natalie's misbehavior in the family's culture and talking about and managing them as primary child-centered family frames. In addition, each time these words are used, they become further "populated" with the voices of family members. Thus, even though these behaviors are negative (some more than others), through repeatedly using the same words to talk about them, family members index their shared past experiences with these words and with each other. Another, perhaps more parent-centered way of thinking about this is that Janet and Steve, in using these words, index an ongoing, everyday part of what being a parent means in their lives: struggling together to manage their child's misbehavior.

Words for the Child's Bedtime Ritual: "Rocks and Rubs"

The word "rocks" and its partner, "rubs," refer to parts of the bedtime ritual for Natalie. I use the term "ritual" here in its noncanonical sense, in the spirit of Goffman's (1967) concept of "interaction ritual"—the idea that everyday social interactions are patterned and carry symbolic import—and corresponding with anthropological perspectives on the ordinary cultural routines of everyday life (Shore 2003:3).[6] "Rocks and rubs" occurred immediately after another required component of the pattern: book reading. It is thus a way of prolonging Natalie's bedtime. Thus the ritual can be viewed as a kind of "discourse of anticipation" that at once "prepares for—yet simultaneously forestalls—the moment of bedtime separation" (Sirota 2006:497). As Steve described to me in an email message approximately five years after the family recorded:

> Rocks and rubs refers to part of our bedtime ritual for Natalie, where, after reading her some books, she'd sit on the lap of whomever was putting her down [to bed] while sitting in a rocking chair for a few minutes, then when we'd transfer her to her crib we'd stand there and rub her back until our arm fell off. If we dared try to leave the room before she was asleep then she'd start screaming bloody murder and we'd have to start over again. Boy did she have us whipped!

"Rocks and rubs," as part of the bedtime ritual, also has the function of keeping Natalie's behavior in check; it is thus linked in some way to temper tantrums.

Though the terms "rocks" and "rubs" frequently occur together on the family's recordings, they occur separately as well. The repeated use of the terms is demonstrated in the following excerpts, which also highlight the connotations of intimacy, comfort, and familyness associated with "rocks" and "rubs." Excerpt 21 shows Natalie complaining that she wants her mother to perform the bedtime ritual as Steve prepares to take her upstairs. This is after Steve and Janet have had an argument, and it seems Natalie is upset about this.

(21)　17　Natalie:　<*whining*> No I want Mommy (read me books).

　　　　18　　　　　　(And I want her to) give me <u>rocks and rubs</u>.>

Later that same evening, Steve helps Natalie brush her teeth and mentions "rocks." Natalie checks to see that she will get "rubs," too, demonstrating that these two words are paired together in the familylect and that the actions are paired together in the bedtime ritual. (Note that when Steve says he is uncertain if Mommy can bend down to give Natalie rubs, he is likely referring to the fact that Janet is pregnant and has been having some pain in her back.)

(22)　1　Steve:　Okay let's brush.

　　　　2　　　　　Natalie let's brush,

　　　　3　　　　　and then Mommy'll give you <u>rocks</u>.

　　　　4　Natalie:　Okay!

　　　　5　　　　　You will give me <u>rubs</u>,

　　　　6　　　　　you will give me <u>rubs</u> too!

　　　　7　　　　　Would you like that?

　　　　8　Steve:　Well I don't know if Mommy can really →

　　　　9　　　　　bend over very well to give you <u>rubs</u>.

　　　　10　　　　　She'll give you nice <u>rocks</u>.

As with the other terms that relate to Natalie, Janet and Steve use the terms "rocks" and "rubs" when talking about Natalie when she is not present. In the next excerpt, Janet was in the process of describing to Steve how she had put Natalie to bed while her friends were over for a dinner party.

(23)　1　Janet:　So somehow we all got up there → ((*"there"* = *upstairs*))

　　　　2　　　　　under the guise of showing everybody her big-girl bed,

3		and- but it was very funny,
4		so I read her books and . she didn't- I- →
5		I tried to avoid <u>rocks</u> just because I was →
6		trying to speed things along,
7		and she didn't say a word about <u>rocks</u>,
8		and just climbed in that bed →
9		and was like. ((*gestures?*))
10		<*laughing*> you know,>
11		she was just- because I thought it might be →
12		a big problem getting her . down,
13		but she was SO tired,
14	Steve:	She was done.
15	Janet:	Yeah,
16		she was done.

In this excerpt, Janet uses the term "rocks" to talk with Steve about an instance in which Natalie's bedtime ritual is modified. The excerpt also reinforces the fact that rocks and rubs are linked to Natalie's misbehavior and wanting to talk and play instead of going to sleep. Steve and Janet have developed a special ritual to calm her down, and there is some risk in modifying this ritual.

The terms "rocks" and "rubs" take on a meaning in this family beyond simply rocking Natalie in a rocking chair and rubbing her back. The next excerpt shows the connotations of affection and caring associated with rocks and rubs. Around the time of recording, Janet's mother, Laura, had been regularly babysitting Natalie while Janet went to work, but had recently become ill. Here Janet is preparing Natalie for staying with Laura on a day when Laura was not feeling well.

(24)	1	Janet:	Yes,
	2		we need to help Boo-Boo today.
	3		Be on our best behavior.
	4	Natalie:	I'm going to help her feel a little better.
	5	Janet:	It will help her feel better if you don't scream,
	6		and you listen when she talks to you,
	7		okay?
	8	Natalie:	I'm gonna help her feel better.
	9	Janet:	I bet you will.

10   [Okay.]
11 Natalie: [Is <u>rubs</u>] gonna help her feel better?
12 Janet: What's that?
13 Natalie: Is <u>rubs</u> gonna help her feel better?
14 Janet: Oh I bet some <u>rubs </u>would help her feel better,
15   that would be nice.
16   ((*short pause*))
17   I bet she'd like <u>rubs</u>.

"Rubs" here is used outside the bedtime ritual context, and outside the parent–child relationship. In this excerpt, "rubs" is something the Neeley-Masons share with their family: Natalie wants to give rubs to her grandmother.

On arriving at Laura's house, the term comes up again. Excerpt 25 further emphasizes the positive emotional connotations with the word. It begins with Laura responding to Natalie's question if she will play with her.

(25) 1 Laura: I'm going to be um not a very active participant today.
      2 Janet: Remember,
      3   Boo-Boo's not been feeling her best right?
      4 Laura: Yeah,
      5   Boo-Boo still has a tummy that's NOT behaving →
      6   itself.
      7 Janet: So we've got to take it a little bit easy with Boo-Boo→
      8   today.
      9 Laura: I think I need a massage though,
      10   do you think you could give me one?
      11 Janet: Oh she was saying she was going to give you <u>rubs</u>,
      12   weren't you?
      13 Laura: Give me <u>rubs</u>?
      14   Oh that'll [help a lot.]
      15 Janet: [<*chuckles*>]

Though Laura uses the term "massage" in this excerpt, Janet uses the word "rubs," which she knows Natalie recognizes. Laura also seems to recognize the term. Thus this familylect term extends to an extended family member in this case. In addition, the word "give" helps to frame "rubs" as a gift for family members.

Both "rocks" and "rubs" surface while Natalie is playing with her dolls and enacting the Mommy role vis-à-vis the dolls. At the beginning of the next excerpt, Steve is reading a book that describes bedtime activities. In line 10, Natalie introduces pretend play.

(26) 1 Steve: <*reading*> And take a bath.>
2 Natalie: Take a bath
3 Steve: <*reading*>Scrub a dub a dub.
4 Put on pajamas.>
5 Natalie: Put on . pajamas.
6 And have <u>rocks</u>,
7 and go to sleep.
8 Have <u>rubs</u>,
9 ((*short pause*))
10 I'll be the momma and you be the dada.
11 I'll pretend . →
12 all of my girls are going to sleep. ((*"girls"* = *dolls*))
13 Steve: Okay.
14 ((*short pause*))
15 You gonna put them down?
16 Natalie: First we have . <u>ro:cks</u>.
17 <u>Rocks</u> first.
18 <u>Rocks</u> first.
19 Steve: Will you g— which one are you gonna give <u>rocks</u> →
20 to first.
21 Natalie: (That girl) who's missing a eye.
22 Steve: Okay.

Here Natalie as "the momma" talks about the bedtime ritual in relation to her dolls. It is clear that "rocks" comes before "rubs," and these words have connotations of care and connection in family usage; in other words, they signal frames of attention and caring. Indeed, bedtime rituals have been identified as a site of "relational work" in families (Sirota 2006). Natalie's bedtime ritual—and the terms used to describe its elements—thus re-create a family culture featuring child-centeredness and connection; Natalie creates a mini-version of this culture in her pretend play.

"Rocks and rubs" is a collocation used by the Neeley-Masons to refer Natalie's bedtime ritual, though each word is also used individually. Like the meaning of "buppie," the meaning of "rocks and rubs" would not be transparent or even decipherable to outsiders of the family. Use of these terms, in addition to those discussed previously, mark the Neeley-Masons as a social group with a unique lexicon containing words linked to the specific contexts of their use—a family culture that revolves, in some sense, around managing the child's (mis)behavior.

Routine Ways of Speaking: Creating Play and Performance

The routinized (or ritual) interactions captured in the Neeley-Mason family's recordings can be viewed as having a binding function among family members; the bedtime ritual was one example. Other rituals revolved more explicitly around talk. Two everyday talk-based rituals especially served to create frames of play and performance in the discourse of this family. Interestingly, it has been observed that ritual is a genre similar to play: Both are framed activities (Shore 1996:90). In addition, ritual is inherently linked to the notion of performance; it is a "manifestation of the essentially theatrical nature of human behavior" (Shore 2003:1). I thus consider recurrent exchanges that move beyond child-centered lexical items, exploring also frames that can be characterized as couple-centered.

"My Love/My Dove" and "My Dear": Paired Terms of Endearment and the Construction of Couple-Centered Frames

I now turn to an everyday ritual that occurs between adults in the Neeley-Mason family: Janet and Steve's repeated use of reciprocal pairs of terms of endearment, "my love"/"my dove," and "my dear"/"my dear," in everyday interaction. I suggest that the ritual (re)creates playful, couple-centered frames, or what (Kendall 2006) calls "couple-centered footings," in the discourse of this family. In contrast to frames that focus on the child, couple-centered frames and footings foreground "non-parental social relations within the family," for instance "married partners" or "lovers" (Kendall 2006:424).

Though terms of endearment were used in all three families, Janet and Steve Neeley-Mason used a particularly noticeable variety of these terms to address one another and to address Natalie. For example, they called one another "dear," "my love," "my dove," "darling," and "lovie." The Patterson/Foleys and the third family, the Shepherd/ Sylvans, did not use any of these terms during their recording periods. Kathy and Sam most frequently used one another's first names (with Sam frequently calling Kathy "Kath"); in the presence of Kira they tended to use the terms "Mommy/Mama" and "Daddy/Dada." They called Kira by name or "Ki-Ki," though she was also referred to as "munkin" (which seems to be a variation of "munchkin") and "baby." Clara Shepherd and Neil Sylvan used a number of terms of endearment when talking to Jason (e.g., Clara called Jason "Jasie," "Jasie-pooh," and "tweeters," and both Clara and Neil called him "sweetie" quite often, and less frequently, "honey"). Clara and Neil did not use terms of endearment when speaking to each other; they used first names. In fact, once during the week of recording, Neil responded when Clara addressed Jason as "cuddle bunny," resulting in shared laughter. In contrast, when Janet addressed Steve as "cuddles," the term was treated as unmarked.

The Neeley-Masons used "sweetheart" more frequently than the Patterson/Foleys and the Shepherd/Sylvans. During their recording period, the Patterson/Foleys used the word "sweetheart" four times (Kathy used "sweetheart" three times when talking to Kira, and once when talking to Sam). In the Shepherd/Sylvan family, the term was used twice, both instances of Clara talking to Jason. In contrast, during the Neeley-Masons' recording period, members of the family used the word 135 times. This included several instances of Natalie using it when playing the role of mommy in role-play. Furthermore, whereas the Neeley-Masons referred to each other using "honey" 337 times, the Patterson/Foleys referred to each other using this term only eighteen times, and the Shepherd/Sylvans used "honey" four times (three times Clara to Jason; one time Neil to Jason). Thus the Neeley-Masons used a wider variety of terms of endearment and produced them a greater number of times. Here I focus on Janet and Steve's use of terms of endearment as reciprocal pairs, demonstrating how this creates playful, family-specific frames. Sam and Kathy did not do this, nor did Clara and Neil.

The first excerpt shows Janet and Steve finishing up a phone call on the second day of recording using the expressions "my love" and "my dove." Janet also uses the term "dear." For this conversation, Steve was at work and Janet was at home. Notice also the repetition of "all right."

(27) 1 Janet: Well I suppose I will talk to you later.
      2 Steve: Yes ma'am.
      3 Janet: And I'll keep you updated →
      4   what our plan looks like,
      5 Steve: Yes ma'am.
      6 Janet: All right <u>my love</u>?
      7 Steve: All right <u>my dove</u>.
      8 Janet: I love you <u>dear</u>.

The "my love/my dove" pair here serves to mark the nearing closure of Janet and Steve's phone call while also sending a metamessage of couple-ness. The repetition and prosody has a playful quality (as does Steve's use of "ma'am"). This was one typical use of paired terms of endearment.

Excerpt 28 shows both endearment pairs, "my love/my dove" and "my dear/my dear." Here, Janet is preparing in advance for a dinner party she will be having with her friends (Steve will be going to one of his restaurant jobs), and she tries to get Steve to help her.

(28) 1 Janet: You have to help me chop garlic and tomatoes and (?)
      2   [<u>My dea::r</u>.]
      3 Steve: [Of course <u>my love</u>.]
      4 Janet: <u>My dea:r</u>
      5 Steve: 'Course <u>my dove</u>.
      6 Janet: Ho!
      7   Something tells me that you're not as helpful →
      8   as you might be.

This shows Janet providing the "my dear/my dear" pair and Steve producing the "my love/my dove" pair. This is interaction is in a particularly playful key. Janet asks for a (small) favor, and Steve agrees (though apparently pretending he will not help, thus prompting Janet's remarks in lines 7–8: *Something tells me that you're not as helpful as you might be*). Both use language that implies a larger imposition than the request really is. They thus joke with one another and perform for each other and possibly also for the researchers who would later listen to the recordings.

Excerpt 29 shows the reciprocal use of "my dear," but the situation is quite different. Janet and Steve talk at the obstetrician's office after having had an argument that morning at home because Steve forgot about the appointment (to which he had said he would accompany Janet). Near the beginning of the excerpt, Steve apologizes for having forgotten about it and explains that in fact he did have the appointment noted in his calendar. Their use of "my dear" introduces the conversational moves of apology and acceptance after an earlier argument (this is the beginning of the longer conversation in which Steve describes Natalie's morning meltdown to Janet [shown in excerpt 14]).

(29) 1   Steve: Hi there. ((*Steve is walking into the office*))
      2   Janet: Hello.
      3   Steve: How are you doing.
      4   Janet: Fine how are you.
      5   Steve: Good.
      6   Janet: <*sighs*>
      7   ((*short pause*))
      8   Steve: <u>My dear,</u>
      9   I'm sorry about this morning,
     10   and I- I did have it in my book here.
     11   Janet: You did?
     12   Steve: Yeah.
     13   Janet: Oh <u>dea:r</u>.
     14   Steve: "See Doctor Brown this morning." ((*reading?*))
     15   Janet: <*laughing*> A:w.>
     16   Yes <u>my dear</u>.
     17   Steve: <u>My dear</u> I'm just—
     18   This is just my- my Achilles heel.
     19   Janet: Why?
     20   Steve: I'm just-
     21   ((*short pause*))
     22   I- I- just have not r- adopted it → ((*"it" = day planner*))

23   into my day-to-day . life,
24   Janet: [Well you must.]
25   Steve: [I- I try to,]
26   I know I must.

As Steve uses "my dear" as a way of beginning to apologize to Janet (line 8), she uses "my dear" to accept this apology (line 16). Whereas in excerpt 27 it marked the nearing of the end of a phone call, here it marks two moves in an apology sequence (apology and acceptance). The couple-ness and playful key associated with the routine are drawn on here to begin to make up after an argument; the repetition shows alignment and cooperation in this endeavor, as does Janet's gentle laughter in line 15.

In a similar way, the next day Janet apologizes to Steve for being upset with him regarding the forgotten appointment and introduces her apology with "my dear." Steve responds starting with "my dear." Here, they had just started driving to their children's theater performance (Natalie is at home with Sylvia). Janet has just remarked that the neighbors are planting some new grass. Then there is a pause in the conversation.

(30) 1   ((*short pause*))
      2   Janet: My dear,
      3   I'm sorry if I'm not as flexible as I might be.
      4   Steve: My dear,
      5   I understand what's going on,
      6   you've got a lot of things going on right now,
      7   and I do understand that and .. →
      8   we just need to take it a day at a time,
      9   that's all.
     10   Janet: That's right.

Steve matches Janet's introduction of her apology with "my dear" by beginning his own acceptance of that apology with "my dear." "My dear" thus works toward transition to a new topic of talk, and a new frame of interaction of a conversation of married persons whose lives are interconnected. Before this conversation started, Janet was commenting on something she saw out the car window. "My dear" thus also marks Janet's attention moving back into the intimate family realm. Steve's matching shows his cooperation in this endeavor.

These excerpts collectively illustrate how endearment term use is patterned between Janet and Steve: They are often used as pairs in interaction, creating a routine of exchanging matching affectionate terms; they are also used to segment interaction (in this way, I suggest that they seem to have a discourse marking function, following Schiffrin 1987). This ritualized way of interacting not only marks closures and transitions in interaction, it is also a humorous strategy that sends a metamessage of rapport and familiarity, creating couple-centered, playful interactive frames. Perhaps for this reason, this pattern often surfaces during the resolution of conflicts; the ritual seems to work as a kind of metaphorical glue, pulling the partners back together. Because each use points to all prior uses, this way of speaking is reinforced as is family membership. By intertextually exchanging terms of agreement, Janet and Steve re-create a family-specific—indeed, a couple-specific—frame that works toward defining and maintaining their relationship.

Speaking in Multiple Voices: Playing and Performing

In addition to repeatedly exchanging terms of endearment in mutual ways, Janet and Steve recurrently use multiple "voices" in their daily talk. Though all individuals speak in "other voices" in their daily lives (e.g., through using constructed dialogue in narrative and other means of reshaping the prior text of others), Janet and Steve frequently manipulated pitch and accent when speaking to each other but not necessarily quoting a particular person. (Bear in mind that Janet and Steve were trained as actors, met through theater, and act on weekends in a children's theater troupe. Thus acting, or speaking in character voices, is a skill they share, and this no doubt contributes to their notable manipulation of pitch and accent in everyday talk.) I illustrate how Janet and Steve do this for the purpose of playing with, entertaining, or encouraging Natalie to do things and for humorous and affectionate effect between the two of them. As a familylect strategy, it reveals linguistic innovativeness, creativity, and playfulness; it repeatedly creates frames of play and performance.

Entertaining and encouraging Natalie through voices.   Janet and Steve frequently engaged in role-play with Natalie during the week of recording. In doing this, they often assume "play" voices. For example, Janet uses a high-pitched voice to signal that she is playing the role of "Natalie" in their frequent role-reversal pretend play (see e.g., Gordon 2002,

2006). Janet also uses marked pitch and/or accent in other types of role-play, for example where she plays the roles of a baby, a British claymation character (Wallace of *Wallace and Gromit*), Natalie's preschool teacher, and a doctor. Steve also manipulates pitch in role-play interactions with Natalie; for instance, he uses a markedly low-pitched voice as he pretends to be a doctor, a high-pitched voice while enacting Natalie's dolls, and a "spooky" voice while pretending to be the Wizard of Oz.

In addition to using marked pitch while engaged in role-play with Natalie, Janet and Steve also use it to entertain her while they accomplish other activities. In excerpt 31, Janet keeps Natalie amused as they are driving to Laura's ("Boo-Boo's") house by pretending to be the pilot of an airplane. Janet uses a monotone, deep voice that sounds muffled as if she has her had held to her nose and mouth to simulate a loudspeaker, and she directs her utterances to the "passengers" of the "airplane." The radio is on in the background, making some of Natalie's utterances difficult to decipher.

(31) 1 ⇨ Janet: <*loudspeaker voice*> Passengers,
        2 ⇨   we'll be landing in about twenty minutes,
        3 ⇨   at Boo-Boo's house.>
        4   Natalie: We're (??)
        5   we're (landing) at Boo-Boo's house.
        6 ⇨ Janet: <*loudspeaker voice*> Yes passengers.>
        7   Natalie: (Let's fly there).
        8 ⇨ Janet: <*loudspeaker voice*>Yes,
        9 ⇨   now we are flying the plane.>
       10   Natalie: Flying the plane.

Natalie contributes to this play framing by repeating Janet's words.

Excerpt 32 shows Janet animating a character voice through pitch manipulation while reading a book to Natalie at bedtime. The book is about the character Elmo from the children's TV show *Sesame Street*. On television, this puppet is animated using a squeaky high-pitched voice, which Janet mimics to perfection.

(32) 1 ⇨ Janet: <*reading, high-pitched like Elmo*> Did you know →

2 ⇨   that furry little red monsters are very ticklish?
3 ⇨   Tickle Elmo's toes.>
4   Can you tickle his toes?
5 ⇨   <*laughs, very high-pitched*> ((*sounds just like Elmo*))
6 ⇨   <*reading, very high-pitched, like Elmo*> [That tickles!]>
7   Natalie: [<*laughs*>]

Other times during the recording week, Janet and Steve read other books to Natalie using appropriate accents and pitches for different characters. For example, Steve reads one book using a Scottish accent, and while reading the story of the three bears, he animates the mother bear using a high-pitched voice and the father bear using a deep voice.

In the next excerpt, Janet manipulates phonology in interaction with Natalie. She uses an Italian accent while trying to get Natalie to leave the playground so they can go home and make pizza for dinner. Janet also sings a funny song, most likely trying to make the idea of pizza sound fun. (The pizza song seems to be part of a family ritual when they make pizza.) Janet and Natalie are playing at the playground in the following excerpt.

(33) 1   Janet: Oh you know what?
     2   It's time for us to go back home!
     3   Natalie: Why.
     4 ⇨ Janet: <*Italian accent*> Because we've got to →
     5 ⇨   make the pizza pie!>
     6   <*singing*> Yoo do do do do do do,
     7   do do do do do do do do.>
     8   Come on,
     9   [we'll go sing] the pizza song.
     10   Natalie: [(???)]
     11   ((*short pause*))
     12   Janet: Do you know how it goes.
     13   Natalie: No.

Janet uses the Italian accent and the pizza song to try to get Natalie to leave the playground without a fuss so they can go home and make dinner. In doing so, she tries to frame the interaction as playful. True to form, Natalie resists, saying in line 13 that she does not know the pizza song, though she does sing it later at home.

Similarly, in the next excerpt, Steve uses a marked voice to try to get Natalie to give Janet a good morning hug and kiss, and he does not succeed, though Natalie is clearly entertained by his antics, responding with laughter. They are in the kitchen on Sunday morning. Natalie has just told Janet that she (Natalie) will be using two spoons to eat her cereal.

(34)	1	Janet:	Two spoons!
	2		<*affectionately*> You funny little love. ((*to Natalie*))
	3		Did I get a morning hug and kiss?>
	4	Natalie:	No.
	5	Janet:	I don't remember.
	6		Do you think I could have one?
	7	Natalie:	No.
	8		After breakfast you can have one.
	9	Janet:	<*pretends to cry*> Boo-oo-hoo!>
	10		No hug?
	11	Natalie:	After breakfast.
	12	Janet:	<*whispers*> Just one!>
	13 ⇨	Steve:	<*"reprimand"*> No prebreakfast hug for the →
	14		Mom-a?>
	15	Janet:	<*whispers*> Just one.>
	16	Natalie:	No!
	17 ⇨	Steve:	<*low-pitched*> Oh! Give her a hug won't ya!>
	18	Natalie:	<*laughs*>
	19	Steve:	Give her-
	20	Natalie:	After breakfast I will.

Steve, like Janet, manipulates voices to entertain Natalie. Here he uses a pretend or false reprimand voice and an extremely low-pitched voice to encourage her to give her mother a hug. Janet contributes to encouraging Natalie by pretending to cry (line 9) and whispering (lines 12, 15). Natalie responds by resisting, thus prolonging the playful interaction.

In sum, the excerpts demonstrate how Janet and Steve repeatedly manipulate pitch or accent to entertain (or perform for) Natalie and to try to win her over when they want her to do something and she resists. This works to create child-centered frames that are also playful in nature. In addition, the use of play voices in interaction with Natalie fits in with other playful strategies this family uses, such as the parents reciprocally calling each other "my love" and "my dove" and using the playful term "choppers." In the next section, I show how Janet and Steve manipulate pitch and/or accent for each other's benefit, performing for each other (and possibly for the researchers) rather than for Natalie.

Voices, humor, and affection among spouses. Janet and Steve's use of marked voices is not limited to entertaining Natalie. In excerpt 35, Steve uses a "theatrical" voice in responding to Janet. The family is eating breakfast on Sunday morning. A radio station playing popular music from the 1980s and 1990s is on in the background.

(35) 1   Steve: Here we come . sweetie. ((*to Natalie*))
    2   Janet: Here we come peaches. ((*to Natalie*))
    3   M- how about some juice?
    4 ⇨ Steve: <*in a theatrical voice*> Why yes!>
    5   Janet: <*laughs*>
    6   Natalie: I want some juice too.
    7   Janet: What baby? ((*to Natalie*))
    8   You want some juice too?

Steve uses a dramatic, overenthusiastic voice to accept Janet's proposal of juice, much to Janet's amusement. This creates humor in an ordinary, nonhumorous situation.

In excerpt 36, Janet and Steve are at a children's theater performance. Janet jokingly chastises Steve for not wearing his "tape player" (his digital recorder for the project) on stage during the show. She does so using a soft, high-pitched voice.

(36) 1   Janet: Now what did you do with your tape player.
    2   How did you—
    3   Steve: I just- I- I propped mine up behind the door.
    4   Janet: You didn't WEAR it?

5	Steve:	No,
6		not on stage.
7		You can HEAR everything.
8		((*short pause*))
9 ⇨	Janet:	<*soft, high-pitched*> My dear!>
10	Steve:	I'm not gonna wear it on stage.

In this interaction Janet manipulates pitch as she pokes fun at Steve for not wearing his recorder on stage (she wears hers), possibly performing not only for Steve but also for the benefit of the researchers. It is also notable that it combines a marked use of pitch with a term of endearment ("my dear"), another feature of their familylect.

In the following excerpt, occurring in the evening of the family's last day of recording, Steve intentionally brushes his teeth directly into the microphone of the recorder, acknowledging the presence of the researchers who will eventually listen to the family's tapes. Janet responds to this by laughing and by using a "stage voice" to playfully chastise him, contributing to his performance.

(37)	1		((*short pause, sound of running water, brushing teeth*))
	2		((*Steve seems to be brushing directly into microphone*))
	3	Janet:	<*laughs*>
	4		All right.
	5		Ha ha!
	6		((*Steve brushes teeth directly into microphone*))
	7		<*laughs*>
	8		((*short pause, sound of running water*))
	9 ⇨		<*high stage voice*> Don't be ridiculous, dear!>
	10	Steve:	I just thought I'd give them a little (brush),
	11		at the very end.
	12	Janet:	Oh boy.

This is not the only instance where Steve and Janet create a performance together for each other and for the researchers. Indeed, this family more than the others used recording as an opportunity to "entertain" those who would later listen to and transcribe their tapes.

Excerpt 38 shows Janet and Steve matching accents. At the beginning, it seems that Janet wants to record a TV show and she is confused because there is no "VCR-plus number" to enter into the VCR. Steve responds to her pointing this out by using what sounds like a stereotyped Southern drawl, and Janet matches it. Note also the "my love/my dove" and "my dear/my dear" routines appear in this excerpt. This combines matching terms of endearment with manipulation of accent and pitch.

(38)	1		Janet:	Now why is there no .. VCR-plus number.
	2			Like some- .. some shows don't have them →
	3			listed.
	4	⇨	Steve:	<*drawl*> Dub dose are not programmed →
	5			m' do:ve.>
	6	⇨	Janet:	<*drawl, high-pitched*> Why <u>me dear.</u>>
	7	⇨	Steve:	<*drawl*> I can't tell you <u>my do:ve?</u>>
	8	⇨	Janet:	<*same accent*> But dat makes me so angry,
	9	⇨		m' [de::ar?]>
	10	⇨	Steve:	[<*same accent*> I know] it does <u>m' do:ve.</u>>
	11	⇨	Janet:	<*high-pitched*> Hmm.>
	12		Steve:	I think it's .. like one offs b-like well, ((*no drawl*))
	13			I don't know.
	14			I have no idea.
	15	⇨	Janet:	<*drawn, high-pitched*>But <u>m' dear</u> dat means .. →
	16	⇨		somehow I gotta do it myself?>
	17			((*long pause*))
	18		Steve:	Did you know (Michael Penn) is forty-one?
	19		Janet:	(What hon.) ((*regular voice*))

Janet and Steve both use a marked accent in this excerpt, presumably for the purpose of showing their affection toward one another while also playing. The accent is combined with both "my love/my dove" and "my dear/my dear." Thus prior text is combined in new and creative ways in this interaction. Janet and Steve vary the routines of using accent and terms of endearment by here using both simultaneously and repeatedly, thus changing the pronunciation of the terms (e.g., "my dear" becomes "me dear"). The drawling accent they are using could be related to the problem at hand: Janet cannot figure out an aspect of the VCR, and the drawl could, through drawing on stereo-types, be intended to imply incompetence.

Janet and Steve do not always create play frames together so seamlessly. Sometimes, play is rejected by one partner. In excerpt 39, Steve speaks with what seems to be a German accent for no apparent reason, and Janet does not respond through laughing or using an accent of her own. They were watching a TV game show, and Steve had left the room to get some medicine for Janet.

(39) 1 ⇨ Steve: <*German? accent*>I brought ze medica:tions.>
      2   Janet: Well I don't need THIS right now
      3   Steve: I (don't) know what you need.

This accent again emphasizes the performance-oriented nature of this family, though Janet does not seem amused. It is possible that her utterance in line 2 ("Well I don't need THIS right now") rejects Steve's prior utterance on two levels, implying that she doesn't need the medication he brought her, and she doesn't need to hear the funny accent. Or, it could mean she is rejecting the play frame.

In sum, collectively these excerpts show how in the Neeley-Mason family, many different "voices" are integrated into everyday talk. High pitch was used in role-play and in playful talk and teasing between spouses, whereas markedly low pitch was used to entertain Natalie. Furthermore, character voices were used, as when Janet read a book using the voice of Elmo. Finally, we saw Janet and Steve use accents, for example when Steve used a German-sounding accent when talking to Janet and when Janet spoke to Natalie with an Italian accent. Thus, speaking in voices extends beyond adult–child role-play in this family and occurs across a range of interactions. It was a part of Janet and Steve's everyday language use.

These pretend voices do not occur in the Patterson/Foleys' family-lect. Though members of the Patterson/Foley family did use marked tones of voice in the everyday interactions that were captured on tape, it was nowhere near the extent to which the Neeley-Mason family did. Instead, the Patterson/Foleys mostly used baby talk rather than speaking in the voices of other characters. As another point of comparison, Clara, Neil, and Jason occasionally used character voices (mostly quoting TV characters), but their main manipulation of voice occurred when Clara spoke to (and for) the family dogs using an extremely high-pitched voice.

Jason also was recorded using high pitch while interacting with the dogs. Thus each family is unique in this regard.

The Neeley-Masons' use of voices works to create several aspects of their family culture. First, because the voices are often used to entertain Natalie, they create child-focused frames and index the child-centeredness of the family. Voices were used by Janet and Steve to amuse Natalie for the sake of her enjoyment (e.g., in role-play) and in an attempt to distract Natalie and get her to comply with their wishes.[7] Second, their use of voices foregrounds their shared identities as performers in children's theater for each other and for the researchers. Third, these voices contribute to the overall playful tone of many of their family interactions: This is a kind of pretend play that adults engage in to add humor and fun to their everyday lives. Finally, the presence of so many different voices in their family conversation points to the variety of voices (and people) that in fact make up their family. Whereas the Patterson/Foleys ventriloquized Kira using baby talk, creating a triad, the Neeley-Masons introduced all sorts of voices into their family, symbolically expanding its boundaries, which they do in other ways as well, as will be shown in chapter 3.

PRIOR TEXT, FAMILYLECTS, AND "FRAMING THE FAMILY"

In his description of Bakhtin's understanding of dialogism and the utterance, Todorov (1984:x) notes:

> The most important feature of the utterance, or at least the most neglected, is its *dialogism*, that is, its intertextual dimension. After Adam, there are no nameless objects nor any unused words. Intentionally or not, all discourse is in dialogue with prior discourse on the same subject, as well as with discourses yet to come, whose reactions it foresees and anticipates. A single voice can make itself heard only by blending into the complex choir of other voices already in place. This is true not only of literature but of all discourse, and Bakhtin finds himself forced to sketch out a new interpretation of culture: culture consists in the discourses retained by collective memory (the

commonplaces and stereotypes just as much as the exceptional words), discourses in relation to which every uttering subject must situate himself or herself.

In this chapter, I examined discourse that was in dialogue with a particular type of prior discourse: prior family discourse, that is, prior words and ways of speaking repeatedly used by family members. Examining words the three families used for child-centered terms showed how familylects can differ on the lexical level. I suggest that these lexical items, as they are used over and over again by all family members, become infused with their voices over time—a single voice blends into the family choir, and a metamessage of family membership is sent.

By examining the Patterson/Foley and Neeley-Mason familylects individually in greater detail, I showed how not only words but also everyday interactive rituals or ways of speaking comprise prior text. Thus, recurring patterns of talk, such as using reciprocal terms of endearment, ventriloquizing, and speaking in "voices," like lexical items, can make up part of a familylect. I also argued that a family's prior text points to not only a distinctive familylect but also a unique family culture or a unique world constructed through the (re)creation of family-specific frames. For example, Janet and Steve's use of voices created frames of playful performance and worked toward creating a family culture that values performance as a skill, language as a source of entertainment, and teasing as an affectionate activity. Likewise, Kathy and Sam's use of reduplicated terms like "nu-nus" and "wa-wa" fits into broader patterns of speaking related to their child's linguistic competency at the time of recording; they created frames that involved their "baby" in family conversations.

The analysis presented in this chapter links Bakhtin's understanding of dialogism as words being "populated" by the voices of others and his view of culture as consisting of mutually remembered discourses; Becker's idea that the grammar of a language involves time, memory, and a set of prior texts; and the notion that ritualized language use in families creates the family as a group with a distinctive culture by creating and re-creating particular symbolically meaningful frames. This brings together intertextuality and framing, suggesting that to understand the notion of familylect and uncover how families are discursively constructed, intertextuality and framing need both be considered and viewed as theoretically interrelated. In addition, my analysis examined segments of two families' relatively lengthy recording periods, identifying recurrent frames over time. Thus, I have also demonstrated how these notions can be brought together methodologically: through the intertextual tracing of not only linguistic and paralinguistic features but also frames.

Both Bakhtin and Becker recognize that social groups are fused not just by a shared language but also by a shared set of experiences and interactions using that language. Sillars (1995:375) observes, "people establish their own moral and social order within close [family] relationships, including private codes and unique sets of rules for interacting." In focusing on two "private codes and unique sets of rules for interacting," I demonstrated how the Patterson/Foleys and the Neeley-Masons create their own unique family worlds and their familyness through everyday talk. By taking an intertextual perspective (or, in Becker's terms, an approach to "languaging" that involves time and memory), I have identified linguistic features making up two familylects and have shown how language use constructs family-specific frames, creates the flavor of family culture, and binds family members together into a socially, linguistically, and emotionally significant (and recognizable) unit.

It is important to point out that, as Nydegger and Mitteness (1988) note, it is not possible to fully comprehend the private language of any family other than our own. I do not claim here to have presented a complete picture of the complex patterns of language use in these families. Nor do I pretend to fully understand every recorded interaction between members of these families; although the linguistic snapshot of the discourse of these families presented here is relatively rich, the repertoire of shared prior texts in these families extends back years (and I do not have access to these prior texts). This chapter has focused on sketching familylect features that were prominent during each family's recording period. In doing this, I also hope to have demonstrated how viewing the familylect as interrelated with the concepts of intertextuality and framing enriches our understanding of why family members repeat one another over and over and how this strategy works toward creating a shared family culture.

THREE

"Tell Uncle Noodles What You Did Today"

Intertextuality, Child-Centered Frames,
and "Extending Family"

The Neeley-Masons were unique among the families participating in the family discourse project in that they not only routinely integrated play voices into their everyday family interactions, as shown in the last chapter; they also integrated other people into their family in ways the other families did not. This chapter explores how two close family friends, Jill and Tim (also called "Noodles"), are linguistically included in the Neeley-Mason family: Through intratextual and intertextual repetition, participants create a symbolic family whose culture consists of frames in which Janet, Steve, Jill, and Tim collaboratively "parent" Natalie.

My analysis thus furthers the argument that intertextuality and framing are productively viewed as fundamentally interconnected through the examination of phenomena that have been widely examined in prior family discourse research: parent-child directives (e.g., Ervin-Tripp et al. 1984; Blum-Kulka 1990, 1997; Tulviste et al. 2002), behavior assessments (e.g., Ochs & Taylor 1992a, 1992b, 1995; Junefelt & Tulviste 1997; Tulviste et al. 2002), and family narratives (e.g., Blum-Kulka & Snow 1992; Ochs & Talyor 1992a, 1992b, 1995; Blum-Kulka 1997). These phenomena have been examined primarily through the lenses of parent-child socialization, speech act theory, linguistic politeness, and the re-instantiation of the family power structure. I explore them from a new perspective, demonstrating how monitoring, directing, and assessing a child's behavior and storytelling can be conceived of as the intertextual (re)creation of child-centered frames. I analyze the construction of frames of child behavior regulation/evaluation and of narrative elicitation/telling in the Neeley-Mason family, with particular attention to the participation of Jill and Tim. Interlocutors' repetitions of words, strings of words, speech acts, and paralinguistic features work to create these frames as well as the footings within them. Importantly, Jill and Tim participate in the discursive construction of child-centered frames by taking up co-parent footings. In this way, they take on parent-like identities and become symbolic members of the family.

Studies of family discourse have recently begun to use frame analysis to analyze situations in which parents use language to attempt to manage or influence children's behaviors, with a focus on a range of different issues, including paternal identity construction (Marinova 2007), trajectories in directive/response sequences and resulting disputes (M. H. Goodwin 2006), and interrelationships between task-based frames and play frames (Sirota 2002; Gordon 2008). Such studies have used frame analysis to provide insights into identity construction, alignment negotiation and the structuring of parent-child talk, and the socialization of children. The analysis I present here builds on these studies, as well as on prior research on teams in interaction, to investigate the linguistic construction of family.

Goffman (1959:8), observing that individuals often do not act as individuals in social interaction, draws on a theatrical metaphor in suggesting that through staging "similar individual performances" or "dissimilar performances which fit together into a whole," interlocutors can function as a team in interaction. Research in discourse analysis on "conversational duets" (Falk 1979) and "interactional teams" (Lerner 1993; Kangasharju 1996, 2002; Gordon 2003) demonstrates how team-building occurs in interaction, while also identifying repetition as playing a central role. In Gordon (2003), for instance, I show how one father and his wife act as a team vis-à-vis his fourteen-year-old daughter by sharing turns at talk, alternating turns parallel in function, conferring with one another, and evidencing the same "knowledge schema" (Tannen & Wallat 1993) in parenting frames, as well as by creating supportive alignments through a range of linguistic strategies identified in prior research as showing support, including repetition of another participant's words. Thus, the parents' use of repetition—of words, of speech acts producing matching conversational moves in parallel turns, and of ideas and expectations—enabled them to create a team composed of members exhibiting what Goffman might call "similar individual performances."

However, team alignments also can entail dissimilar performances that fit together, as Goffman suggests. For example, two rival "suitors" might "duet" in the presence of the woman for whom they are competing (Falk 1979). Although this is a different understanding of what is commonly thought of as teamwork, the competitors share a role in the conversation and jointly build one floor. Similarly, "format tying" (Goodwin & Goodwin 1987; see also M. H. Goodwin 1990 and Sacks 1992)—where participants repeat words or sentence structures drawn from another speaker's prior turn, thereby linking turns together—is sometimes used by family members as they disagree with one another (C. Goodwin 2006; M. H. Goodwin 2006). These participants are somewhat team-like in the sense that they collaboratively engage in and construct a frame of conflict (as in the duet example), although they enact different "sides." In an argument involving an adolescent boy and his father, for example, the boy linguistically transforms a prior utterance by his father in a way that allows him to "use Father's own words to contradict what he just said" (C. Goodwin 2006:450). Repetition can thus create teams in interaction characterized by support and positive affect, as in the parental team example; however, it can also construct discord and negative affect, as in the example of the son and father. Importantly, in either case, repeating can be viewed as a means of binding participants together: Participants are linked in a shared activity and into their shared unfolding history of talk (even if that history is not always positive). In the interactions examined in this chapter, Janet, Steve, Jill, and Tim are bound together in overwhelmingly harmonious team alignments through repetition at various levels of linguistic structure occurring both intertextually and intratextually; furthermore, although their "performances" are not always identical, they always fit into what Goffman might describe as "a whole." Also, overwhelmingly, the adults act as teammates that are on the same side of the conversation.

The Neeley-Masons know Jill and Tim (Noodles) because Jill had been engaged to Janet's brother for approximately one year (five years before taping); despite the fact that Jill and Kevin called off their engagement, Janet and Jill remained close friends. Tim and Jill became a couple approximately three years before taping.[1] Jill and Janet are particularly close: They talked on the telephone on three of the recording days (the other four days, Jill was out of town), and Jill was going to host the baby shower for the new Neeley-Mason baby. When Jill called on the phone to speak with Janet, Natalie wanted to speak with her as well; Steve occasionally worked as a waiter with Jill (a caterer). Jill and Tim were close enough with the family that they got regular updates about Natalie's progress in potty-training. The family friends are referred to as "Auntie Jill" and "Uncle Noodles." When I asked Janet and Steve by email about where the name "Noodles" came from, Steve gave me the story behind it. Jill and Tim brought Natalie to a play that Janet and Steve were performing in as part of their children's theater troupe, and in that play there was a line about "noodles" that Tim repeated over and over, making Natalie laugh. Natalie then started calling him "Noodles," as did Janet, Steve, and Jill. (Steve reports that this nickname has followed Tim into his other social circles as well.) The couples also refer to one another as "the friendlies" and "friendly friends" when talking to and about one another (this was captured on tape and also described in an email message Steve sent me). In addition, Janet and Steve encourage Natalie to call Jill and Tim "Auntie Jill" and "Uncle Noodles," respectively; in Natalie's presence, it is not uncommon for the adults to refer to one another, and sometimes address one another, using kinship terms from Natalie's perspective. For instance, when Jill was painting Natalie's nails, she asked Steve if he could keep track of drying time by saying, "Daddy could we get a little timer?"

In contrast to many others with whom Janet, Steve, and Natalie interacted during their recording period, Jill and Tim produced and showed comprehension of familylect vocabulary (recall that members of the extended family did as well, to varying degrees; for example, Janet's brother was familiar with "meltdowns," whereas Steve's sister was unfamiliar with "boppy"). Comprehension of familylect words and phrases alone suggests that Jill and Tim are in some way insiders to this social group; additionally, both Jill and Tim were captured producing the phrases "rocks and rubs" and "brush choppers" as well as the term "tinkles" in interactions with the Neeley-Masons. As mentioned in the last chapter, Tim sang the "brushing choppers" song with Natalie. Jill also used the term "meltdown" to refer to Natalie's tantrum behavior and "boppy" and "buppie" in a conversation with Janet and Natalie.

The analysis that follows examines how Jill and Tim act—and are treated—as symbolic members of the Neeley-Mason family; specifically, it considers interactions between the Neeley-Masons and "the friendlies" that occurred one day of recording when they spent a relatively lengthy period of time together. On that day (Thursday, the second day of recording), Janet, accompanied by Natalie, met Jill at a mall to shop and socialize; later Jill and Tim spent the evening at the Neeley-Mason home. Particularly interesting about these interactions is how Janet, Steve, Natalie, Jill, and Tim create a family built around Natalie through their participation in child-centered behavior regulation and evaluation frames, as well as in narrative frames. Both Jill and Tim act as members of a parenting team along with Janet or Steve in behavior regulation/evaluation frames; in narrative frames Jill and Tim also take up co-parent footings. Natalie plays the child role in these frames. Numerous kinds of repetition—of speech acts, words, and aspects of prosody, specifically pitch, volume, and duration—are used intertextually to create child-centered parenting frames and the adults' co-parenting footings within them; the symbolic family is created through the linguistic construction of these footings and frames.

A DAY WITH THE FRIENDLIES

The data I consider in this chapter consist of one afternoon and evening's worth of recording that captured Janet, Steve, and Natalie interacting with Jill and Tim. Activities occurring include a shopping mall trip (Janet, Jill, and Natalie), driving home from the mall (Janet and Natalie—Jill drove separately), and conversations at the Neeley-Mason house that evening (involving Janet, Steve, Natalie, Jill, and later, Tim). Before turning to the analysis, I briefly sketch out the events of the day in more detail.

Early in the day, Janet decided that she and Natalie would meet Jill at the mall after Natalie's naptime. Natalie expresses excitement about the mall visit; she is interested in seeing Jill and very enthusiastic about playing in the mall's children's play area or "kid pit." On arriving at the mall, they greet Jill; then Janet uses the restroom while Jill talks with Natalie, asking her what her favorite foods are (Janet left the recorder with Jill). Next, all three participants go to get a snack, stopping to toss pennies in a fountain along the way. Janet buys a chocolate croissant for her and Natalie to share (although Natalie wants her own). Then they walk to the kid pit, during which time Janet and Jill chat and attend to Natalie. Once they arrive, Natalie goes to play and Jill begins to tell

Janet a story about her (Jill's) brother, which is interrupted multiple times by Natalie's misbehavior, which is later described by Jill to Tim and Steve as a meltdown. Janet and Jill jointly deal with this meltdown and discuss Natalie's misbehavior. Natalie repeatedly interrupts Janet and Jill as they try to talk, crying and whining because another child in the kid pit took a balloon she was playing with and because she wants some of her mother's half of the croissant. Eventually, Natalie's misbehavior leads the adults to decide that it is time to leave the kid pit, at which point the recording ends. When the next tape starts, the participants are still at the mall, and Jill is pretending to be a doctor examining Natalie. The trio walks to a children's store, and Jill is finally able to finish telling the story about her brother. Janet and Jill comment on items for sale in the store, then go to a clothing store where Janet tries on bras; finally, they go to a shoe store where Jill helps Natalie try on shoes. Throughout this time, Janet and Jill both monitor Natalie's behavior. Finally, they decide to go back to the Neeley-Mason house but stop at the restroom first. Jill and Janet each take a turn going in while the other stays with Natalie. Then, just prior to leaving the shopping mall, Natalie announces that she wants to "go potty," too; Janet and Jill are skeptical (because Natalie has never used a "potty" away from home before, except at preschool), but determine that Natalie does intend to do so. They help Natalie go potty; her success is met with approval and congratulations. Then, Janet and Natalie drive home. Jill drives separately to the Neeley-Mason house.

On arriving at the house, Janet, Jill, and Natalie find that Steve has just arrived, too. Tim, Steve informs them, will be late. They stand outside and talk about Natalie's "tinkles at the mall," then go into the house. Jill talks with Natalie as Steve and Janet discuss what to order for dinner and look at menus. Steve continues to look at menus as Jill plays with Natalie. Natalie continues to want to play as all three adults confer about which Chinese restaurant to order dinner from and what to order. Tim arrives (with much celebration by Natalie) and the "tinkles at the mall" story is told to him. Steve orders the Chinese food; this takes time because he ends up having to call two different restaurants (the first one they call no longer offered delivery; Steve has a difficult interaction with an employee at the second restaurant). During this time, Tim plays with Natalie, Jill and Janet intermittently play with her, and Janet discusses the difficulty with the Chinese restaurant with Steve. Steve, Natalie, Jill, and Tim chat; then Janet and Steve talk in the kitchen. Jill joins Janet and Steve in the kitchen; Tim continues to play with Natalie. Janet announces it is time to go upstairs for bedtime; Tim and Natalie go up and the others follow. Tim and Janet get Natalie to put her nightgown on. The doorbell rings (it's the food delivery) and Steve goes to answer it. Tim and Natalie "brush choppers"; Janet and Jill chat in another room about the bras Janet bought at the mall (Tim and Natalie are still audible in the background). Steve comes back upstairs. Janet and Jill go downstairs to unpack the Chinese food and talk when Tim begins to read Natalie bedtime stories (with Steve also present). Janet and Jill talk about the food that has arrived, Natalie's misbehavior, and Janet's other friends; meanwhile, Tim does "rocks" with Natalie (with Steve present). Steve helps Natalie say her prayers. Tim says goodnight and goes downstairs; Steve talks with Natalie for a short amount of time and then joins the others downstairs. The adults eat dinner and talk.

The mall visit lasted approximately one hour and forty-five minutes; it is followed by the car trip home (twenty minutes). Before Tim arrives, Janet, Natalie, Steve, and Jill are home together for approximately thirty minutes. The remainder of the evening consists of two hours and five minutes of recording, although the recorders stopped taping before Jill and Tim left.

PARENTING IN TEAMS: CO-DIRECTING AND EVALUATING NATALIE'S BEHAVIORS

Family friends Jill and Tim linguistically participate in parenting frames, or situations in which what is taking place is the monitoring, directing, or evaluating of Natalie's behavior. Intertextual analysis reveals that their participation in these frames as co-members of a parenting team is parallel to ways Janet and Steve together parent Natalie: Like Janet and Steve, the family friends use intratextual repetition of words and speech acts to construct co-parent footings within these frames. The adults all produce directives that attempt to elicit action from Natalie, assessments that evaluate her behavior, requests that aim to elicit information from her, and assertions that convey information (usually to provide Natalie with encouragement, explain someone else's behavior to her, or justify a directive). In participating in the production of such speech acts[2] directed at Natalie, Jill and Tim take up "parental" alignments vis-à-vis the child and "co-parent" alignments vis-à-vis

Janet and Steve. They act, and are responded to, as symbolic family members.

Janet and Steve: Parenting Team

Janet and Steve are co-parents, and thus in some sense they always constitute a team of parents. However, in individual interactions, they also act as teammates by reinforcing one another's parenting behaviors. This occurs frequently as Janet and Steve try to manage Natalie's recurrent misbehavior and temper tantrums.

Excerpt 1a shows Janet and Steve interactionally working as a team one morning as they try to get Natalie to open her mouth so Steve can brush her teeth; how they do this corresponds to how the family friends co-parent Natalie. Janet and Steve both produce directives as Natalie resists their wishes; to do so, they repeatedly utter the word "open" as well as the phrase "open wide." They thus alternate turns parallel in function—they produce matching speech acts—as they deal with Natalie's resistance. (Note that each adult's intratextual repetition of another's words is highlighted in the excerpts presented in this chapter with underscoring; additionally, in the transcripts that follow, the basic speech acts produced by the parents are indicated when they are an analytical focus.)

(1a)	1		Steve:	Okay.
	2	*Directive*		Natalie please <u>open</u>.
	3			((*short pause*))
	4	*Directive*	Janet:	<*clears throat*>
	5			<u>Open wide</u>.
	6		Natalie:	<*whines/cries*>
	7	*Directive*	Janet:	<u>Open wide</u>.
	8		Natalie:	<*whiney*> No!>
	9		Janet:	<*clears throat*>
	10	*Directive*	Steve:	<u>Open</u>, please.
	11		Natalie:	<*yelling*> No!>
	12	*Directive?*	Janet:	[Natalie,]
	13		Steve:	[Thank you.]
	14			When you scream nice and loud →
	15			that's good,
	16			because your mouth is <u>open wide</u>.

In this excerpt, Janet and Steve take turns countering Natalie's resistance with directives. In repeating one another's words, they evidence a supportive alignment vis-à-vis one another as they co-parent their daughter.

As this conversation continues (shown in 1b), Steve again encourages Natalie to scream to make it easier for him to brush her teeth. When Natalie screams again, Janet criticizes Steve's parenting behavior:

(1b) 1   Steve: Scream.

      2   Natalie: <*screams*>

      3 ⇨   Janet: Uh!

      4 ⇨   Oh God,

      5 ⇨   don't tell her to scream.

      6   Natalie: <*whiney*> No no [no] NO!>

      7   Steve: [Done.]

Janet's criticism of Steve is similar to an alignment I identify in my analysis of the discourse of one blended family (Gordon 2003). In that case, the father counseled his daughter about how to ask a boy to a dance at her all-girls school. The father told the daughter that if she did not ask the boy she wanted to ask to the dance that day, it would be too late; his wife, in front of the daughter, reproached him (suggesting to him that perhaps the daughter should not ask the boy at all, since she had never even had a conversation with him). This, I demonstrated, is one way they show that they are a team in interaction: They confer among themselves regarding what they should jointly be telling the daughter to do; the goal of such conferring seems to be to resolve a difference of opinion so that they can present a unified parental front. Although their performances at such moments are dissimilar, the parents can be viewed as jointly working to "fit" their performances "together into a whole" (Goffman 1959:80). Similarly, Janet's side comment to Steve about appropriate parenting actions (whether it is a good idea to tell their daughter to scream) evidences their membership on the same team (of parents) in the interaction. And, this strategy, too, is intertextually reenacted by the family friends (especially Jill).

Excerpt 2 provides another example of Janet and Steve directing Natalie's behavior and dealing with her resistance as a team. Here,

Natalie and Steve have just awakened Janet one morning. Natalie enthusiastically jumps on her mother, and both Janet and Steve direct her to not do this.

(2)	1		Janet:	OO:w.
	2		Natalie:	Mm [mmm.]
	3	*Directive*	Janet:	[Please please,]
	4	*Assertion*		I can't breathe.
	5	*Directive*	Steve:	Careful,
	6			careful,
	7			sweetie.
	8	*Assertion*		Mommy can't breathe.
	9	*Assertion*	Janet:	Honey I can't breathe,
	10	*Directive*		you can't jump on me.
	11	*Directive*	Steve:	Don't jump on Mommy.
	12		Natalie:	<*noises*>
	13	*Assertion*	Steve:	Mommy's (???) in the morning.
	14		Natalie:	No.
	15		Janet:	<*gagging noises*> ((*pretending it seems*))
	16		Steve:	<*laughs*>
	17		Natalie:	Ah,
	18			NO!
	19	*Directive*	Janet:	Come on sweetie,
	20	*Assertion*		Mommy's gotta get up.
	21	*Directive*	Steve:	Let Mommy get up.
	22		Natalie:	Uh huh,
	23			no:::!
	24			No:::::::!

Janet and Steve act in tandem; they repeat one another's words while instructing Natalie what to do and what not to do by producing directives in parallel. In addition, they both produce assertions that justify their directives. For instance, when Janet explains to Natalie *I can't breathe* (line 4), Steve reinforces her: *Mommy can't breathe* (line 8). Then, when Janet tells Natalie *you can't jump on me* (line 10), Steve reproduces this directive in the form of *Don't jump on Mommy* (line 11). Likewise, when Janet accounts for why Natalie should not jump on her in line 20 with *Mommy's gotta get up*, Steve supports her by directing

Natalie to *Let Mommy get up* (line 21). Repetition is thus a fundamental strategy in the construction of co-parenting footings in this excerpt.

Excerpt 3 shows Janet and Steve jointly encouraging positive behavior rather than managing misbehavior. In the excerpt, they encourage Natalie to demonstrate two basic positions of ballet she learned earlier that day in her ballet class (called plié and relevé). First, Janet suggests that Natalie demonstrate a plié for Steve (*Show him how you did your- your um plié? Show Daddy a plié*, lines 1–3). Note that Janet's introduction of this is much like a pattern identified by Ochs and Taylor (1992a, 1992b, 1995) in their studies of family discourse—the mother prompts the child to tell a story and designates the father as the primary audience—although Natalie is asked to perform a ballet position, rather than produce a narrative. Following Tannen (2001, 2003), I suggest that this strategy is used by Janet as a way of creating involvement among family members. When Natalie resists performing the ballet moves, Steve encourages her as well (*I'd love to see one*).

(3) 1   *Directive* Janet: Show him how you did your- your →
     2   um plié?
     3   *Directive*   Show Daddy a plié.
     4   Natalie: (I don't want to.)
     5   Janet: You don't want to.
     6   [What about-]
     7   *Directive* Steve: [I'd love to] see one.
     8   *Directive* Janet: What about a relevé.
     9   Natalie: Ee::.
    10   *Directive* Steve: Can you show me a relevé?
    11   ((*short pause*))
    12   Natalie: Daddy look!
    13   *Assess.*   Janet: Oh::m!
    14   Natalie: Relevé.
    15   *Assess.*   Steve: <u>Mmmmm.</u>
    16   Janet: <*chuckles*>

Janet and Steve jointly direct Natalie to demonstrate ballet moves for Steve, and when she at last cooperates (line 11), both parents respond with the same speech act (assessment, which is abbreviated as *Assess.* in this and other excerpts), matching one another's drawn-out production (lines 13 and 15).

In addition to performing as a team through collaborative parenting in individual interactions—that is through jointly monitoring, directing, and evaluating Natalie's behaviors with repetition as a central structuring feature—Janet and Steve also regularly co-parent in another way. One parent attends to Natalie while the other is occupied with another task or activity. For instance, they take turns managing Natalie's bath time, and Steve entertains Natalie early one morning so Janet can sleep in, and she returns the favor the next day. In this way, Janet and Steve share parenting duties not only through actually co-parenting Natalie turn by turn in interaction but also through taking turns with parenting duties.

Janet and Jill as a Symbolic Parenting Team

Much like Janet and Steve, Janet and Jill act as a parenting team the afternoon when they meet at a shopping mall to spend time together and with Natalie. They effectively co-parent Natalie throughout the afternoon as they use repetition in jointly monitoring, assessing, and directing her behaviors. Listening to and transcribing the entirety of the mall trip, I was immediately struck by how Janet and Jill collaboratively looked after Natalie; indeed, I noted in my transcription notes that they seemed to "double-team" her. They do this in a number of ways. For one, Janet and Jill take turns taking care of Natalie: Each takes a turn watching her while the other uses the restroom, and Jill watches Natalie while Janet tries on clothes in a dressing room. Likewise, both adults independently issue directives to Natalie when all three participants are together. For instance, Jill tells Natalie to watch out for a vacuum cleaner cord in one store by saying "Careful of the cord, baby;" similarly, when Natalie begins to wander away from them, Janet directs her, "Come on babe!" and "Over here babe!" However, what I focus on in this section is how the two friends act as a duet or in tandem when all three participants are together. Intratextual repetition structures co-parental footings in interactions involving Janet and Jill just as it does in conversations involving Janet and Steve.

First, Janet and Jill often simultaneously or sequentially issue directives to Natalie, sometimes using the same words to do so, much like the example of Janet and Steve collaboratively encouraging Natalie to open her mouth so Steve could brush her teeth. Excerpt 4 shows

Janet and Jill simultaneously telling Natalie to not touch a door as they leave a store.

(4) 1 *Directive* Jill: [No no sweetie,]
     2 *Directive* Janet: [No no no,] leave the door alone!

Likewise, when it is time to leave a second store, both adults encourage Natalie to leave and they repeat one another's words to do so. In line 2 of excerpt 5, Natalie seems to be referring to a movie poster she sees.

(5) 1 *Directive* Janet: Let's go:!
     2   Natalie: It's the (chicken) movie!
     3   Janet: Oh yeah,
     4   we saw that didn't we.
     5 *Directive*   Come on babe.
     6 *Directive* Jill: Come on little girl,
     7   let's go:!

Notice in this excerpt the immediate repetition of *Come on*, but also the more displaced intratextual repetition of *Let's go!* (lines 1, 7), including the elongated "o" in "go." Thus, Janet and Jill not only encourage Natalie using the same words, they also say them the same way, showing an attentiveness to one another's words and their coordinated alignment.

These excerpts show that Janet and Jill intermittently parent Natalie as a team. In several situations at the mall, the women engage in long sequences of co-parenting with Natalie. I analyze two of these in detail: one regarding Natalie's misbehavior in the children's play area at the mall (the "kid pit" or "baby pit"), and the other involving Natalie using the potty. Both of these situations are co-managed by Janet and Jill and extend beyond the issuing of directives; both also show a variety of linguistic and paralinguistic features being repeated to construct co-parent footings. In addition, both situations provide material for narratives told to Steve and Tim later that day.

Monitoring Natalie's Behavior at the Kid Pit

Janet and Jill use repetition as a means of jointly dealing with Natalie's misbehavior at the children's play area of the shopping mall; their linguistic behavior constructs them as a symbolic team of parents.

Natalie had been anticipating playing in the kid pit since her mother introduced the idea of going to the mall; however, while there Natalie has what is later described as a "meltdown" when a little boy takes away a balloon she had been playing with (she later takes it back). In presenting this interaction, I demonstrate how Janet and Jill deal with this meltdown as a team, creating parental alignments vis-à-vis Natalie and supportive alignments vis-à-vis one another through uses of repetition. Thus, I show how Jill acts as a member of the family—she acts in parallel with Janet—and takes up co-parenting footings. Reciprocally, Janet acts in tandem with Jill, thus contributing to this construction.

The situation unfolds as follows: Jill is telling a story about her brother to Janet when Natalie, who had been playing nearby in the kid pit, approaches them, whining and crying. As the adults respond to Natalie, they participate in similar ways, performing speech acts in tandem. In this way, they use repetition to produce turns parallel in function, a feature that is indicative of team alignments in interaction.

(6a)	1	*Request*	Jill:	<u>What's</u> wrong sweetheart?
	2		Natalie:	<*cries*>
	3	*Request*	Janet:	<u>What's</u> the matter?
	4		Natalie:	<*whiney*> He took the balloon.>
	5	*Directive*	Jill:	Well <u>you've got to</u> share honey.
	6		Janet:	Sweetie,
	7	*Directive*		<u>you've got to</u> [use your words.]
	8		Natalie:	[I want the] balloon.
	9	*Directive*	Jill:	Well <u>go</u> ask [[(?? ??)]]
	10	*Directive*	Janet:	[[Say "I was playing]] →
	11			with that."
	12	*Directive*		[<u>Go</u> grab the orange one.]
	13		Natalie:	[<*cries/whines*>]
	14			<*cries/whines*> ((*sounds forced*))

Janet and Jill both address Natalie's crying and whining. Interestingly, Jill seems to lead this activity. First, both adults request information as to what the problem is. As the interaction continues, when Natalie explains that a little boy took a balloon she had been playing with (line 4), they both respond by addressing Natalie using a term of endearment (Jill: *honey*, Janet: *sweetie;* lines 5, 6) and by suggesting how she should deal with the situation: Jill suggests sharing in line 5; Janet suggests talking to the boy—*you've got to use your words*—in line 7. Although the adults' suggestions are not exact matches, they together make a whole: they collaboratively constitute the "parental" side of the conversation that requests information and issues directives. Furthermore in line 9, Jill seems to shift to match Janet's directive to talk to the boy by using the word "ask" (most of Jill's utterance is inaudible, however, because Janet produces overlapping talk). Despite the adults' coordinated efforts, Natalie only responds by crying and whining.

As the interaction unfolds as shown in excerpt 6b, Janet and Jill continue to address Natalie as a team, though they also have a brief exchange between the two of them regarding Natalie's behavior that highlights Janet's role as mother: Jill asks Janet how she tolerates the misbehavior (line 21), and Janet replies in line 22 with a frustrated and drawn-out *Uh*. In this way, they stop parenting Natalie momentarily to commiserate about the nature of Natalie's behavior. (Note that Steve and Janet do this frequently in interaction.) However, Janet and Jill soon resume co-directing Natalie how to deal with the situation, this time with Janet leading the way. In addition, both provide her with encouragement to go talk to the boy about the balloon.

(6b)	15		Janet:	Honey,
	16		Natalie:	<*cries/whines*>
	17		Jill:	[(?? ?crying?)]
	18		Janet:	[It's okay,]
	19			look he's–
	20		Natalie:	<*cries/whines*>
	21		Jill:	How do you deal with this. ((*to Janet*))
	22		Janet:	U:h. ((*to Jill, as if frustrated*))
	23		Jill:	<*laughs*>
	24		Natalie:	<*whiney*> I want the balloon.>
	25	*Directive*	Janet:	Can you go get an orange one? ((*to Natalie*))
	26	*Directive*		Go get the orange one,
	27	*Directive*		[run!]
	28		Natalie:	[<*whiney*> No,]
	29			I want those ones!>
	30	*Directive*	Jill:	Well you go ask him if you can play →

31			with him.
32	*Directive*		Go ahead,
33	*Assertion*		<u>you can</u> do it!
34		Natalie:	<*whines loudly*>
35			<*whiney*> I can't!>
36	*Assertion*	Janet:	<u>Sure you [can.</u>]
37	*Assertion*	Jill:	[<u>Sure you]</u> can.
38		Natalie:	<*whiney*> No I can't,
39			I want those,
40			those are MINE.>
41		Jill:	Natalie,
42			why do you say no you can't,
43	*Assertion*		you can.
44	*Assertion*	Janet:	<u>You [can</u> tell] him.
45		Natalie:	[<*whiney*> No!>]
46			<*whiney*> No!>
47		Janet:	Why honey?

Notice that in addition to performing the same speech acts vis-à-vis Natalie in this segment, Janet and Jill also repeat one another's words. When Janet assures Natalie that she can go talk to the boy about the balloon (lines 32–33) and Natalie whiningly states that she can't (line 35), Janet and Jill repeatedly reassure her through assertions: When Janet tells her *Sure you can* (line 36), Jill repeats her words exactly (line 37). Likewise when Jill tells Natalie *why do you say no you can't, you can* (lines 42–43), Janet reinforces her, saying *You can tell him* (line 44). In this way, they show their shared alignment, much like how Steve and Janet did in the interaction in which Natalie jumped on her mother.

As the conversation continues to unfold, Jill suggests what Natalie might say to the little boy; in this instance, however, Janet critiques her suggestion.

(6c)	48	*Directive*	Jill:	Go up to him and <u>say,</u>
	49			"<u>excuse me sir</u>, may I play →
	50			[with the balloon too?"]
	51	⇨	Janet:	[<*laughing, quietly*> "<u>Excuse me sir</u>,">]
	52	*Directive*	Jill:	"<u>Excuse me</u> little boy,
	53			can I play with the balloon too?"

| 54 | *Directive* | Janet: | <u>Say</u>, "<u>let's play together!</u>" |
| 55 | *Directive* | Jill: | "<u>Let's play together.</u>" |

When Jill tells Natalie to approach the little boy and indicates what she should say (lines 48–50), Janet laughingly repeats part of Jill's suggestion under her breath, *"Excuse me sir"* (line 51). She uses this repetition to comment on Jill's directive (though in a lighthearted way); in this sense, this could be viewed as an instance of parental conferring as Janet gently criticizes Jill's parenting directive, leading her to modify it. Janet follows this with the simpler directive *Say, "let's play together!"* (line 54), which Jill repeats to Natalie (line 55). Thus Janet and Jill present a unified front.[3]

However, Natalie does not follow Janet and Jill's suggestions and starts doing something else (it is not clear from the recording exactly what it is, but it soon becomes obvious that one thing she has done is taken the balloon from the little boy). Janet and Jill both comment on Natalie's behavior, again simultaneously parenting her:

(6d)	56	*Directive*	Janet:	Uh oh,
	57			don't—
	58			<u>No</u> no no,
	59	*Directive*	Jill:	Oh <u>no no</u>.
	60	*Directive*	Janet:	<u>no</u> no no.
	61		Jill:	*<laughs>*
	62		Janet:	Oh boy. ((*to herself?*))
	63	*Directive*		No Natalie,
	64	*Directive*	Jill:	[Play together.]
	65	*Directive*	Janet:	[throw it to him,]
	66			there you go.
	67		Natalie:	*<screeches/cries>*
	68		Jill:	O:h.
	69	*Directive*	Janet:	Come here.
	70	*Directive*		Sweet heart you've got to share the →
	71			balloons.
	72		Natalie:	*<whiney>* No I want (to) balloon.>
	73	*Assertion*	Janet:	[Well he was] gonna throw it to you!
	74		Jill:	[Natalie,]
	75	*Assertion*		he's just learning how to throw,
	76			he's gonna try okay?

In this segment of conversation Janet and Jill repeat one another's words as both say "no" to discourage Natalie's behavior. Next, in lines 64–65 Janet and Jill simultaneously issue directives to Natalie that are also very similar in content, though not form; each suggests she play with the boy. They then both explain what they perceive the little boy's intentions to be by making assertions—that he is trying to throw the balloon (lines 73, 74–76)—thus maintaining similar footings vis-à-vis Natalie in the interaction.

Natalie then begins to share the balloon with the little boy, and Jill and Janet positively evaluate her behavior. In so doing, they use the same paralinguistic feature—high pitch—marking their shared orientation.

(6e) 77 *Assess.*   Janet: *<high-pitched>* Almost!>
      78 *Assess.*   Jill: *<high-pitched>* Woo!>
      79 *Assess.*   Janet: *<high-pitched>* That's very nice!>
      80 *Assess.*   Jill: *<high-pitched>* Yeah!>

This time, Janet and Jill take up a different parental alignment. Instead of issuing directives to try to control Natalie's behavior, they jointly praise it. Instead of using the same words to do so, they use the same speech act (positive evaluation/assessment) and the same paralinguistic cue (high pitch). This is similar to how Janet and Steve praised Natalie's demonstration of ballet moves (excerpt 3) through matching drawn-out sounds.

Soon, however, Natalie ceases "playing nicely." Janet and Jill try to make her understand that the boy is younger than she is: Both point out the fact that the boy is "little" (these lines not shown). Then Janet and Jill both continue to praise and direct Natalie as she plays nicely with the boy. As in excerpt 6e, Jill and Janet act here as a parenting team that praises.

(6f) 98   *Assess.*   Jill: There you go, ((*to Natalie*))
      99   *Directive*   now go play with the little boy,
      100 *Assess.*   Janet: There you go! ((*to Natalie*))
      101 *Directive* Jill: ask him what his name is.
      102 *Assess.*   Janet: There you go!
      103 *Assess.*   Jill: There you go.
      104 *Assess.*   Janet: *<laughing>* Aw, there you go.>
      105 *Assess.*   Jill: How nice!
      106 *Assess.*   Janet: That's a girl!

Through the repetition of "there you go," Jill and Janet function as a team evaluating Natalie's behavior.

After playing nicely with the boy for a short time, Natalie comes over to Jill and Janet to eat some of the snack they have bought, a chocolate croissant, which Janet and Natalie are sharing. Several moments later, Natalie finishes one piece of her croissant and wants some of her mother's piece (though Natalie still has two pieces of her own remaining). She repeats "gimme gimme" in a whiney voice over and over again and Jill and Janet again form a team with one another to monitor and direct her behavior. One particularly interesting moment occurs when they use the same strategy in dealing with this situation: Jill asks Natalie why she wants another piece of her mother's croissant when she has two pieces of her own, and Jill herself provides an answer to this question, animating Natalie in a humorous way using constructed dialogue (line 176). Janet follows suit (line 177).

(6g)   173   Jill: Why do you want another one → ((to Natalie))
           174   if you already have two.
           175   ((short pause))
           176   ⇨   "Because I'm three and I'm not logical."
           177   ⇨   Janet: "Because I want everything Mommy has."
           178   Natalie: <whiney> (?? ?[? ??)>] →
           179   Janet: [No that's it!] ((to Natalie))

A team alignment is again constructed through the linguistic strategy of repetition. Janet repeats the beginning of Jill's utterance (Because I; lines 176–177), and both Janet and Jill respond to Jill's question (which Natalie does not answer) by speaking as if they were Natalie, or by animating or ventriloquizing her (one of the rare instances of ventriloquizing the child in this family). In this way, the women again match one another's participation through a form of repetition, taking an adult perspective here in constructing dialogue to discuss possible motivations for Natalie's insistence on having another piece of her mother's half of the croissant. In addition, they seem to be using this strategy to create humor together.

Excerpts 6a–g together illustrate how Janet and Jill perform as a parenting team when Natalie misbehaves at the mall's play area. I show one more extended sequence in which a parenting team occurs at the mall—involving Natalie having to use the toilet—because this experience contributes to showing the range of prior texts repeated in co-parenting while also providing the basis for a story that is later shared with Steve and Tim.

Helping Natalie "Go Potty" at the Mall

After Jill, Janet, and Natalie leave the kid pit, they go into a few stores. Then, before leaving the shopping mall to go home, Janet and Jill take turns using the restroom. Natalie subsequently announces that she wants to "go potty," and Janet and Jill deal with this situation as a team. First, they determine if she really wants to go potty at the mall, or if she means that she wants to go when they get back to the house. (Recall that Natalie is not yet fully potty-trained; in addition Natalie has never used a public restroom before, except at preschool, where child-size toilets are available.)

Although Janet and Jill collaboratively determine that Natalie does intend to use the toilet at the mall and together bring her into the restroom (lines 21–68, not shown here), Natalie subsequently resists Jill coming into the stall. She does allow Janet to come in, though she resists help. Both Janet and Jill end up helping Natalie, despite her opposition. The main struggles with the situation seem to result from the adults' (particularly Janet's) concerns about the germs Natalie might come into contact with in the public restroom. Janet initially tries to hold Natalie above the toilet (later described to Steve by Jill as "hovering" and by Janet as "a TOTAL disaster"), but in the end Janet and Jill decide that covering the toilet seat with toilet paper is sufficient, and Janet allows Natalie to sit down. Of particular interest is how in the excerpt Jill criticizes Janet's idea of hovering (lines 77–79); this is similar to Janet criticizing Steve about how he was brushing Natalie's teeth (by encouraging her to scream) (excerpt 1b, lines 3–5) and Janet gently criticizing Jill's suggestion about how Natalie should deal with the little boy who took her balloon (excerpt 6c, line 51), in that one parent or parental figure tries to influence the behavior of the other vis-à-vis Natalie.

(7a) 69   Natalie: Don't help me Mommy.
     70   Jill: She's got to help you, ((*to Natalie*))

71			because it's a BIG potty.
72		Janet:	*<laughs>*
73		Jill:	(??? in there,)
74			what can we use?
75	*Assertion*	Janet:	Okay we'll put some paper down,
76		Natalie:	What?
77	⇨	Jill:	She's just learning, ((*to Janet*))
78			there's no way she can go that way →
79			with you holding her.
80		Janet:	*<laughing>* Okay!*>*
81		Natalie:	Why you gonna put .→
82			[some toilet paper down.]
83	*Assertion*	Janet:	[We put some toilet paper on,]
84	*Assertion*	Jill:	We put paper down →
85			so that it's nice and sanitary.
86		Janet:	Right.
87			*<under her breath>* Oh God.*>*
88		Natalie:	(?? ?)
89		Janet:	*<laughs>*

In addition to jointly concluding that putting paper down is the best course of action, in part through the conferring resulting from Jill's criticism, Janet and Jill also act as a team by sharing a turn at talk, as they both answer Natalie's question *Why you gonna put . some toilet paper down* (lines 81–82) and repeat one another's words in responding (lines 83, 84).

As the interaction continues, Jill and Janet both direct Natalie's behavior and praise her, repeating one another's words and speech acts.

(7b)	90		Jill:	[Okay,]
	91		Janet:	[Okay] we're doing great,
	92			*<laughs>*
	93		Jill:	You've never used a potty outside before,
	94		Janet:	It's okay, ((*to Natalie*))
	95	*Directive*		sit down,
	96	*Directive*	Jill:	Sit-
	97	*Directive*	Janet:	sit down,

98			<u>sit</u> down,
99	*Assess.*		that's a <u>girl</u>.
100	*Assess.*	Jill:	Good <u>girl</u>!
101			[Now (??)]
102	*Assess.*	Janet:	[There we go!]
103			Mommy's got you!
104		Jill:	Okay.
105		Natalie:	(Why are you) holding my hand?
106		Jill:	Okay.
107		Janet:	We're just helping you. ((*to Natalie*))
108			Let us know when you make your →
109			tinkles okay?
110			((*short pause*))

Janet's use of the pronouns *we* and *us* (lines 107–108) contributes to the co-parent footings constructed in this excerpt by making clear that both she and Jill are helping Natalie.

Next, Jill and Janet use matching voice qualities as a way of encouraging and supporting Natalie: They talk about (but not to) Natalie using a tone of voice that sounds child-directed, positioning her as an intended overhearer. Thus they create matching alignments vis-à-vis Natalie as they continue to interact with her.

(7c)	111	⇨	Jill:	<*child-directed voice*> She's a VERY big girl,
	112	⇨		making b- tinkles in the mall!>
	113	⇨	Janet:	<*child-directed voice*> I kno:w!>
	114		Natalie:	Yeah.

This excerpt shows co-parenting and also provides an example of Jill using the familylect term "tinkles," a term Janet used just moments before (in 7b, line 109).

After several moments of Janet and Jill chuckling and asking Natalie when she is going to "make tinkles" (these lines not shown), Natalie finally does. This is met with laughter by all as well as praise from both Jill and Janet.

| (7d) | 133 | Janet: | [<*laughs*>] |
| | 134 | Natalie: | [<*laughs*>] |

135		Jill:	[<laughs>]
136		Natalie:	<laughs>
137		Janet:	I heard something! ((to Natalie))
138	Assess.	Jill:	<stage whisper> She's a <u>big girl</u>,
139			we've got to flush it.>
140	Assess.	Janet:	Oh my goodness!
141	Assess.		<whisper> What a <u>big girl</u> you are!>
142	Assess.	Jill:	Good job Natalie.
143	Assess.	Janet:	What a <u>big gi:rl</u>!
144			You're going to be wearing underwear→
145			in no time.
146			You're going to be wearing <u>big girl</u> pants →
147			in no time.
148	Assess.	Jill:	Good job Natalie!

In this excerpt, in addition to both adults praising Natalie, we see phrasal repetition: "Big girl," first uttered by Jill here (line 138), is repeated by Janet two times as a noun (lines 141, 143) and once as an adjective (line 146). In addition, Jill uses a stage whisper voice, positioning Natalie as overhearer to the praise (lines 138–139); though Janet does not create the same alignment vis-à-vis Natalie as she talks directly to Natalie, she does match her volume to Jill's in that she whispers (line 141).

In the remainder of the episode, the women project a future time when they (Jill, Janet, and Natalie) will tell Steve and Tim about this experience. Jill and Janet also help Natalie wash her hands and continue to praise her. Thus, throughout the public potty experience, Jill and Janet collaboratively parent Natalie and successfully manage the situation. Jill, through her use of speech acts (especially directing and evaluating), words, and ways of speaking that are redundant with Janet's, takes up parental footings vis-à-vis Natalie and supportive co-parent footings vis-à-vis Janet. Janet similarly echoes Jill's verbal behaviors. This use of intratextual repetition by the women intertextually echoes strategies Janet and Steve use to co-parent Natalie in everyday interaction. Janet and Jill's conferring about parenting decisions also affects alignment construction by working to frame Jill as a parental member of the symbolic family centered on Natalie.

Thus far I have considered a parenting team created by Jill and Janet. However, on arriving home, where Steve has just arrived and Tim later arrives, other parenting teams are constructed: Jill and Steve, Janet and Tim, and Steve and Tim. Though none of these are enduring as the team created by Janet and Jill, they are revealing of how both Jill and Tim interact with Natalie and her parents in parenting frames; I show three short excerpts in which Tim assumes the co-parent footing through repetition.

Janet and Tim as a Symbolic Parenting Team

Later in the evening, a parenting team develops involving Tim and Janet when they jointly try to get Natalie to put on her nightgown before bedtime (referred to as PJ's, which is short for "pajamas"); both also ask her if she wants to "go potty." Thus, they perform speech acts in parallel as they prepare Natalie for bed. Jill is also present. (Note that in the excerpt [lines 30–31], Natalie talks to herself and seems to be looking at a book.)

(8a)   1   Tim: <u>All right,</u>
       2 *Directive*   let's put on the <u>PJ's!</u>
          ((*lines 3–27: Jill and Janet sing; talk about a 1980s musical group*))
       28   Janet: <u>All right,</u>
       29 *Directive*   come get your [<u>PJ's.</u>]
       30   Natalie: [(the mama bear,)]
       31   [["you have to (go ??)]]→
       32 *Directive* Tim: [[Let's put on the <u>PJ's!</u>]]
       33   Natalie: [all by yourself,"]
       34 *Request* Janet: [<u>Do you want to</u> try] and <u>use the potty?</u>
       35   ((*short pause*))
       36   Tim: Oh yeah,
       37 *Request*   <u>do you want to use the</u> [<u>potty?</u>]
       38   Natalie: [Mnm mnm] →
       39   mnm mnm. ((*negative*))
       40 *Request* Tim: [You don't] have to go?
       41 *Request* Janet: [No?]
       42   Natalie: Mnm mnm. ((*negative*))
       43   Jill: We had one triumph today.
       44   Janet: Right.

While collaboratively directing Natalie to put on her pajamas and inquiring if she wants to use the potty, Janet and Tim repeat one another's words. This parenting team alignment, which creates a sense of familyness, is reinforced by a comment Jill makes at the end of the excerpt: She describes Natalie's use of the potty at the mall as a "triumph" to be shared by all by using the pronoun *we* (line 43).

Following this excerpt, Janet continues without success to encourage Natalie to put her nightgown on. Then, Tim makes an attempt: Using a funny military-sounding voice, he instructs Natalie to "report for PJ inspection" (thus he tries to blend the task with play, a parenting strategy used occasionally by Steve and frequently by Janet; see Gordon 2008). Finally, Natalie comes over; she has trouble putting her nightgown on but nevertheless resists help. Then, Janet and Tim, as a team, instruct her how to do it.

(8b)	352		Janet:	Natalie,
	353			maybe you should try it like this.
	354	*Directive*		Put your arms through it—
	355			I don't know, ((*to self? to Tim?*))
	356			how do you teach a kid to dress.
	357			Okay,
	358	*Directive*		<*chuckling*> come here.>
	359	*Directive*	Tim:	Put your head through,
	360	*Directive*	Janet:	Put your- come put your head through here,
	361	*Assess.*		that's it,
	362	*Assess.*	Tim:	There you go.
	363	*Assess.*	Janet:	There you go,
	364	*Directive*		now put your [arms through,]
	365	*Directive*	Tim:	[Now put] your arms →
	366			through,

The repetition in the discourse of Janet and Tim is particularly striking in this excerpt: The two adults often repeat one another's words exactly in back-to-back turns; in addition, Tim sometimes leads in this activity (in lines 359, 362). Through repetition of words and speech acts, Tim and Janet collaboratively accomplish the parenting task of getting Natalie in her nightgown for bedtime.

Steve and Tim as a Symbolic Parenting Team

Steve and Tim also function as a parenting team. I show one example that occurs as they put Natalie to bed (Jill and Janet have gone downstairs to unpack the Chinese food dinner). Natalie selects Tim to read her books and to give her "rocks." After Tim does "rocks," sitting in the rocking chair with Natalie and talking with her about the books they just read (for 98 lines), with Steve also present, Steve moves the bedtime events along, with Tim acting as Steve's teammate in parenting.

(9)	383		Steve:	Can we give—
	384	*Directive*		You <u>give</u> Noodles <u>a big hug and a kiss.</u>
	385	*Directive*	Tim:	<u>Give</u> me <u>a big hug and a kiss.</u>
	386			Mmmm mm <*kissing sound*>
	387			I love you.
	388		Natalie:	(Gimme) rubs.
	389		Tim:	Okay.
	390		Natalie:	Daddy could you give too?
	391		Steve:	Sure.
	392	*Request*		Here you <u>want your blankie?</u>
	393	*Request*	Tim:	<u>Want your blankie?</u>
	394		Natalie:	He bankie.

Here Steve and Tim co-participate in Natalie's bedtime ritual; this in itself points to Tim's special status in the family. In addition, Natalie gives both Steve and Tim a hug and kiss goodnight after they direct her to do so. They repeat one another's words to ask Natalie to hug Tim (lines 384, 385); they further function in tandem to request information—to see if Natalie wants her special blanket ("blankie," lines 392, 393)—and they agree to both give her "rubs" (lines 389, 391). In this way, through their participation in this intimate interaction, Tim and Steve function as a parenting team, similar to how we saw parenting teams consisting of Janet and Steve, Janet and Jill, and Janet and Tim. Importantly, Steve and Tim co-parent in such a way as to include Tim seamlessly in the bedtime ritual. In addition, Natalie treats the two adults in parallel ways, for instance asking if both will do "rubs" (lines 388, 390).

Parenting Teams in Family Interaction

I have illustrated how parenting teams composed of Janet and Steve, Janet and Jill, Janet and Tim, and Steve and Tim are linguistically constructed and enacted in conversation with Natalie. Similarly, Steve and Jill also participate as a team at times; for instance, they collaboratively try to determine what Natalie wants for dinner, and they also try to get her to sit down while using scissors. In summary then, monitoring, directing, and evaluating Natalie's behavior—in other words, taking up parental footings in parenting frames—are actions not limited to parents only. Jill and Tim co-parent along with Janet and Steve: The adults construct themselves as a team by creating supportive alignments through the strategy of repetition of words, syntactic patterns, and paralinguistic features and by acting in tandem by repeating one another's speech acts. Thus, intratextual repetition is an intertextual family-building strategy in parenting frames. In addition, the adults confer with one another about parenting decisions (e.g., how to direct Natalie to play nicely with the little boy at the mall). In these ways, parenting work is distributed outside the realm of the nuclear family, and family friends linguistically become part of the family.

Note, however, that although all four of the adult participants collaboratively parent Natalie, they often do not participate in exactly the same way. As confrontations with Natalie worsen, the family friends often cease to participate verbally, and Natalie's parents take over. For instance, when Steve and Jill jointly tried to get Natalie to sit down to use scissors and Natalie continued to contradict them, after several turns Jill ceased to verbally participate.

NARRATIVE FRAMES: ELICITING AND TELLING
FAMILY STORIES

Child-centered narrative frames, by which I mean situations in which stories about the child are elicited and told, also evince repetition both within and across them; these frames are used as a context to construct Jill and Tim as honorary family members. I examine patterns of narrative introduction, specifically a version of what Ochs and Taylor (1992a, 1992b, 1995) refer to as the "father knows best" phenomenon: Janet and Jill prompt Natalie to tell about her day, with Steve and Tim as primary story recipients. Following Tannen's (2001, 2003) interpretation of this pattern in light of her earlier theorizing on gendered patterns of interaction and the ambiguity and polysemy of linguistic strategies in terms of power and solidarity (Tannen 1994), I suggest that Jill and Tim encourage Natalie to tell about the events of her day as a way of creating involvement between interlocutors comprising the symbolic family. I also analyze intertextual patterns of co-narration of stories that revolve around Natalie, particularly by the adults. Co-narration, as a means of creating and displaying solidarity (Mandelbaum 1987; Eder 1988), contributes to the construction of rapport in interaction. Furthermore, telling family stories can metaphorically be understood as a type of social glue (Byers 1997). As an example of this, I demonstrate how Janet and Jill (and to a lesser extent, Natalie) co-narrate stories about Natalie "going potty" at the mall. My analysis thus extends research on how story co-narration is negotiated and accomplished linguistically, and on the interactive consequences of doing what Mandelbaum (1987) refers to as "sharing stories." In co-narrating, Janet and Jill not only share the task of telling, they also construct what has been called a "story world" (e.g., Schiffrin 2006) in which they function as characters making up a parenting team; they do this through repeatedly representing themselves as a "we" that acts vis-à-vis Natalie's story world character.

Through these patterns of interaction in narrative frames, members of the symbolic family, particularly Janet and Jill, linguistically work toward (re)creating the family. Because these stories revolve around Natalie, they reaffirm her position as the center of the narrative frames, and the center of the family itself.

Eliciting and Telling: "Tinkles at the Mall"

Telling and retelling Natalie's public restroom experience help to create the symbolic family. A first telling about this event occurs immediately on Janet, Jill, and Natalie's arrival to the Neeley-Mason house after the mall visit. The three chat with Steve outside (he has also just arrived home). After everyone exchanges greetings, Steve explains that Tim is running a little late. Then, Janet and Jill prompt Natalie to tell Steve about her earlier successful potty experience.

(10a) 1 ⇨ Janet: <u>Tell Daddy</u> the news!
     2 ⇨ Jill: <u>Tell Daddy</u>.
     3   Natalie: Tinkles!

4 ⇨	Janet:	Guess <u>where</u> she made tinkles [Daddy!]
5	Steve:	[Where did you-]→
6		where did you make tinkles?
7	Natalie:	Tinkles, potty!
8	Steve:	On the potty?
9 ⇨	Jill:	<u>Where</u>?
10 ⇨	Janet:	At the .
11 ⇨		(<u>Where</u>.)
12	Jill:	<u>Where</u> were we?
13	Natalie	Mall!
14	Janet:	At the mall!
15	Steve:	The mall!?

Here Janet and Jill co-introduce the "tinkles" story, designating Natalie as primary teller and Steve (the only participant who did not experience the event narrated) as the story recipient; they also collaboratively prompt Natalie to provide the pivotal detail of where the potty was (lines 9, 10–11, 12). Natalie participates by giving minimal responses to Janet and Jill's repeated prompting (e.g., *Tinkles!*, line 3; *Tinkles, potty!*, line 7; *Mall!*, line 13). However, as the interaction continues, Janet and Jill take over narrating what happened and Natalie is no longer a teller.[4]

(10b)	16	Natalie:	[Yeah.]
	17	Jill:	[Oh] [it was—]
	18	Steve:	[The mall] has a [pot—]
	19	Jill:	[We thought-] we →
	20		thought she was [(??)]
	21	Janet:	[She went] on the toilet [dear].
	22	Jill:	[Yep,]
	23		yeah.
	24	Janet:	Her first public bathroom.
	25	Jill:	We thought she [was bluffing.]
	26	Steve:	[How did she do.]
	27		[<*chuckles*>]
	28	Janet:	[<*laughing*> It was squishy.]

(The term "squishy" [line 28] seems to imply that the situation was uncertain or touch-and-go.) When Janet affirms that Natalie *went on the toilet* (line 21), Jill contributes through supportive minimal responses (*Yep, yeah*, lines 22, 23). When Janet emphasizes that this was Natalie's *first public bathroom* (line 24), Jill adds another detail, thus contributing to the telling (*We thought she was bluffing*, line 25). In using "we" to refer to herself and Janet, Jill also emphasizes their co-presence in the actual event and portrays their shared uncertainty. In fact, because claiming knowledge of another person's thoughts can be viewed as a display of intimacy (Mandelbaum 1987:162–163), Jill's utterance displays solidarity and closeness in this regard, in addition to contributing to the co-telling. Thus, although this excerpt does not include much repetition, through other linguistic means Janet and Jill's co-narrator status is constructed in this frame, as is their co-parental status in the story world.

After four lines of talk in which Steve mentions that his recorder batteries are dead (not shown here), the adults continue talking about the potty experience at the mall, with Jill and Janet continuing to depict themselves as a parenting team in the story world while also sharing in narration. In excerpt 11c, Janet reintroduces the topic by expressing appreciation that Jill was with her, using the kinship term "Auntie" to refer to her (line 33). (Note that near the end of the excerpt, in line 53, Jill seems to be responding to an earlier indecipherable utterance by Natalie in line 51; it is unclear exactly what they are talking about, but Janet finishes telling the story to Steve as Jill attends to Natalie.) In the excerpt, "we" is used repeatedly, emphasizing Janet and Jill's conjoined participation as parental characters in the story world.

(10c)	33	Janet:	Thank God Auntie was there.
	34		[We each went to the bath- <*laughs*>]→
	35	Jill:	[Well she thought she was gonna hover,]
	36	Janet:	<*laughs*>
	37		We each went to the bathroom,
	38		and she goes "I have to go,"
	39		or she said →
	40		[something,]
	41	Jill:	[Something] like ["I'm gonna go potty".]
	42 ⇨	Janet:	[And we were like,]

43		"are you sure?"
44		And she was like "yes."
45 ⇨		And we were like "okay,"
46 ⇨		so we get her in the bathroom,
47		[and she's—]
48	Steve:	[(?) that diaper] looks pretty full right now.
49	Janet:	Oh, I think it—
50		Well,
51		she wouldn't let me change her after [naptime.]
52	Natalie:	[(??)]
53	Steve:	Ah.
54	Jill:	[Dog? That's another new dog.] ((to Natalie))
55	Janet:	[So, that's another story.]
56		But um, so it was very squishy going.

In co-narrating this story, Janet begins to describe what happened (*We each went to the bath-*, line 34), and Jill overlaps with another detail (*Well she thought she was gonna hover*, line 35). When Janet uses constructed dialogue to animate what Natalie said (*and she goes "I have to go," or she said something*, lines 38–40), Jill adds her version of the constructed dialogue (*Something like "I'm gonna go potty,"* line 41). Janet continues to share with Steve how the interaction between the three of them unfolded. She depicts herself and Jill as members of a team by using the term *we* to refer to them (lines 42, 45, 46). The lines of dialogue Janet constructs throughout the excerpt contribute to this effect: Janet and Jill provide one side of the conversation and Natalie provides the other side. In addition these lines also support Jill's earlier statement that *We thought she was bluffing* (excerpt 10b, line 25).

After Janet summarizes the restroom experience at the mall (*But um, so it was very squishy going,* line 56), Steve offers to help carry something, and they go into the house and discuss what kind of food to order for dinner. Natalie asks when Tim will arrive. Jill and Janet both answer this question, and then Jill reintroduces the topic of Natalie using the potty at the mall by saying that they all are proud of her (lines 82–83). This exchange shows Janet and Jill together telling the story's resolution; it also again shows Jill using the familylect word "tinkles."

(10d)	79	Jill:	He's coming.
	80		(???)
	81	Janet:	He's coming sweetie. ((*to Natalie*))
	82	Jill:	Natalie,we are →
	83		SO PROUD of you doing your tinkles in the potty!
	84	Natalie:	[<*squeals*>]
	85	Janet:	[<*high-pitched*> Tinkles!>]
	86	Jill:	Good job!
	87	Janet:	(Big) girl!
	88	Jill:	[(Janet) thought it would be a good] idea to →
	89		hover first.
	90	Janet:	[I said, "She (??) wearing—"]
	91	Steve:	Uh uh.
	92	Janet:	Yeah,
	93		so that was a TOTAL disaster,
	94		Natalie's like "Uh, <*laughing*> u::h.">
	95		[So—]
	96	Jill:	['Cause] she was HOLDING her over the toilet.
	97	Janet:	<*chuckles*>
	98		So that didn't work.
	99		So- so Jill's like "Let's just put some paper down."
	100	Jill:	And that worked!
	101	Janet:	And it worked!

Both Janet and Jill praise Natalie (lines 86 and 87), and Jill launches back into the narrative, explaining that Janet's initial idea was to hold Natalie over the toilet so she wouldn't have to actually sit on it (using the word *hover*, line 89). Janet and Jill collaboratively explain that that was unsuccessful, and Janet then credits Jill with coming up with the solution of *put [ting] some paper down* (line 99. Note, however, that although Janet and Jill are portrayed as having different ideas in the story world, they are also portrayed as sharing the same goal: helping Natalie use the public toilet. Then Jill and Janet explain to Steve that Jill's strategy was successful, repeating one another's words to do so (Jill: *And that worked!*, line 100; Janet: *And it worked!*, line 101). Thus they jointly provide the story with a positive outcome that demonstrates a successful co-parenting experience.

The "tinkles at the mall" story resurfaces later in the evening, when Tim arrives. Its prompting and retelling show intertextual similarities with the excerpt in which Janet prompted Natalie to tell Steve the story (excerpt 10a, line 1). Immediately after everyone greets Tim, Jill directs Natalie to tell Tim about what happened at the mall (line 1).

(11)   1 ⇒ Jill: Tell Uncle Noodles your exciting news!
       2   Tim: What's the exciting news I hear?
       3 ⇒ Jill: Tell Uncle Noodles what you did today!
       4 ⇒   [In the] mall!
       5   Natalie: [(?)]
       6   Tim: What'd you do.
       7   Natalie: Tinkles!
       8   Tim: TINKLES!
       9   Janet: Tinkles at the mall!
      10   Tim: At the ma::ll! ((*clapping*))
      11   In the potty?
      12   Jill: [Of COURSE in] the potty.
      13   Natalie: [(?? ma:::ll!)]
      14   Tim: All right!
      15   Steve: In a public potty!
      16   Tim: Wo::w!
      17   Janet: Her first public [bathroom experience!]
      18   Natalie: [Ya::y!]
      19   Tim: [Wo:w!] ((*clapping*))
      20   Janet?:   [Woo hoo!]

Jill initiates the sharing of the day's details with Tim, likely to build solidarity among interlocutors. In fact, all present do participate in the telling about Natalie having used the toilet at the shopping mall; they also use familylect vocabulary to do so (*potty*, *tinkles*). Further, the adults jointly praise Natalie for this accomplishment. They thus construct "familyness" through retelling and responding to Natalie's success story.

The "tinkles at the mall" story resurfaces approximately twenty minutes later and is once again used to create a sense of familyness. Natalie has left the living room for a couple of minutes to get something from Janet in the kitchen, and Tim asks Jill about what happened at the mall. Jill describes Natalie's "meltdown" in the children's play area and the potty experience. In telling about these events, Jill represents herself and Janet acting as a parenting team in the story world frame. Steve is also present to hear this story.

(12)	1	Tim:	So what happened at the mall?
	2	Natalie:	For the party! ((*from the other room*))
	3	Jill:	Oh nothing really,
	4		we- Natalie had a meltdown in the baby pit →
	5		though,
	6		not really crying, ((*Natalie talking in background*))
	7		just being all irrational because y'know →
	8		she's not logical like an adult,
	9		she's logical [like a baby!]
	10	Steve:	[<*chuckles*>]
	11 ⇨	Jill:	But um y'know she just- she- everything we→
	12		suggested was,
	13		"No! I don't want to!"
	14 ⇨		So we suggest the opposite,
	15		"I don't want to!"
	16		So anyway,
	17		after that it was fine,
	18		and then we were getting ready to leave and →
	19		we made a pit stop in that bathroom →
	20		by the Gloria Jean's?
	21 ⇨		And um- we- we both went in the bathroom,
	22 ⇨		different times so we could keep an eye on her,
	23		RIGHT as we're leaving,
	24		[she said,]
	25	Natalie:	[We're back.] ((*Natalie returns to the living room*))
	26	Jill:	"I have to go the potty too."
	27	Natalie:	We're back everybody.

28 ⇨	Jill:	And we were like, "yeah, yeah, [whatever,"]
29	Tim:	((*to Natalie*)) [You are?!]
30	Jill:	"No, I have to go the potty,"
31 ⇨		so we went [(?)]
32	Natalie:	[Like it?] ((*to Jill it seems*))
33	Steve:	[<*chuckles*>]

In this short narrative, Jill describes how she and Janet jointly dealt with Natalie's tantrum. She uses the familylect term "meltdown" (line 4), then repeatedly refers to herself and Janet using the pronoun "we," portraying the duo as jointly making suggestions to Natalie (lines 11, 14), as taking turns *keep[ing] an eye on her* (line 22), as collaboratively questioning Natalie's intentions to use the toilet (line 28), and as doing something inaudible (line 31). Though this story is not co-narrated, it works toward constructing the family in multiple ways. Like the co-telling in excerpt 11, it simultaneously allows Jill to portray herself in the story world as a co-parent with Janet and share the details of their day with Tim and Steve the way that mothers have been observed to do in research by Ochs and her colleagues. Also similar to excerpt 11, here Natalie is positioned at the center of the story world and of the symbolic family; like the nuclear family, this symbolic family struggles to manage Natalie's misbehavior, and the parental figures are bound together though this struggle.

Through repetition and co-narration then, Janet and Jill describe their coordinated alignment in the story world while also enacting a coordinated alignment in the telling world. Through prompting telling about the "tinkles at the mall" experience, Janet and Jill enact an interactional pattern common in the discourse of some families in which mothers facilitate the sharing of everyday events in children's lives with fathers. By co-narrating stories and using familylect vocabulary and kinship terms, they create solidarity. In portraying themselves as co-parents, as a "we" vis-à-vis Natalie in the story world, Janet and Jill further create a sense of familyness. Everyone's enthusiastic responses to these stories that revolve around Natalie suggest that they create a kind of family solidarity.

Family Narratives

As narrative is a powerful means of creating family (in the sense of "nuclear family" or "extended family"), so, too, is it a primary means of creating this symbolic family, as revealed through an intertextual frame analysis. Indeed there is a great deal of research in a variety of fields identifying narrative's many important functions in family discourse. For instance, research has shown that storytelling in family discourse is a means for exerting social control (e.g., Langellier & Peterson 1993), reinforcing a family's hierarchical structure (e.g., Erickson 1990; Ochs & Taylor 1992a, 1992b, 1995), building and maintaining solidarity (e.g., Byers 1997), socializing children (e.g., Blum-Kulka 1997), helping children develop a sense of well-being (e.g., Fivush et al. 2004), constructing cultural or ethnic group identities (e.g., Blum-Kulka 1997), creating a family's beliefs and values (e.g., Ochs, Smith, & Taylor 1996), and constructing a unique family culture (e.g., Langellier & Peterson 1993). The examples I have presented can be viewed from any of these perspectives. We saw adults exerting control over Natalie by scaffolding her participation, family hierarchy being reinforced as parents portrayed themselves as directing (or trying to direct) Natalie's behavior in story worlds, participants building solidarity through patterns of co-narration and the sharing of narrative details, interlocutors collaboratively socializing Natalie into using the toilet, and "American" child-centeredness in that Natalie was in many ways the hub of these interactions. However, most interesting for my purposes is how in both the telling world and the story world adult participants used repetition to act as co-parents, weaving discourse that on two levels sends the metamessage "We're a family." To do this, participants repeatedly create a narrative frame in which a gendered, family interactional pattern recurs (Janet and Jill introduce a story about Natalie and position Steve and Tim as primary recipients), they repeatedly use familylect words (e.g., it is always "tinkles"; other words—like "pee" or "pee-pee"—never surface), they repeat each others' words in co-telling, and they respond in coordinated ways.

To uncover these patterns, I looked at narrative frames intertextually, thus finding similarities in how Janet and Jill prompt child-centered narratives, in how repetition is used in co-narration across retellings, and in how pronouns and parallelism are used. These strategies collectively enable Janet and Jill to portray themselves as a team of parents not once, but over and over again, and for Tim and Steve to respond positively to stories in which familyness is portrayed. Focusing on narrative as a frame highlighted the footings participants take up, thereby revealing how familyness emerges in interaction and encompasses family friends.

EXPANDING FAMILY BOUNDARIES

During the week of recording for the Neeley-Masons, Janet, Natalie, and Steve interacted with a number of people beyond the nuclear family. They conversed with Janet's mother, Janet's brother, Steve's mother, Steve's sister, Jill, Tim, other friends, as well as co-workers and strangers (e.g., in service encounters). In the presence of some individuals (e.g., extended family, Jill and Tim), a certain sense of familyness came through in the talk. This was particularly true in conversations with Jill and Tim, family friends who exhibited familiarity with family-lect lexical items even more so than extended family members and were referred to using kinship terms.

In this chapter, I considered the creation of a symbolic family to which Janet, Steve, Natalie, Jill, and Tim all belong. I demonstrated how the adults took up alignments vis-à-vis Natalie that can be characterized as parental, as well as supportive co-parent or parenting team alignments vis-à-vis one another in two recurrent frames in the family context: frames of child behavior direction/evaluation and frames of narrative. The analysis thus provided insight into how family is created moment by moment through discourse.

How and why the linguistic strategies used by these interlocutors work to create a family is related to the notion of intertextuality in a number of ways. First, this analysis was strongly motivated by the identification of repetition, both within and across conversations: I examined linguistic patterns (often, patterns of intratextual repetition) that occurred not once or twice but repeatedly over the course of several hours and several locations. This led me to focus on frames in which child behavior is managed and evaluated and frames of narrative elicitation and telling. Second, many of the individual excerpts I identified were also rich with intratextual repetition, sometimes (from my perspective) astonishingly so; this played centrally in the analysis. Third, I took an intertextual perspective in the sense that I looked across stretches of talk to compare Natalie's parents' parenting behaviors and the behaviors Tim and Jill manifest in interaction with the Neeley-Masons. This enabled me to draw parallels in the ways Janet and Steve parented together, how each of them parented in tandem with a family friend, and how Janet introduced and told stories and how Jill did. Finally, Bakhtin and Becker's theorizing about intertextuality, specifically the idea that members of cultural or social groups are bound together through reshaping words and ways of speaking others have used before, shaped my understanding of the Neeley-Mason family as consisting of a polyphony, a choir, of intertwined voices. Conceptualizing the family as a distinctive, discursively constructed world of talk led me to focus on family talk itself, not just on the talk of members of the nuclear family.

Intertextual examination of frames of co-parenting and of narrative was facilitated by the depth of the data set; the study's methods of data collection enabled me to identify this symbolic family, a family that would likely not be recognized in the analysis of an isolated conversation involving only nuclear family members. Thus, my findings, I believe, have methodological implications: If we are to view families as constructed through everyday interaction, recording a gathering of nuclear family members only, and over a short period of time, is perhaps too limiting. Indeed the larger study from which my data were drawn, as well as an interdisciplinary family research center at the University of California, Los Angeles (CELF), both use lengthy recording, involve ethnographic observation, and capture family members interacting not only with nuclear family members but with co-workers, friends, and others in their social networks (see Tannen and Goodwin 2006 for overviews of these projects). My analysis, along with others growing from these projects—like Pash's (2008a, 2008b) study of same-sex parent-headed families and parental ties to the community, for instance—give important insights into how families self-create and extend beyond traditional family boundaries.

The examples presented here not only show the interactional construction of a family and reveal how methodology shapes the object of analysis; in doing so, they also demonstrate how extending family boundaries enables a distribution of parenting "work"—such as preparing a child for bedtime, monitoring her behavior in a public place, and helping her in the process of toilet-training—beyond the parental unit. In fact, the parents in all three families with young children that participated in this study all relied on, to some degree, non-family members to care for their children (preschool teachers, day care workers, and/or babysitters). They also drew on outside or public sources of information (e.g., parenting books, day care providers) in making private, everyday parenting decisions (see Tovares 2005). Furthermore, private family conversations (in particular, conflicts) sometimes played out in public (see Tannen 2006). Thus no family has absolute, definitive discourse boundaries—the voices of non-family members surface in what might be thought of as family discourse. However, the Neeley-Mason family was the only one participating in the study to use language to "invite" non-family members into the family and include these interlocutors as honorary members of the family in actual interaction with and about the family's center—the child.

This expansion of family boundaries not only allows a wider distribution of parenting work, it also distributes the relationship work of the family. Strategies for creating family solidarity—prompting the co-telling of family narratives, using familylect vocabulary and kinship terms, participating in the child's bedtime ritual—are used by multiple interlocutors. Thus, the discursive extension of the family whose talk is analyzed here suggests that understanding how contemporary families function may entail looking beyond nuclear and traditional family boundaries to the many other voices that surface in and shape family talk.

FOUR

"You're the Superior Subject"

Layering Meanings by Creating Overlapping and Embedded Frames

The analyses presented in chapters 2 and 3 demonstrated how bringing intertextuality and framing together sheds light onto the processes of creating a family's culture and identity and expanding its boundaries; analyzing webs of interrelated interactions revealed the role of repetition and framing in the linguistic construction of family. This chapter and the next one shift focus from family-making to meaning-making, demonstrating how reshaping shared prior text serves as a resource for creating meanings in specific family interactions. Although the theory of intertextuality conceptualizes meaning-making as a process that extends across interactions, how this works moment by moment in conversation has been only minimally explored. I demonstrate how bringing intertextuality together with framing in the context of a chain analysis of linked conversations provides new insights into how prior interactions relate to meanings made in later ones.

This chapter builds on Goffman's (1974, 1981) observation that frames are often laminated in discourse, illustrating how intertextually reshaping another family member's words enables participants to laminate frames—and meanings—in two different ways, which I refer to as *overlapping* and *embedded*. Goffman describes lamination (or layering) in quite general terms, noting that laminations occur through the transformation and rekeying of activities (1974:82) and observing that participants often keep multiple frames and footings in play (1981:155–156). The analysis that follows builds on, delves into, and works toward specifying Goffman's (1974:157) idea that "Every possible kind of layering [of frames] must be expected." In addition, I draw on Bakhtin's (1984) discussion of dialogicality, particularly his notion of double-voiced discourse—the idea that on some occasions, people repeat the words of another person in such a way that "the sounding of a second voice *is* a part of the project of the utterance" (Morson & Emerson 1990:149).

The examples of intertextual repetition presented in this chapter consist of five pairs (and two trios) of interactions wherein one family member repeats words uttered previously by another in a specific prior family interaction. When reproduced by a new speaker and embedded in a new situational and interactive context, the words take on new meanings, comment on their own prior use(s), and invoke frames that are laminated, either overlapping or embedded (or sometimes, both). For each pair of excerpts, I present one conversational excerpt, then go back to consider it in the context of a particular prior excerpt of interaction that provides essential prior text. I do this to emphasize the importance of having access to (i.e., sharing) prior text in discerning layers of meaning and in constructing these two different types of laminated frames.

OVERLAPPING FRAMES

By the phrase "overlapping frames," I mean an utterance is situated in (at least) two frames at once. Put another way, the utterance refers "simultaneously to two contexts of enunciation: that of the present enunciation and that of a previous one" (Todorov 1984 [1981]:71). Following Bakhtin's perspective, I suggest that when family members repeat shared prior text in the presented excerpts, they create words that are "populated" by at least two voices: The voice of the current speaker, and the voice of the family member who originally uttered the words. Bringing dialogicality and framing together shows how in situations where double-voicing occurs there are two definitions of what is taking place in the interaction, with the double-voiced words situated in both frames. In this way, two frames are created and interrelated in an overlapping configuration.

Utterances creating overlapping frames point to two different contexts: one current conversation, and one prior. However, they do not always do so for the same reasons. Bakhtin points out that in using another's words, an author or speaker can create a range of evaluative stances toward those words. According to Morson and Emerson's (1990) and Todorov's (1984 [1981]) readings of Bakhtin's work, passive double-voiced words exist on a continuum according to how the words are evaluated by the current speaker and what they are used to do.[1] The two poles of the continuum of passive double-voiced words are unidirectional (showing agreement/admiration) and varidirectional (showing disagreement/mockery). To give concrete examples: In this study, I recontextualize quotations from numerous scholars whose words I agree with and find essentially "in accordance with the task to be accomplished" (Morson & Emerson 1990:150), my task being an analysis of intertextuality and framing in family discourse. In contrast, when the tasks of the current speaker/writer and the original speaker/writer are not the same or are at odds with one another, the other's discourse is subjected to "harsh treatment" (Morson & Emerson 1990:152); an example of this is parody. In this type of discourse, the audience is "meant to hear both a version of the original utterance as the embodiment of its speaker's point of view (or 'semantic position') *and* the second speaker's evaluation of that utterance from a different point of view" (Morson 1989:65).

The primary task parents in these families accomplish through intertextually repeating one another to create double-voiced words is to comment on one another's linguistic behavior in past situations, while also doing something in the present situation (often commenting on the spouse's current behavior). However, as will soon become apparent, it is not always easy to discern how harshly or admirably the words are being treated in the construction of overlapping frames. This is likely because Bakhtin's ideas were developed primarily with reference to literary contexts, not naturally occurring talk; I believe this also points to the complexity of the function of repetition in general and the nuanced nature of family conversation in particular.

"Inordinate Amount of Accidents": Kathy and Sam

It is early one evening at the home of the Patterson/Foley family; Kathy is feeding Kira dinner at the kitchen table while Sam is an adjacent room working on the family's computer. On the tape, there is the sound of

Kira falling from her chair and wailing loudly. Then, as Kira continues to cry, the following occurs.

(1a) 1   Sam: Kath? ((*from another room*))
      2   Kathy: Oh oh, she fell!
      3   Sam: Did she hit her same spo:t?
      4   Kathy: She just fell off the chair,
      5   she's all right.
      6   Sam: Did she hit the back of her head, ((*entering kitchen*))
      7   or her lip again?
      8   Kathy: She hit her head.
      9   ((*short pause, loud cries from Kira*))
     10 ⇨ Sam: <*smile voice*> How come she always seems to have→
     11 ⇨   an inordinate amount of accidents →
     12   [with Mom.>]
     13   Kathy: [(Oh you were waitin')] →
     14   for that.
     15   Sam: <*laughs*>
     16   Kathy: <*annoyed?*> No:, she got excited —>
     17   <*soothing voice*> It's all right, ((*to Kira*))
     18   it's all right.
     19   You fell off the chair.>

Here Sam seems to take a critical alignment toward his wife and her ability to care for their child; this might seem uncalled for, given that children have accidents even in the charge of competent caregivers. Considered in the context of this isolated interaction, Sam's "smile voice" seems inexplicable—Is something funny about the child falling from her chair? (Although Kira was crying loudly, she was not seriously injured.)

To help us understand this interaction and the layers of meaning it involves, we need access to a prior interaction that occurred several hours earlier that same day that is linked to the later one through intertextual repetition. Excerpt 1b shows that interaction. Sam is at home with Kira (who is taking a nap). Kathy phoned home from work to check in; in the conversation, Sam reveals that Kira fell down and hurt her lip while he was out walking with her earlier in the day. (The two sides of the conversation were put together by listening to both Sam's and Kathy's tapes.)

(1b)	1	Kathy:	Are you there.
	2	Sam:	Yea:h.
	3	Kathy:	What time did she go to bed.
	4	Sam:	Just now.
	5	Kathy:	Is she all right.
	6	Sam:	Well,
	7		*<laughs>* she was.
	8	Kathy:	Yeah?
	9		Did she melt? (("*melt*" = *have a tantrum*))
	10	Sam:	*<rising>* No,>
	11		she was good,
	12		but she was running back from McDonald's,
	13		and she fell and her- split her lip.
	14	Kathy:	*<louder, annoyed>* What!>
	15	Sam:	She got- cut her lip.
	16	Kathy:	*<small sigh>*
	17 ⇨		How come a disproportionate amount of injuries →
	18 ⇨		[and accidents . occur when . she's under your care.]
	19	Sam:	[*<chuckles>*]
	20		*<smile voice>* 'Cause we have more fun.>
	21	Kathy:	FUN equals injuries and accidents?
	22	Sam:	*<higher tone, "justifying">* She was running,
	23		and she was holding onto my finger,
	24		and she was pulling me,
	25		and then . she fell down.>
	26	Kathy:	*<sighs>*

(As the conversation goes on, Kathy verifies that Sam took proper care of Kira's injury—that he put ice on it, and so forth, which he did.) The interaction in 1b makes it apparent that Sam's comment in 1a, *How come she always seems to have an inordinate amount of accidents with Mom?*, is not a simple case of criticism. Instead, it is as an echo of—and comment on—Kathy's earlier criticism (in 1b) occasioned both by that prior criticism and by the interaction where Kira falls down while Kathy is supervising her (1a). This means that in excerpt 1a Sam repeats Kathy's earlier criticism; though he does not use the exact words she used, the similarities are clear:

(from 1b) Kathy: <u>How come</u> <u>a disproportionate amount of</u> injuries
                    and <u>accidents</u> occur when she's under your care.
(from 1a) Sam: <u>How come</u> she always seems to have <u>an inordinate</u>
                    <u>amount of accidents</u> with Mom.

Through repeating a version of Kathy's utterance and reshaping it to the new context in 1a, Sam simultaneously comments on both the current situation and Kathy's earlier criticism of his ability to care for Kira. However, it remains unclear how seriously either criticism should be taken; Sam's utterance in particular seems intended to be humorous. (When asked about this pair of excerpts, Kathy and Sam reported that they were joking.) More important for my purposes is the fact that it is the participants' shared past and their abilities to call up this past that enable them create these layers of meaning. The design of the study allowed me, as the analyst, to uncover this fundamental layer of meaning.[2]

To conceptualize how Sam's utterance works to layer frames, I provide a visual representation. I suggest that Sam's utterance can be conceived of as creating overlapping frames, as shown in figure 4.1. The rectangles in the figure represent frames of interaction; bold phrases in the corners of the rectangles represent the metamessages that define each frame and signal how the utterance should be interpreted. The figure represents the reshaped utterance containing word repetition in the center of the figure; the reshaped material signals two frames through sending two metamessages about what is going on in the interaction: here, (1) commenting on Kathy's caregiving, and (2) commenting on Kathy's earlier criticism.

This figure visually represents how Sam's utterance cues and is situated in two frames at once; however, note that the visual representation is overly static and flat (as any visual, paper-based representation of framing would be), as these frames represent a fleeting moment in unfolding conversation. One of these frames consists of Sam commenting on the fact that Kira got hurt while Kathy was watching her, criticizing (jokingly, perhaps) her caregiving abilities; the other consists

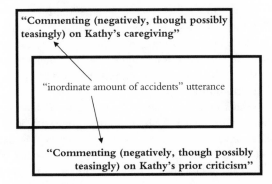

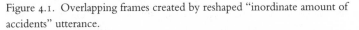

Figure 4.1. Overlapping frames created by reshaped "inordinate amount of accidents" utterance.

of Sam parodying or mimicking (or perhaps criticizing) Kathy's prior criticism of him, thus humorously implying she was wrong to have criticized him.

It is worth noting that within the conversation in which Sam repeats Kathy's criticism (excerpt 1a), there are clues that point to the relevance of prior experience and interaction. For example, Sam refers to Kira bumping *her same spot* (line 3) and *her lip again* (line 7). Sam's use of a smile voice while uttering the criticism also suggests that there might be more going on in the interaction than a simple comment on his wife's caregiving—and indeed there is. Prior text crucially affects the interpretation of the later text; through it Sam layers meaning, as if to say, "Remember when you criticized my caregiving? Now it's your turn!" Kathy's barely decipherable comment, *Oh you were waitin' for that* (excerpt 1a, lines 13–14), supports this interpretation. It is possible too that there is another layer of meaning here; perhaps the joint construction of this routine creates bonding through recreating a shared style of interacting.

"Superior": Steve and Janet

The phenomenon of one parent reshaping prior words of the other across interactions is not unique to the Patterson/Foley family. The Neeley-Masons echo one another's words back to each other as well. In contrast to the example drawn from the tapes of Kathy and Sam, the next example involves a pair of conversational excerpts that is less ambiguous in terms of its key or tone: It is more obviously closer to joking or teasing than serious criticism. In addition, the topic of talk is far less serious: the couple's participation in the family discourse study, specifically which of them is the better "subject" for research.[3] However, here intertextual repetition extends to a third interaction, and the last excerpt shows the prior text being reshaped in a conversation that takes a more serious turn.

First, consider excerpt 2a, occurring on Thursday morning. Janet, who is at home with Natalie, is talking on the phone with Steve, who is at work. The conversation was captured by the recorder the family had hooked up to their home phone. In the conversation, Janet and Steve talk about the batteries for their portable recorders for the study. Janet had been explaining that her batteries have not been lasting as long as she expected. She summarizes this in line 1 of the excerpt. (It was discovered later by the researchers that the recorder Janet used did malfunction and consumed batteries at an accelerated rate.)

(2a) 1   Janet: Yeah I've not had good battery luck today.
      2   Um so I don't know what's going on there.
      3   Steve: Boy.
      4   (No) I've had- I've had great luck with this.
      5   Janet: Gee!
      6   Well!
      7 ⇨   You're- you're the <u>sup</u>— <*chuckles*>
      8   Steve: I mean for a little while I- I plugged it in but,
      9 ⇨ Janet: You're the <u>superior</u> <*laughing*> subject.>
     10   <*laughing*> I'm just kidding.>
     11   Steve: I just have the <u>superior</u> batteries apparently.
     12   Janet: Right,
     13   well that's good.
     14   Um,
     15   Steve: It's funny though sometimes because when I had →
     16   the regular batteries in it?

Here, Janet explicitly (though humorously) positions Steve as the "superior" research subject, teasing him after he emphasizes the luck he has been having with recording that day. The frame of this interaction is playful, as cued by Janet's laughter accompanying her utterance *You're the superior subject*, as well as by her metacomment in line 10, *I'm just kidding.* (Note however that the metacomment also suggests that Janet's attempt at play needed to be overtly pointed out to Steve.) As the interaction continues from line 15 and following, Steve describes to Janet a few taping troubles of his own—this move can be considered one of solidarity and "matching" and could be used to address any perceived power or status imbalances.[4]

As in the example from the Patterson/Foley family, understanding the complexity of framing in this conversation depends on having access to prior text, because the word "superior" as it pertains to the research project did not "originate" in this interaction. In an interaction occurring the day before the conversation shown in 2a, the word surfaces as a way of playfully negotiating who is the "better" research subject, that is, who more closely follows the directions given by the researchers. On the first day of taping for Janet and Steve (Wednesday), the interaction shown in 2b occurred the moment Janet started recording. In this excerpt, she is trying to make sure her recorder is working, and she seems to be talking to herself in lines 1–9 as she fiddles with it. The "cheat sheet" she refers to consists of a simplified set of instructions for operating the tape recorder given to all participating families.

(2b)	1	Janet:	Okay, ((*to self it seems*))
	2		there we go.
	3		Start I D—
	4		Oh now that's you're supposed to hit something,
	5		when- when it's flashing that.
	6		(Oh) I forget what,
	7		we gotta go get that cheat sheet.
	8		Oh, now it's not doing that.
	9		Okay.
	10	Steve:	I'm not having any troubles.
	11	Janet:	Well of course you're not.
	12 ⇨	Steve:	I must be <u>superior</u>!
	13	Janet:	O:h boy.
	14		((*short pause*))
	15		Yes you must be.
	16		Did you—
	17		Oh, oh it's Wednesday . morning, ((*reporting*))

18		at seven fifty-five.
19		Did you announce your time? ((*to Steve*))
20	Steve:	Why yes of course I did.
21	Janet:	<*laughing*> Oh well,
22 ⇨		you really are <u>superior</u>!>
23		<*clears throat*>
24		Okay peaches, ((*to Natalie*))
25		we've got to brush those choppers!

Steve, perhaps "showing off" for the researchers who will eventually listen to the tapes, jokingly describes himself as the "superior" participant in the study in line 12. This contrasts with and responds to Janet struggling with verifying that the recorder is working and her considering consulting the cheat sheet. In line 16, Janet seems to recall that they were instructed to say the date and time at the beginning of each audiotape; she reports this information into the recorder in lines 17–18, and then asks Steve if he did this (line 19, *Did you announce your time?*). When Steve confirms that he did, the term "superior" surfaces again, with Janet laughingly exclaiming to her husband, *Oh well, you really are superior* (lines 21–22) before getting on with the morning activity of brushing Natalie's teeth ("choppers").

This pair of excerpts of conversation between Janet and Steve suggest that Janet's use of the word "superior" in the phone conversation with Steve on Thursday finds its source in Wednesday morning's episode, where Steve teasingly called himself superior (and Janet teasingly confirmed his superiority). When the topic of "taping and the troubles associated with it" resurfaces, so does a word and an associated stance used in the original conversation about it—"superior." (It may be worth pointing out here that though Steve positions himself or was positioned as the "superior subject," he was in fact, at least from the perspective of the project, not necessarily "superior": As noted earlier, he inadvertently recorded over a number of his own tapes, thereby erasing previously recorded data.) When Janet repeats Steve's comment *I must be superior* in the form of *You're the superior subject*, her words are double-voiced in Bakhtin's sense: They work to respond to the interaction where Steve jokingly claimed superiority (excerpt 2b) via teasing. Additionally, Janet's utterance is a comment occasioned by Steve's immediately prior remark that he was not having problems with his batteries when Janet was, and her utterance responds to that. Janet's

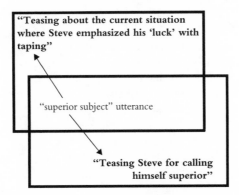

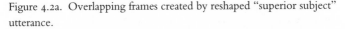

Figure 4.2a. Overlapping frames created by reshaped "superior subject" utterance.

repetition of Steve's words thus creates two meanings; her words can be described as polysemous. This duality of meaning is represented in figure 4.2a, which illustrates how the intertextual repetition creates overlapping frames.

Interestingly, a similar use of *superior* reappears in one later interaction between Janet and Steve and adds an additional layer of meaning. This use occurred on Sunday. Natalie has just used the potty, and Steve cleans up around the toilet. Janet is also present. Suddenly there is a loud noise on the tape; Steve has knocked down a picture. Minutes earlier he had broken a glass jar that belonged to Janet. Steve reacts to his knocking down of the picture in line 1.

(2c)	1	Steve:	Jesus!
	2	Janet:	Uh oh!
	3		What was that?
	4	Steve:	A picture.
	5	Janet:	Huh?
	6	Natalie:	Daddy . what was that?
	7	Steve:	<*louder, possibly irritated*> Just a picture!>
	8	Janet:	Why are you Mister Clumsy today.
	9	Steve:	[No!]
	10	Natalie:	[Daddy] what was that? .
	11		Daddy what was that?
	12	Steve:	<*sounds less irritated*> A picture.>

13	Janet:	Is it all right?
14	Steve:	Yes it's fine.
15		It comes off all the time.
16	Natalie:	Is it all right?
17	Steve:	It's fine honey thanks.
18		It's very close to the rail,
19	Janet:	I've never . knocked down—
20	Steve:	Of course you haven't.
21 ⇨		You are far <u>superior</u>.
22	Janet:	<*laughs*>
23		I'm just saying you first broke that, ((*the glass jar*))
24		now you are knocking down pictures.

This excerpt of conversation is in some ways a replay of excerpt 2b. Although the topic of talk is no longer recording, some of the same language plays into both interactions, in particular the words "of course" and "superior" and their surrounding syntax. In 2b (lines 10–12), Janet had been describing some troubles she had been having with her recorder when Steve told Janet he was not having problems with his (*I'm not having any troubles*). Janet had then responded, *Well of course you're not*, and Steve jokingly replied, *I must be superior!* In 2c (lines 18–21), Steve gives a possible reason why he knocked a picture down (*It's very close to the rail*), Janet says *I never . knocked down* and is cut off, and Steve responds: *Of course you haven't. You are far superior.* This conversation also links back to the one shown in excerpt 2a, where Janet jokingly called Steve the superior subject (line 9). The tenor of excerpt 2c is more agitated and less playful than excerpts 2a and 2b—perhaps because breaking family objects is a more serious offense than bragging about one's ability to operate a recorder for a research study, and it is face-threatening to refer to someone as "Mister Clumsy." However, there is perhaps humor and bonding here too: *Mr. Clumsy* is the name of a popular children's book by Roger Hargreaves, so Janet might be making an intertextual reference to this book that she thinks Steve will recognize. In any case, Steve seems upset to have earlier broken Janet's glass jar, he apologizes to her, and they end up involved in a playful exchange, as is typical in this family: Janet laughs about Steve's use of "superior" (line 22), and moments later asks in a child-like voice, "Don't we love each other a

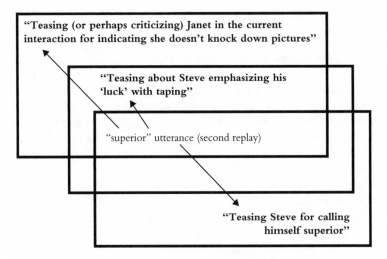

Figure 4.2b. Overlapping frames created by re-reshaping of "superior" utterance.

little bit?" Steve jokingly replies, "Well we're satisfied." Then Janet laughs again. The repetition of prior text as shown in excerpt 2c can be viewed as creating overlapping frames as show in figure 4.2b.

Figure 4.2b demonstrates how multiple frames can be conceptualized as overlapping. It aims to capture how, in referring to Janet as superior, Steve's utterance recalls not one but two prior interactions (although the repetition does link more closely to the prior text occurring in excerpt 2b). The utterance thus responds to something in the current interaction (Steve knocking down the picture and Janet emphasizing she has never knocked it down). It also responds to her prior uttering of these words to tease Steve about his recording successes. Finally, it in some way subjects Steve's own prior use of the word *superior* (in excerpt 2b) to "harsh treatment" in the sense that it contradicts it: In 2b Steve had (jokingly) proclaimed *I must be superior*; here, he describes Janet as *far superior* to him. In these ways, Steve's use of *superior* in the last excerpt, 2c, carries traces of his and Janet's voices from both prior interactions, creating not two but three overlapping frames.

"PIZZA!": Steve and Janet

The first two sets of excerpts considered in this chapter showed over-lapping frames being created to direct two simultaneous meanings to one's co-interlocutor: commenting (negatively, though teasingly) on caregiving abilities and one's earlier utterance about caregiving abilities (Kathy and Sam) and commenting (negatively, though teasingly) on recording abilities and prior reference to one's self as superior in this regard as well as being superior in one other (less humorous) context (Janet and Steve). In these first examples, intertextual repetition can be viewed primarily as a means of negotiating footings or alignments between spouses (criticizer/criticized, teaser/teased). The next two pairs of excerpts show a slightly different phenomenon that surfaced in the conversations of these families: Overlapping one frame of commentary with another frame of "doing something" in the current interaction beyond commenting on the behav-ior of one's spouse. The first pair of excerpts is drawn from the discourse of the Neeley-Masons. Whereas in the "superior" example shown in 2a, Janet repeated prior text to create two overlapping teasing frames, here she repeats shared prior text to tease Steve (commenting on his behavior in a humorous way) while simultaneously accomplishing the action of testing the phone recorder the family was using as part of their participation in the family discourse study.

In excerpt 3a, Janet and Steve were talking in the kitchen one evening. This was the evening when Jill and Tim had come over for dinner; Natalie was in the next room playing with them. At the beginning of the excerpt, Steve apologizes to Janet for behavior he exhibited earlier while ordering Chinese food for dinner: He had loudly yelled while on the phone, as we'll see in excerpt 3b. In 3a, Janet describes this behavior using the familylect term "meltdown" (line 2). Then, Janet and Steve speculate about whether Steve's "misbehavior" was captured by the recorder they had hooked up to their home phone. Janet subsequently tests the recorder, shown in lines 45–47.

(3a) 1 Steve: I'm sorry I had a- . a vocal display.
      2 Janet: A- a scary meltdown?
      3 Steve: Oh my God.
      4 Janet: In front of all of our friends?[5]

5	Steve:	It was- it was bad.
6	Janet:	It was bad.
7		There's no . questioning that it was bad.
8		Does this go together somehow? ((*[glass?] object?*))
9	Steve:	No, ((*sound of glass clinking*))
10		that's totally separate. ((*sound of glass clinking*))
11	Janet:	Oh.
12		((*short pause*))
13		Okay.
14		((*short pause*)) Well this will just renew →
15		everyone's enthusiasm for pizza.
16	Steve:	<*laughing*> Yea::h.>
17	Janet:	<*chuckles*>
18		((*short pause*))
19		<*chuckles*> I wonder if that conversation got taped.
20		Did you notice?
21	Steve:	Oh I didn't even.
22		((*short pause*))
23	Janet:	That would be really humiliating.
24		[I don't] really think it did.
25	Steve:	[(?)]
26		Yeah.
27		I- I don't know what's with that thing. ((*re: recorder*))
28		((*short pause*))
29		[(Yes.)]
30	Janet:	[Are] you sure that you're not supposed to hit record →
31		when it- when like you start talking?
32	Steve:	No,
33		that's why it's hooked into that remote thing.
34		Y- you have record already pushed,
35	Janet:	Right.
36	Steve:	and then it- I mean,
37		pick up the phone,
38		and- and um get a dial tone,
39		and you'll see it'll start,

40		but then [it'll stop.]
41	Janet:	[Oh it will?]
42	Steve:	Yeah.
43		((*sound of phone picking up*))
44		((*short pause*))
45 ⇨	Janet:	<*falsetto*> Yes,
46 ⇨		I'd like to order some Chinese food.
47 ⇨		<*louder*> Pi:::zza::::!>>
48	Steve:	<*chuckles breathily*>
49		(Well) is it working?
50	Janet:	Seems to be.
51	Steve:	Oh that's good.

((*discussion continues: how the telephone recorder works; joking about how embarrassed they are to have a prior conversation caught on tape*))

In the lines 45–47, Janet tests the phone recorder by picking up the receiver and talking into the phone. However, she does not utter something that might be expected when testing recording equipment, such as *testing, one, two, three*. Instead she uses a playful falsetto voice to announce that she would like to order Chinese food, and then pretends to yell *pizza*, drawing out the word. To understand the meaning of Janet's utterances, access to prior text is necessary, for they have meaning beyond simply testing the recorder. The word *pizza* and its manner of production, as well as its juxtaposition with the action of ordering Chinese food, "originated" approximately ten minutes prior to the interaction shown in excerpt 3a in excerpt 3b, a conversation that involved Steve ordering Chinese food on the phone. Its use in 3a thus constitutes an instance of intertextually repeated prior text.

Some background information is necessary to understand the development of the extreme frustration that Steve displays in excerpt 3b. Janet, Steve, Jill, and Tim had decided to order Chinese food instead of the usual delivery dinner they have when they get together—pizza (everyone was tired of pizza). Everyone (including Steve) was hungry. Steve had called a Chinese restaurant and discovered that they no longer offered delivery. Then, during his call to the next Chinese restaurant, he has a very difficult interaction with the person who answered the phone. This seems to be due in part to Steve having trouble understanding the restaurant employee's heavily accented nonnative English as well as the fact that Steve and the employee are apparently looking at different versions of the menu. As Steve's frustration develops during his telephone interaction, Janet reacts by chuckling and reporting Steve's lack of progress ordering to their friends. Steve's frustration reaches a crescendo when he desperately (and self-mockingly) calls out "Pizza!" loudly during the call (he was on hold at that time, though Janet did not know this). The transcript begins several minutes into the difficult phone call and shows what Janet and Steve both hear. The utterances produced by the restaurant employee, which are not relevant for the analysis here, are not shown. In line 47, Steve tries to order vegetarian soup for himself and Jill (as Steve is a vegetarian and Jill often eats vegetarian food).

(3b)	47	Steve:	What kind of vegetarian soup do you have.
	48		((*short pause*))
	49		Do you- do you have spinach and bean curd.
	50	Janet:	<*chuckling*> It's not going well.> ((*to Jill and Tim*))
	51	Steve:	How many sizes do you have it in.
	52	Janet:	<*chuckling*> It's just not going well.>
	53	Steve:	Okay.
	54		For one person?
	55		It serves one.
	56	Tim:	When in doubt,
	57		order a calzone.
	58	Jill:	Ugh I don't want pizza products!
	59 ⇨	Steve:	<*very loudly, but not into phone*> PI:::ZZA:::::::::::::::::::!>
	60	Janet:	Did you just hang up? ((*to Steve*))
	61	Steve:	NO. ((*to Janet*))
	62		It's for two? ((*into phone*))
	63		Okay I'll take [that.]
	64	Janet:	[You're] screaming "<u>pizza</u>" in the phone?!
	65	Jill:	And you're getting taped?
	66	Steve:	Egg drop soup for one,
	67	Janet:	Oh my God,
	68		he's (???)

((*Steve continues to order for several more minutes*))

Steve, having grown increasingly frustrated as he struggles to place his order, yells "pizza" while he is on hold, perhaps demonstrating for the others that ordering pizza would be simpler. Janet immediately reacts to the yelling, quickly asking if he had hung up (he had not). When Steve tells her this, Janet responds with surprise, perhaps playing to the audience of their friends and/or the researchers, uttering *You're scream-ing "pizza" in the phone?!* (line 64). Jill then references the fact that their interactions were being recorded (line 65).

Approximately ten minutes later, the conversation where Janet pretends to order Chinese food and reproduces Steve calling out "pizza" occurs (shown in excerpt 3a). For this conversation, Janet and Steve seem to be largely out of earshot of Jill and Tim, who are playing with Natalie in the other room. As Janet repeats Steve's prior telephon-ing behavior, she actually picks up the phone to test the recording equipment to see if the yelling was captured by the recorder (it was). However, Janet does not simply reenact Steve's phone call to check the recording equipment; she simultaneously comments on the appropri-ateness of his earlier behavior, in essence teasingly pointing out its ridiculousness. She does this by speaking in a falsetto voice and by juxtaposing two central interactional moves: the polite initial request to order Chinese food (which one would expect to hear from someone talking on the phone with a stranger in a service encounter), and the subsequent (unexpected) loud, elongated calling out of "pizza," which mimics Steve's production of that word.

Janet calling out "pizza" performs multiple projects at once: It has a dual orientation and as a repetition it is double-voiced. First, it creates a frame relevant to the current interaction where Janet undertakes the action of testing the recording equipment. Simultaneously, she is able to comment on (via teasing) Steve's prior yelling of "pizza." This is illustrated in figure 4.3.

Through intertextual repetition, Janet creates a polysemous utter-ance. Both meanings of Janet's words (i.e., both frames signaled by her words) are accessible to the participants because they were jointly involved in the prior interaction. Another way of thinking about this is in terms of the centrality of intertextuality in meaning-making in the excerpt: Reshaping linguistic material from a shared prior experience enables the participants to create and discern multiple, overlapping meanings.

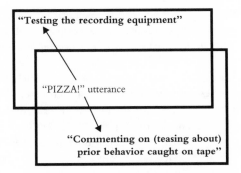

Figure 4.3. Overlapping frames created by reshaped "PIZZA!" utterance.

"Are You Gonna Let Me Burn Your Popcorn?": Kathy and Sam

The next pair of excerpts was drawn from conversations of the Patterson/Foley family and shows Sam recycling shared prior text to create a duality of meaning that creates overlapping frames. Like Janet's use of prior text to simultaneously tease and test the recording equipment, Sam's repetition of prior text in this example accomplishes both teasing (though he seems to be teasing about or making fun of himself, not Kathy) and an action (agreeing to do a task for Kathy).

In excerpt 4a, occurring Sunday evening, Sam, Kathy, and Kira are in the kitchen at home. *Star Trek: The Next Generation* is on the television in the background, and Kira seems to be showing interest in her bottle (*ba-ba*, lines 1–3) and in Sam's pen (*Dada pen,* lines 4–5). Kathy is making popcorn. Kathy indirectly asks Sam if he will watch the popcorn in line 7, and Sam agrees in line 10.

(4a)	1	Kira:	Ba-ba!
	2	Kathy:	Ba-ba!
	3	Kira:	Ba-ba, (pop.)
	4	Sam:	Dada pen?
	5		Dada pen?
	6		((*short pause*))
	7	Kathy:	<*quietly*> (?? real quick.)
	8	Sam:	<*chuckling*> Yeah you can you can-> [oh, the popcorn.]
	9	Kathy:	[<*chuckles*>]

10 ⇨ Sam: Are you gonna let me <u>burn</u> your <u>popcorn</u>?
11   Kathy: I'll be out before that happens.
((*Kathy leaves the room, possibly to go to the bathroom*))

In line 10, Sam verifies that he will watch the popcorn that Kathy is making while she leaves the room (to go to the bathroom, it seems). However, instead of saying something to the effect of "yes, I'll watch the popcorn," he asks if she is going to let him burn her popcorn. This utterance is actually a reference to a prior conversation that occurred three days before.

Excerpt 4b shows the prior conversation, where Sam burned popcorn after a long argument with Kathy about who made better popcorn and whether Sam had burned popcorn in the past.[6] At the beginning of the excerpt, Kathy is in the kitchen, and Sam is calling to her from another room where he is with Kira. (The terms *burn* and *popcorn* are repeated throughout this argument; particularly relevant lines are arrowed.)

(4b)   10   Sam: Ka::th! ((*calling out from another room*))
11   Kathy?
12   Kathy: What?
13   Sam: Let's switch.
14   Kathy: Why.
15   Sam: I don't know, ((*coming into kitchen*))
16   you take care of her,
17   I'll do whatever you're doin'.
18   Kathy: I'm making <u>popcorn</u>.
19 ⇨   But you always <u>burn</u> it.
20   Sam: No, I don't!
21 ⇨   I never <u>burn</u> it,
22   I always make it perfect.
23   ((*short pause*))
24   You making <u>popcorn</u>?
25   In the (big) pot, [or?]
26   Kathy: [Yes,] but you're going to ruin it.

27   Sam: No, I won't!

28   I'll get it just right.

((*lines 29–40: Kathy talks about diapers and "poo-poo"*
with Kira))

((*lines 41–49: Kathy tells Kira that they will make*
popcorn and not allow Sam to do it))

50   Sam: I can make popcorn better than you can!

51   Kathy: Daddy (?)

52   Sam: I cook every kernel.

53   Kathy: (No,) you (don't)!

54   Sam: (I do!)

55   (I do!)

56   ⇨   It's never burned!

57   ⇨   It always burns when you do it! ((*popping sound*))

((*lines 58–64: Kathy talks to Kira about popcorn and*
about changing Kira's diaper))

65   Kathy: Don't make excuses for yourself. ((*to Sam*))

66   Sam: (????) the trick.

67   Kathy: I know the trick!

68   Sam: No, you don't,

69   ⇨   'cause you always burn it.

70   Kathy   <*high, exasperated*>I do NO::T!

71   What are you, crazy!>

((*lines 72–75: Kathy talks about "pee-pee" with Kira*))

((*lines 76–89: Kathy leaves the kitchen, and Sam comes*
into the kitchen))

((*line 90: Kathy returns to the kitchen where Sam is*
making popcorn))

((*lines 91–110: Kathy instructs Sam to heat the popcorn;*
Sam rejects her instructions; Sam talks to Kira, telling her
to help Kathy put the dishes away))

111   Kathy: (You gotta) take the trash outside. ((*to Sam*))

112   Sam: I ca:n't,

113   I'm doin' the popcorn.

114   Kathy: I'll DO it,

115		I'll watch it.
116		You take the trash out →
117		and come back in a few minutes and—
118	Sam:	(No,)
119 ⇨		because it'll <u>burn</u>!
120		Take the . water.

((lines 121–125: Sam tells Kira to help Kathy put the dishes away))

126	Sam:	Now it's popping.
127		Hear it?
128		[(??)]
129	Kathy:	[I make] it perfect.
130 ⇨	Sam:	I've NEVER <u>burned</u> it.
131	Kira:	<wail-sings>

((lines 132–142: Kathy talks to Kira while emptying the dishwasher))

143 ⇨	Sam:	(??) get <u>burned</u>.
144	Kathy:	Fine, but if it starts smoking you have take it →
145		off the oven.
146 ⇨		Remember last time you <u>burned</u> it?
147		That's what happened.

((lines 148–165: Sam burns the popcorn; Sam blames the pot, and Kathy blames Sam))
((line 166–187: Kathy tells Sam that the popcorn is inedible and instructs him to throw it away, while Sam continues to blame the pot Kathy selected))

This long excerpt, which is filled with intratextual repetition regarding burning popcorn, makes it apparent that Sam's utterance about popcorn "originates" in this interaction (and certainly has a family history farther back that was not captured on tape, though for the purposes of this analysis, 4b will be considered the original). In 4a, where Sam intertextually repeats the words *burn* and *popcorn* in agreeing to watch the popcorn by saying, *Are you gonna let me burn your popcorn* (line 10), Sam's utterance does not seem to refer to any one utterance from the previous interaction, but rather to that interaction as a whole. Nevertheless, in recalling this prior exchange through repetition, Sam's utterance creates two separate frames. First, what is going on in the interaction is that Kathy leaves the task of popping the popcorn in Sam's hands, and he agrees to take on this task. Second, Sam is commenting on the previous interaction in which he and Kathy argued about who would make the popcorn, and he ended up burning it. Sam thus uses these words to make fun of his prior burning of popcorn and Kathy's prediction of his burning "her" popcorn, as well as to indirectly apologize for the earlier incident by admitting fault whereas previously he insisted it was her fault (she chose the wrong pot). He takes up an apologetic and slightly self-mocking footing. Sam's utterance thus creates frames as shown in figure 4.4, thereby capturing these meanings.

Sam simultaneously acknowledges that he will watch the popcorn and calls attention to the prior popcorn argument, which included Kathy accusing him of burning popcorn (an accusation that turns out to be valid). The single utterance involving intertextual repetition of two key words from a prior interaction (*burn* and *popcorn*) works to create a layering of meaning captured by Goffman's concept of frame lamination, which in this pair of excerpts of interaction I suggest is best conceptualized and represented as overlapping frames.

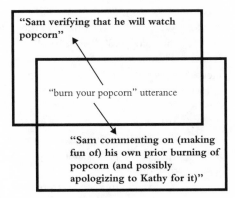

Figure 4.4. Overlapping frames created by reshaped "burn your popcorn" utterance.

"When You Make Tinkles in Those, the Colors Will Disappear": Janet and Natalie

The last example I present of the construction of overlapping frames involves a child—Natalie Neeley-Mason—laminating frames in this manner. Because children often repeat what they hear (both within and across conversations), it is perhaps not surprising that Natalie, an especially talkative child, uses language to link two disparate conversations together and layer meanings. This particular example has to do with her ongoing toilet training.

The scene is at a local K-Mart one early afternoon. Janet and Natalie are at the checkout with their purchases. Natalie tells the (female) cashier about some pull-ups[7] (special toilet-training diapers that look like underpants) that Janet is buying for her. Here, Janet is a listener who is ratified but not addressed by Natalie, who directs her utterances to the cashier.

(5a)   1   Natalie: Hi.
       2   Cashier: Hi.
       3   Natalie: We got those (things) [(from) back there.]
       4   Cashier: [You have a one-fifty,]
       5   nice price.
       6   Janet: <chuckles politely>
       7   ⇨ Natalie: When you make <u>tinkles</u> in those, ((to cashier))
       8   ⇨   the colors will <u>disappear</u>.
       9   Cashier: They will!?
      10   Janet: <laughs>
      11   Cashier: They do!?
      12   Natalie: Yeah.
      13   ⇨   When you keep them <u>dry</u>,
      14   ⇨   they won't [<u>disappear</u>.]
      15   Cashier: [Keep them dry,]
      16   they don't.
      17   You trying to keep them real dry?
      18   That's a good girl.
      19   One of these days you won't need them,
      20   (????)
      21   Janet: <chuckles>

In this excerpt, Natalie explains to the cashier how, if one wets the pull-ups (if you "make tinkles"), the colorful flowers on them will vanish. (This feature of the pull-ups is intended to motivate the child to keep them dry.) Natalie takes on a teacher footing vis-à-vis the cashier, who readily cooperates with this somewhat humorous interaction. As it turns out, in this excerpt, Natalie is intertextually reshaping her mother's words from a conversation that occurred about ten minutes before.

In that conversation, Natalie is first introduced to the special toilet-training diapers with the colorful flowers that disappear. Although Natalie has other pull-ups at home, this type is new to her. Janet has just found a box of these new pull-ups in Natalie's size and begins to explain to Natalie how they work. Natalie shows interest, asking questions, requesting that Janet talk further about them, and intratextually repeating her mother's explanations. (Notice that we also saw Natalie intratextually repeating Janet in excerpt 2c, in which Steve knocked down the picture. Indeed Natalie frequently repeated the words of her mother across the family's taping week; see, e.g., Gordon 2007b)

(5b)	1	Janet:	These pull-ups,
	2		guess what THEY do.
	3	Natalie:	What do THEY do.
	4	Janet:	They are pretty special.
	5		You know why?
	6	Natalie:	Why.
	7	Janet:	Because . what they do is,
	8		whoa. ((*something falls it seems*))
	9		They . .
	10	Natalie:	They what.
	11 ⇨	Janet:	Um . . they have <u>flowers</u> on them,
	12 ⇨		and if you keep your pull-ups <u>dry</u>,
	13 ⇨		then <u>the flowers</u> stay there.
	14 ⇨		But if you w- make a <u>tinkles</u>,
	15 ⇨		then <u>the flowers</u> <u>disappear</u>!
	16	Natalie:	Why if I make a <u>tinkles</u> <u>the flowers</u> will <u>disappear</u>.
	17	Janet:	Because they're trying to—
	18		They're trying to get you to keep them nice →
	19		and <u>dry</u>.
	20	Natalie:	Why—

21		Can we talk about these?
22		Can we talk about these specials?
23	Janet:	Sure.
24 ⇨	Natalie:	I want to say they- when you make a <u>tinkles</u> in →
25		them,
26		they <u>disappear</u>.
27		((*short pause*))
28	Janet:	Well because the point is to keep your →
29		pull-ups <u>DRY</u>.

Here Janet is teaching Natalie about the pull-ups, with Natalie in the role of enthusiastic learner. When Natalie repeats these words in her talk with the cashier, there are some changes: *The flowers* (5b, lines 13 and 15) becomes *the colors* (5a, line 8), for example. However, key words (e.g., *disappear*), syntactic frames (*if/when X, Y*), and the basic meaning are retained. Thus, in doing the reshaping, Natalie re-creates the teaching frame she experienced with her mother, this time taking on the teacher footing. In addition, by repeating Janet's prior words in her presence, Natalie not only endorses Janet's use of these words in a Bakhtinian sense, she also demonstrates to her mother that she understands the new training diapers. This is illustrated in figure 4.5.

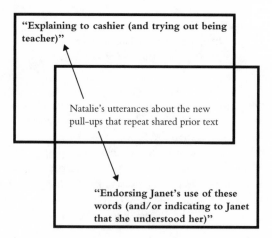

Figure 4.5. Overlapping frames created by Natalie's words about pull-ups echoing prior text.

In this example, Natalie repeats her mother's words to speak to a third party, the cashier at the store. However, there are many examples of Natalie repeating Janet's words intertextually in conversation between the two of them and layering frames in a similar manner. Many of these examples are those in which Janet has taught Natalie about something or is socializing her into something, and Natalie repeats words related to this teaching or socializing back to Janet across interactions. (Other instances involve intertextual repetition in role-play; an example of this is examined in the next section of this chapter.) Examples of intertextual repetition creating overlapping frames in conversations that involved Natalie frequently pertained to potty-training. For instance, one afternoon Natalie "made poopy" in her pull-up and got upset (note that this is one of the few instances where the term "poopy" is used instead of the more common familylect term "poops"). Janet asked her if she was upset because she didn't use the toilet: "Did you want to try to use the potty, and- and you couldn't quite get there?" and Natalie concurs: "I wanted to y- I wanted to use the potty and I couldn't quite get there." Later in the day, Natalie successfully uses the potty, and she recalls the earlier conversation, telling her mother: "When I made poopy in my pull-up, I didn't get here on time." Her words show an understanding of the current situation (in which she realized she had to use the potty and successfully did it); in addition, by using her mother's words, Natalie creates a dialogic relation of agreement regarding how these words should be used and in what circumstances. This example, similar to the conversations about grapes (*You just pop them in*) that I discussed in chapter 1 as well as the flower pull-ups excerpts just shown, demonstrates how intertextual repetition serves as a resource for creating overlapping frames.

EMBEDDED FRAMES

Whereas the overlapping frames configuration features two (or more) frames, each with its own (distinct) metamessage, one relating to a current context and at least one to a context prior, what I call "embedded frames" refers to a situation in which a frame with a more specific metamessage is completely embedded in a frame with a more general metamessage. In his discussion of the lamination of frames, Goffman (1974: 82) introduces the phrase "rim of the frame"; the rim "tells us just what sort of status in the real world the activity has, whatever the complexity of the inner laminations." In what I call embedded frames, there is only one rim, with one overall definition of the situation. However, there is at least one inner lamination within that frame's rim.

To illustrate this phenomenon, I analyze two parent–child pretend play episodes in the Neeley-Mason family and the original interaction on which the role-play is based. My analysis of this trio of excerpts builds on Goffman's (1974:182–183) observation that any "strip of activity" can sustain many "transformations," particularly in theatrical, novelistic, and cinematic works, for instance Shakespeare's play within a play in *Hamlet*, or the book within a book in William Goldman's *The Princess Bride*. These embedded frames share one general rim (e.g., as identified by the frame "this is a theatrical performance," or "this is a novel"), which means that the embedded frames work to further specify the nature of the broader activity identified by the rim. As in previous pairs of examples, to emphasize the integral role of prior text in utterance interpretation and frame identification, I first present the excerpts showing reshaping, then the earlier interaction whence from the prior text was drawn.

First, I want to give a little bit of background on the types of play that occur in the Neeley-Mason family. As we have already seen in chapter 2, Janet and Steve are generally playful people. They frequently play with Natalie: They play with toys and dolls with her, they play games like hide and seek, and during the recording week they even tried to teach her to play the card game go fish. However, the kind of play they participate in most with Natalie is pretend role-play, in which, for instance, Natalie pretends to be "Mommy" and Janet plays the role of "Natalie" or Natalie plays the role of a doll's mother and Steve plays the role of a doctor. This is a kind of play Natalie greatly enjoys, and her parents generally participate with enthusiasm (or feigned enthusiasm). (The fact that Steve and Janet act in children's theater may help explain their willingness to engage in extended pretend play sequences with Natalie, and, as we saw in chapter 2, in frames of play more generally.) These role-plays (like all instances of play) depend fundamentally on framing, as framing is crucial to the joint understanding of utterances as pretend.

Past work on children's role-play (e.g., Garvey 1976; Fein 1981; Corsaro 1983; Cook-Gumperz 1992; Bergman & Lefcourt 1994; Kyratzis 1999; Paugh 2005) has considered role-play to represent a child's basic social understanding, e.g., how mommies and daddies talk, and has suggested that it serves as a means of identity experimentation. Although these observations are critical to understanding the role of play in children's lives, most studies have focused largely on play as consisting of one and only one play frame (exceptions include Hoyle 1993; Gordon 2002, 2008). However, play can also be analyzed as composed of specific instances of prior text that are used to create and embed multiple play frames. The set of excerpts I present illustrates how "particular prior texts" that are "acquired from particular sources" (Becker 1995:86) are used to create meaning in discourse. Though this new conceptualization of role-play as made up of embedded frames helps elucidate the complex nature of such play, my larger purpose is to illustrate how the reshaping of prior text works to embed frames in family interaction, that is, how intertextuality is central in the process of embedding frames and creating meanings.

Elsewhere (Gordon 2002), I illustrate how frames are embedded in two role-plays between Janet and Natalie through metamessages sent by the participants' in-role utterances (e.g., those using in-role terms of address) and out-of-of role utterances (e.g., Natalie explicitly telling Janet to "be Natalie"). Here, I focus on how specific instances of repeated prior text used as in-role speech embed frames in two role-plays not analyzed in Gordon (2002). I show that by repeating the words drawn from utterances from a prior interaction in their play, Janet and Natalie, and Steve and Natalie, send metamessages that evoke and embed the frames in which they are operating.

"Sit on Your Bottom": Steve, Natalie, Janet

To elucidate how embedded frames are created, I first present two excerpts of role-play which are based on a particular previous interaction that provides a "script" and "lines" for these role-plays; the role-plays involve Natalie and Steve (excerpt 6a) and Natalie and Janet (excerpt 6b). Then, I present the real-life interaction occurring minutes before (excerpt 6c), which serves as the source of the prior text that is reshaped (6c involves Natalie and both parents). All three of these excerpts occur as Janet and Steve take turns sitting with Natalie as she takes a bath, making sure she washes thoroughly and helping her wash and rinse her hair. These bath time role-plays can be conceived of as performed narratives wherein the participants together reenact specific episodes and use specific instances of prior text from their shared past, embedding frames.

In the role-plays, several basic events occur; these events are based on the prior experience that will be shown in 6c. First is the "sitting properly in the bathtub" event. Here in the play Mommy or Daddy tells Natalie to "sit on her bottom," appealing at times to the "rules" of the bathtub, while Natalie says "no" and argues that she wants to "sit on her knees" (kneel). A second event occurring in this play linked back to the original episode is "rinsing," where Daddy rinses Natalie's hair by "counting buckets," or pouring buckets of water over her head while counting. This also includes Daddy or Mommy suggesting that Natalie should put a washcloth on her face (to keep water off of it) and look up (so her head would tilt back and the water wouldn't run into her eyes). Despite the fact that Natalie does not like to get water into her eyes or on her face, she rejects her parents' suggestions, repeatedly saying no and explaining that she wants to look down, then crying and relenting. (This script is consonant, of course, with Natalie's tendency to resist her parents across the week of recording.)

In the first excerpt (6a), Natalie is playing in the bathtub with Steve supervising. Natalie introduces a pretend play frame by assigning roles to herself and her father. This play is, as mentioned previously, based on a prior interaction, and lines that are particularly close reformulations from that interaction are indicated by arrows with key words underlined. Before this excerpt starts, Natalie is playing with a doll she calls "Fishie," while Steve tries to get her to attend to bath-related tasks such as washing her legs. (In Kendall's [2006] framework, Natalie attends the "social encounter" frame while Steve attends a task frame.) This excerpt was recorded by Steve. When he leaves with his recorder to replace its batteries, Janet takes his place, and the interaction continues on her tape (thus, we see an example of sequential co-parenting here). In line 10, "she" refers to Natalie's doll.

(6a)	10	Natalie:	Can we play she's gonna get- →
	11		get water in her face?
	12	Steve:	Uhmm.
	13	Natalie:	Now?
	14	Steve:	Yeah.
	15	Natalie:	I wanna play . that.
	16		Mm I'll take you . Daddy you,
	17		she is- . she is Natalie,

18		and . and you- and you,
19		andyou're Mommy.
20	Steve:	Ok.
21 ⇨	Natalie:	She's gonna rinse.
22	Steve:	Okay,
23 ⇨		Natalie you need to look up! ((*to doll*))
24		((*short pause*))
25 ⇨	Natalie:	She says "I wanna look down!"
26 ⇨	Steve:	Well fine then you can look down,
27 ⇨		but then you'll get water in your face.
28		((*short pause*))
29	Natalie:	Why . you talk to . Natalie?
30		She's- she's gonna get water in her face.
31		Why?
32		Wh- why Mommy?
33 ⇨		Mommy why does she have to look up?
34 ⇨	Steve:	Well if she looks down,
35 ⇨		then she gets water in her face.
36 ⇨		Well if she looks up,
37 ⇨		then water's just . runs off her head.

((*several moments later Steve leaves the bathroom, and Janet replaces him as bath giver*))

Several minutes later, Natalie re-creates this play with Janet after Steve has left the room and in doing so repeats some of the same language appearing in 6a. This is shown in excerpt 6b. In lines 1–37, not shown here, Natalie assigns and reassigns roles for the play to herself, her doll, and Janet. In the excerpt, she assigns Janet the role of "Mommy," thus Janet is "being Mommy," a role she holds in real life. In this excerpt, Natalie tries to create play where she washes the hair of her doll. Music is playing in the background.

(6b)	38	Natalie:	You'll be Mommy,
	39		and I'll be . Daddy,
	40		you'll- and she's- ((*"she" = doll*))
	41	Janet:	I'm . →

42		Natalie:	Daddy too-
43		Janet:	I'm confused, who am I?
44		Natalie:	You're Mommy,
45			and I'm . Daddy,
46		Janet:	Okay.
47		Natalie:	and she's Natalie.
48		Janet:	OH!
49			<*play voice*> Daddy,
50			is Natalie taking a bath?>
51		Natalie:	She is taking a bath
52			and she has . (to swim).
53		Janet:	<*play voice*> Oh!>
54		Natalie:	You're Mommy.
55		Janet:	I'm Mommy?
56		Natalie:	I'm Daddy and you're Mommy,
57		Janet:	Yeah.
58		Natalie:	and she::'s . Natalie.
59	⇨	Janet:	<*play voice*> Natalie, do you wanna hold →
60	⇨		a <u>wash cloth</u> over your <u>face</u>→
61	⇨		when we <u>rinse</u>?>
62	⇨	Natalie:	She says "<u>no</u>!"
63	⇨	Janet:	But Natalie the <u>water</u> will get in your <u>face</u>!
64			Daddy what should we do?>
65		Natalie:	Why she doesn't want the <u>wash cloth</u>?
66		Janet:	<*play voice*> I don't know Daddy.
67			Maybe you can ask her.>
68		Natalie:	(She's-) Natalie,
69	⇨		do you want the <u>wash cloth</u>?
70		Janet:	<*play voice*> What did she say?>
71	⇨	Natalie:	She said "<u>no</u>!"
72		Janet:	<*play voice*> Well how are we gonna <u>rinse</u>, Daddy?>
73	⇨	Natalie:	I asked her and she said "<u>no</u>!"
74		Janet:	<*play voice*> Oh boy!
75	⇨		Well I guess you just have to get <u>water</u> →
76	⇨		in your <u>face</u> Natalie!
77	⇨		Here comes the <u>buckets</u>.

78	⇨		Help Daddy <u>count</u> the <u>buckets</u>.
79	⇨		<u>One</u>, [<u>two</u>::, <u>three</u>,>]
80	⇨	Natalie:	[<u>Two</u>:, <u>three</u>::.]
81	⇨		Do you want the <u>wash cloth</u>?
82	⇨		I asked her and she said "yes!"
83		Janet:	*<play voice>* Oh she does want it now.
84			Here we go.
85			((*short pause*))
86			There you go Natalie,
87	⇨		that will keep it out of your <u>face</u>.>
88	⇨	Natalie:	That will keep it . out of your . <u>face</u>!
89		Janet:	Oh. ((*as if sitting down*))
90		Natalie:	(???)
91		Janet:	*<sings quietly with music playing>*
92	⇨	Natalie:	<u>One</u>,
93	⇨	Janet:	*<yawning>* [<u>Two</u>.]>
94	⇨	Natalie:	[<u>Two</u>.]
95			Here Mommy,
96			and she doesn't want the <u>wash cloth</u>.
97	⇨	Janet:	*<play voice>* Natalie if you don't have →
98	⇨		the <u>wash cloth</u> honey,
99	⇨		it gets in your <u>face</u>.
100			[And I know you don't want that.>]
101	⇨	Natalie:	[If you don't have the <u>wash cloth</u>] Natalie,
102	⇨		it will get in your <u>face</u>.
103		Janet:	*<play voice>* Does she want it now Daddy?>
104		Natalie:	No!
105		Janet:	*<play voice>* Aw,
106			I guess we just have to <u>rinse</u>, Daddy,
107			and she'll just have to get it in her <u>face</u>,
108			right?
109			That's all we can do.
110			We gotta <u>rinse</u> the shampoo out.
111			Right Daddy?>
112		Natalie:	NO!
113		Janet:	NO?

114   Natalie: We can't do it.
115   Janet: <*play voice*> We can't do it Daddy?>
116   Natalie: We can't (get shampoo.)
117   Janet: <*sighs*>
118   Natalie: She got it in her <u>face</u>.
119   Janet: <*yawning*> Did she cry?>   .
120   Natalie: She cried.
121   Janet: <*yawns*> <*play voice*> Oh Natalie!
122   We tried to tell you!>
123   ((*short pause*))

The play interaction continues with Natalie making her doll (who continues to stand in as "Natalie" for the role-play) do something purposely disobedient: "stand on her knees" (kneel).

(6b)   ((*continued*))
124 ⇨ Natalie: She's standing on her <u>knees</u> in the bath!
125 ⇨ Janet: <*play voice*> Oh-oh Natalie that's not <u>the rules</u>.
126 ⇨   [On your bottom Natalie!>]
127   Natalie: [<*laughs*>]
128 ⇨ Janet: <*play voice*> Daddy tell her <u>on her bottom</u>!>
129   Natalie: <*laughs*> No.>
130   Janet: <*play voice*> N- Daddy!>
131   Natalie: <*laughs*>
132   Janet: <*laughing*> Daddy!>
133   Natalie: <*laughing*> What?>
134   Janet: <*play voice*> Daddy you're supposed to help →
135   with <u>the rules</u>!>
136   Natalie: She can't <u>sit on her bottom</u> because she's →
137   a little baby.
138   Janet: Because she's a little baby?
139   Natalie: When she is a big girl she (can) <u>sit on her</u> →
140   bottom very well.

141 Janet: *<yawning>* (Oh.)>
142 Natalie: And now I'm Mommy and you're Daddy →
143   and I'm gonna play . m—
144   Mommy I wanna . play you're Daddy,
145   and I'm [Mommy.]
146 Janet: [Oh now—]
147 Natalie: and she is Natalie.
148 Janet: All right now I am Daddy?
149 Natalie: Now you're Daddy and I'm Mommy,
150 Janet: Okay.
151 Natalie: and she is Natalie.
152 Janet: *<play voice>* Mommy?>
153 Natalie: What?
154 Janet: *<play voice>* How's Natalie's bath coming along.>
155 Natalie: Good.
156   I wanna play she's . getting <u>water</u> in her <u>face</u> →
157   Mommy.
158 Janet: *<play voice>* Oh all right.>
159   (Oh I thought I was Daddy.)
160   Am I Daddy?
161 Natalie: Yes.
162 Janet: Very confusing.
163   Okay I'm Daddy.
164   *<play voice>* Mommy, why don't you <u>rinse</u> →
165   Natalie.>
166 ⇨ Natalie: She does not have a <u>wash cloth</u>.
167 Janet: *<play voice>* Natalie you heard your Mommy,
168 ⇨   if you don't have the <u>wash cloth</u> →
169 ⇨   then it will get in your <u>face</u>.>
170   ((*short pause, sound of water splashing*))
171 Natalie: Um it got in her <u>face</u>,
172 ⇨   and she- she didn't <u>look up</u>.

173 ⇨ Janet: <*play voice*> She didn't <u>look up</u>?>
174   Natalie: No.
175   Janet: <*play voice*> Is she crying tears Mommy?>
176   Natalie: Yes.
177   Janet: <*play voice*> Oh Natalie!
178 ⇨   We tried to tell you that would happen!>
179   ((*short pause*))
180   <*sings along with song playing in background*>
         ((*they play with Natalie's doll, Natalie gets out of the tub to go potty*))

In excerpts 6a and 6b, Natalie role-plays first with her father and then with her mother. Though the roles played are assigned to different interlocutors each time, the basic plot of the role-play is the same: Mommy and Daddy are giving Natalie a bath; Natalie will not sit on her "bottom," and Mommy and Daddy reprimand her; Mommy and Daddy rinse Natalie's hair with buckets of water, and Natalie refuses to use a washcloth to protect her eyes, gets soapy water in her face, and cries. In fact, these role-plays, one building on the other, are based on an interaction occurring minutes earlier where this happened in real life, and both draw language from this prior interaction.

This prior interaction appears in excerpt 6c and involves Natalie and both of her parents. Again, Fishie is the doll that Natalie later uses in the role-play to play the role of Natalie.

(6c) 1   Natalie: I brought another friend in.
      2   Steve: I see.
      3   Natalie: Her name is Fishie.
      4   Steve: Her name is Fishie?
      5   Natalie: She's not (?).
      6   wa::ter (?).
      7 ⇨   Steve: Why don't you <u>sit on your bottom</u> please,
      8 ⇨   instead of your <u>knees</u>.

9	⇨	Natalie:	<u>No</u> on my [<u>knees.</u>]
10	⇨	Janet:	[No we <u>sit</u>] on our bottom in the bath!
11	⇨	Steve:	<u>Sit on the bottom</u> Nat!
12	⇨	Natalie:	<u>No</u>!
13		Steve:	[Natalie!]
14		Janet:	[Natalie!]
15		Steve:	One—
16		Natalie:	Na:::!
17		Janet:	Okay.
18		Steve:	There you go.
19			Thank you!
20	⇨	Natalie:	<u>No, no</u>.
21		Janet:	Natalie!
22	⇨	Natalie:	<u>No</u>.
23	⇨	Steve:	Sweetheart you need to <u>sit on your bottom</u>!
24	⇨	Janet:	That's <u>the rule</u>!
25			((*short pause*))
26		Natalie:	She's got some,
27		Steve:	(Don't criss-cross up with us.)
28	⇨	Natalie:	<u>No</u>.
29	⇨		<u>No</u> I don't wanna (criss-cross up with-)
30	⇨	Janet:	Well you need to <u>sit on your bottom</u>,
31	⇨		That is <u>the RULES</u> of tub.
32			Thank you.

((lines 33–67: *Natalie plays with her doll (not role-play), Steve gets Janet's recorder from the other room*))

68	⇨	Steve:	What are we saying about <u>sitting on your bottom</u>?
69			Thank you.
70		Natalie:	Da—
71		Steve:	Natalie I need to clean your legs now.

((lines 72–138: *talk about Janet's pregnant belly and the messy kitchen. Natalie asks if one of her toys is a bathtub toy; Steve gives the toy to her*))

139 ⇨	Steve:	On your bottom please!
140 ⇨	Janet:	On your bottom!
141 ⇨	Natalie:	<*whiney*> No:::!>
142 ⇨	Janet:	That's the RULES of the bath!
143 ⇨	Natalie:	<*whiney*>No!>
144		((*short pause*))
145		<*cries/whines*>
146 ⇨	Janet:	Help Daddy count buckets.
147	Steve:	You don't even have any water in your eyes silly.
148 ⇨		Here, hold the cloth over your eyes.
149 ⇨	Janet:	Hold the cloth,
150 ⇨		and help Daddy count the buckets.
151	Natalie:	No.
152 ⇨	Janet:	Well it's gonna get in your face,
153 ⇨		if you don't have your wash cloth there.
154 ⇨		O[ne,]
155 ⇨	Steve:	[One,]
156 ⇨	Janet:	Tw[o:::::,]
157 ⇨	Steve:	[Oo:::,]
158	Natalie:	Ah.
159	Janet:	Baby!
160 ⇨		You've got to look up!
161 ⇨	Natalie:	No.
162 ⇨	Steve:	Look up silly-billy.
163 ⇨	Natalie:	I want to look DOWN.
164 ⇨	Janet:	Well if you look down,
165 ⇨		you get water in your face.
166 ⇨	Natalie:	<*whiney*> I wanna look down,
167 ⇨		I wanna look down!>
168 ⇨	Janet:	Well you go right ahead!
169 ⇨		But then you'll get water in your face.
170	Natalie:	<*crying*> No:::!>
171	Janet:	Natalie, I'm not gonna tell you again.
172 ⇨		We sit on our bottoms [in the bath.]
173 ⇨	Steve:	[Sit on your bottom!]
174	Natalie:	<*cries*>
175	Steve:	Then bath time will be over.

176		Natalie:	*<crying>* O:::,
177	⇨		I don't wanna sit on my bottom!>
178			[*<whines>*]
179	⇨	Janet:	[That's the rules!]
180		Steve:	Why not?
181	⇨	Natalie:	I wa-, I wa- I wanna sit on my- on my- on →
182			my knees!
183	⇨	Janet:	It's not- that's not the rules.
184	⇨		[The rules are on the bottom.]
185	⇨	Natalie:	[I don't want- I want on my knees.]
186		Janet:	It's not our fault,
187	⇨		it's the rules.
188		Natalie:	Of what?
189	⇨	Janet:	It's the rules of the bath.
190	⇨	Natalie:	NO!
191		Steve:	Daddy's sitting on his bottom.
192		Natalie:	*<laughs>*
193	⇨	Janet:	That's the rules!
194	⇨	Natalie:	No.
195		Janet:	Can't do anything about some rules.
196		Natalie:	I wanna play with . Fishie,
197			and I wanna get her- get some water in her face.

((*Janet goes into the other room; role-play with Steve begins as shown in 6a*))

When events in 6c are re-created in play in 6a and 6b, conversational moves and speech acts are reproduced. In addition, in producing these speech acts, key words are repeated. For example, related to rinsing Natalie's hair, in the original episode Janet directed, *You've got to look up* (line 160) and Steve said *Look up silly-billy* (line 162), and Natalie responded by saying *No I want to look DOWN* (line 163). In the role-play where Steve plays Mommy and Natalie animates her doll as Natalie (excerpt 6a), Steve issues the directive *Natalie you need to look up* (line 23) and Natalie replies (speaking for her doll, who is "Natalie"), *She says "I wanna look down."* These reshaped conversational moves and strings of words, and others like them, send metamessages that embed frames in this play. This means that intertextually repeated sequences of words within speech acts send metamessages, such as "I'm who you were several minutes ago in our previous interaction." In the context of an

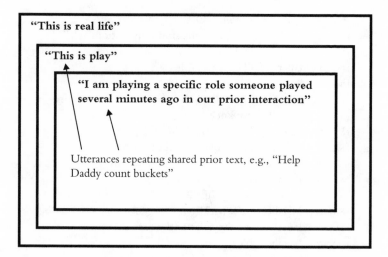

Figure 4.6. Embedded frames created by repeated prior text in bathtub role-play.

already-established play frame—which in these examples is introduced by Natalie assigning pretend-play roles—reshaping material from a prior interaction works to establish a frame wherein the participants' roles are reversed from that interaction. Thus, Janet, Steve, and Natalie's play is framed not only by the metamessage "this is play" but also by the repetition of shared prior text, which cues at least one more specific frame. This is illustrated in figure 4.6.

As an example of constructed dialogue or lines in a dramatic narrative reenactment, utterances repeating shared prior text serve to link Janet, Steve, and Natalie's pretend play roles to the roles in real life on which they are based, framing their play as a reenactment of a specific shared past experience. This specifies the nature of the larger overall activity. As Goffman (1974:182–183) notes, any "strip of activity" can sustain multiple transformations, particularly those that are theatrical in nature. Such is the case with the parent–child role-play shown here, although there is no written dramatic script. In addition, although I have not discussed the idea of overlapping frames as it pertains to this example, in repeating one another's words, Janet, Steve, and Natalie also necessarily take an evaluative stance toward how the words were used in the past. This creates overlapping frames as well.

This set of excerpts from the Neeley-Mason family's conversations shows how frames are embedded through the recycling of prior text in two back-to-back instances of parent–child role-play; these are not the only examples of embedded frames in role-play however (see Gordon [2002] for two other examples). In all of these examples, (at least) one frame is completely enclosed within another, more general frame. Thus, one rim is present in embedded frames. Further, those frames within the rim are not identifiable without access to and recognition of repeated prior text. In the ensuing discussion, I delve more into the differences and commonalities between what I have called overlapping and embedded frames. However, I also emphasize that in both cases, the repetition (and recognition) of shared prior text layers these frames, thus highlighting the linkage between intertextuality and framing.

LAYERING FRAMES IN FAMILY DISCOURSE

In sum, building on Goffman's observation that frames can be laminated in discourse, I have shown how the notion of lamination can be captured through understanding frames as being either overlapping or embedded. I have described how these configurations of frames are created through the intertextual repetition of shared prior text, specifically through the metamessages sent by the repetition. Additionally, my analysis extends Bakhtin's discussion of dialogicality and double-voiced words to everyday family interaction in illustrating that prior text is necessary for meaning-making, arguing that without access to (and recognition of) prior text, entire layers of meaning would be opaque to the participants (and the analyst).

It is important to note that as Becker has argued, all utterances are in some sense composed of prior text, and all language use or "languaging" is the reshaping of old language into new contexts (this also is captured in Bakhtin's broadest use of the word *dialogicality*). However, the instances I have analyzed in this chapter are a particular type of prior text: cases where participants hear words or strings of words embedded in a particular kind of speech act in one shared interaction, and then repeat the word(s) in a later interaction (or two later interactions) in which the repetition can presumably be recognized as a kind of quotation. In these instances, the repeated words become double-voiced. In addition, the analysis focused on examples that showed evidence of this sharing; that is to say, an original occurrence and its repetition were captured on the recording.

Furthermore, although I have argued that repeating shared prior text creates overlapping and embedded frames, I do not want to suggest that this is the only way to create these frame configurations. Elsewhere (Gordon 2002), I discuss other strategies used in role-play to embed frames, such as uses of pitch and address terms. In addition, in storytelling, where the specific instances of prior text may not be shared, frames are embedded as storytellers take on different voices. For instance, one evening Janet describes an episode of Mommy-Natalie role-play to her friends and embeds frames (see Gordon 2006). In telling this story, she uses constructed dialogue that requires her to speak (1) as herself, (2) as herself playing the role of Natalie, (3) as Natalie, and (4) as Natalie playing the role of Mommy. Thus, other linguistic strategies besides the recycling of specific instances of shared (and remembered) prior text, such as constructed dialogue— where the audience may or may not have access to the actual prior text— clearly relate to the creation and lamination of frames in interaction.

Embedded frames are thus created when broad activities (such as "play") become specified or more fine-tuned through the repetition of shared and remembered prior text. In contrast, the necessity of evaluating reshaped words in some way (e.g., as something worthy of emulating or mocking, or as something in between) manifests in the form of overlapping frames. Sorting out exactly how to characterize this evaluation in everyday discourse is a complex task. In addition, the interactive effect is somewhat difficult to pin down in that even if a repetition is intended to be "harsh," as for instance when one interlocutor repeats the words of another clearly for the purpose of mocking that other, it still identifies the original as worth repeating and presumes shared recognition. Morson (1989:73) gets at this in his interpretation of parody: "Even a true parody cannot help paying one compliment to its original, namely, that the original is important enough to be worth discrediting." In the context of family, repeating identifies an original as worth repeating, too, regardless of the evaluative stance the speaker takes toward the words he or she repeats. In this sense, repeating in these examples of family discourse always points to members' shared history of words and thus has an interpersonal binding function as it simultaneously works to laminate frames.

FIVE

"Kelly, I Think That Hole Must Mean Tigger"

Blending Frames and Reframing in Interaction

A s the last chapter identified and described the linguistic construction of overlapping and embedded frames, highlighting the role of intertextual repetition in creating these laminations, here I investigate the notion of blended frames and examine the process of reframing.[1] I also focus on a different type of prior text that is intertextually reshaped—words from children's books. I demonstrate how Janet recontextualizes bits of text from a storybook much loved by Natalie as a means of creating blended frames in conversation with her, specifically combining frames of play with task-based frames. I also show how both Natalie and Janet interweave bits of text from this children's storybook with those from another to repeatedly reframe what is occurring in one extended interaction. As in chapter 4, repetition of specific bits of prior text is identified as a strategy for meaning-making in conversation. However, here multiple repetitions are considered; although these repetitions do not occur as frequently as the familylect lexical items examined in chapter 2, they are repeated more than once or twice, creating a longer intertextual chain or even comprising a web of interrelated texts. The prior text also has a written (rather than a spoken) source, and a source that is more "public" than prior family conversations. However, through reshaping this prior text in particular ways, the participants use it for their own purposes and in some sense make it their own by imbuing it with new meanings.

In identifying blended frames, I further delve into and specify Goffman's discussion of laminated frames. In describing them, I compare and contrast this configuration with what I have called *overlapping* and *embedded frames* while also demonstrating the fundamental role of intertextuality in creating a multiplicity of meanings. In exploring reframing, I build on prior research that considers how frames—and the keying of frames—shift moment by moment while also illustrating how intertextuality serves as a resource in this process. In addition, I identify storybooks as a productive source of prior text in creating frames in parent–child interaction. I conclude by discussing how laminated frames—particularly blended frames—relate to research in cognitive linguistics that has explored meaning-making through the notion of conceptual blending (e.g., Coulson & Fauconnier 1999; Coulson & Oakley 2000; Fauconnier & Turner 2002; Sweetser 2000; Sinha 2005; Turner 2006). I suggest how reframing and laminating frames—that is, transforming interaction and creating overlapping, embedded, and especially blended frames—can be viewed not only as part of frames theory but also as interrelated to conceptual blending, a theory of meaning-making that has a cognitive—rather than social—focus.

THE (INTERTEXTUAL) ROLE OF BOOKS IN THE NEELEY–MASON FAMILY

Natalie Neeley-Mason lives in a family that values reading and books. While visiting the family's home, I observed that there were many children's books in Natalie's bedroom, as well as elsewhere in the house. These books included a variety of types: Those based on TV programs (like *Sesame Street*) or movies (like Disney's *The Lion King*), books centered around holidays (like Christmas and Halloween), books about animals (for instance, a snake, a pelican, a spider, dinosaurs), nursery rhyme books, a book about new babies (recall that Janet was pregnant with the couple's second child), and so on. Books played a central role in Natalie's bedtime and naptime rituals. During the family's recording week, Natalie's parents read her somewhere between three and five books that she selected before naptime and another three to five before bedtime; at bedtime this was followed by "rocks and rubs." Storybook reading was a central, expected, and insisted-on part of naptime and bedtime; talk about storybooks also sometimes entered the bedtime ritual as part of "rocks" (as it did the night Tim did "rocks" with Natalie, for example, as discussed in chapter 3). At naptime, Natalie not only listened to a parent (typically her mother) read books aloud but also looked through books by herself, which she was allowed to do quietly if she wasn't tired (of course, instead of doing this, she often performed "shenanigans"). In addition, Natalie asked her parents to read books to her at other times during the day and to talk about storybooks, and they often complied. Such talk occurred in a variety of contexts, such as while members of the family were out walking, playing at the playground, engaging in pretend play at home, and in the car. Thus, Natalie was frequently exposed to storybooks and participated in talk about books; when her parents read to her, they were providing linguistic material that they and Natalie were subsequently able draw on in other kinds of interaction. This fits in with prior research noting that in families that value books and reading, children learn to use literary language across interactional contexts (Wolf & Heath 1992); it also relates to the observation that preschool children use material from books to "fuel play" with one another and interact socially (Rowe 1998).

One way of thinking about the phenomenon of drawing on what one has read (or what one has heard read aloud) in interaction is through the lens of intertextuality. This type of intertextual reshaping can be conceived of as what Tovares (2005) in the context of family discourse has called "intertextuality in action." She coined the phrase to refer to the phenomenon of parents taking what they learn about from a "public" text—such as a book, magazine, or television program—and applying it in a "private" context—specifically, performing actions related to child-rearing. Tovares's analysis considers interactions drawn from the same larger study that I draw my examples from (although the excerpts I consider are of a different type and are not considered in her study). Tovares observes, for instance, that Janet and Steve use language and objects to reward Natalie for positive behaviors, a strategy known as positive parenting and written about in parenting books they read and try to follow (such as Fraiberg's *The Magic Years*). One example of this is verbally praising Natalie and rewarding her with small chocolate candies when she successfully uses the potty (and not punishing her when she soils her diaper); the colorful pull-ups discussed in chapter 3 also fit into this parenting approach, as the child is rewarded for positive behaviors (if the child keeps the pull-ups dry, the colorful flowers remain) (Tovares 2005). In this way, an idea from a parenting book is intertextually put into action. I suggest that the excerpts I examine herein can also be viewed as a type of intertextuality in action—interlocutors draw on material from one context (a storybook) to do something (such as play and socialize) in another. In reshaping words and phrases from storybooks in face-to-face conversation, the participants create blended frames and reframe interaction. I consider the process of blending first.

BLENDING TASK–BASED FRAMES WITH PLAY FRAMES

As mentioned, in the Neeley-Mason family, the parents frequently engaged in pretend role-play with Natalie. One pattern that caught my attention across the week of recording was that in role-play between Natalie and her mother, characters called "Kelly" and "Carl" were repeatedly enacted, with Natalie playing the Kelly role and Janet pretending to be Carl. Not being familiar with the source of these characters, I was missing relevant prior text in interpreting these play episodes. I therefore emailed the family asking about the source of these character names; Steve responded to my query and informed me that Kelly and Carl are characters (sister and brother) in a book called *I'll Share with You* by Linda Apolzon. The family also reported that this book was one of Natalie's early favorites as well as the first one she memorized word for word. I subsequently purchased the book. The story is about a day in the life of two young children, Kelly and her older brother, Carl, that highlights how happy they are when they play cooperatively and share their toys and how they experience a conflict that Mommy must help resolve when Kelly refuses to share. Although specific elements of this plot are not reshaped in role-play between Janet and Natalie, the character names are; I focus on how Janet uses these characters as a means of blending play frames and task-based frames.

Role-play as a means to accomplish a parenting task is a strategy used repeatedly across the recording week, as Natalie frequently wanted to role-play various characters while Janet had another agenda. Thus, Janet regularly agreed to play with Natalie, but at times she used the play as a way of accomplishing parenting work; we saw for instance in chapter 2 that Janet pretended to be an airline pilot talking over a loudspeaker to keep Natalie entertained in the car. This section focuses specifically on the Kelly and Carl role-play, which occurred repeatedly on two days of recording (Thursday and Tuesday). I demonstrate how the names from the children's storybook are recontextualized in a wide variety of interactions in which two frames are simultaneously present and blended together: Frames of parenting work (e.g., getting Natalie to leave the playground, getting her into her car seat, getting her to speak and act in conventionally polite ways) and frames of Kelly and Carl role-play. I provide four excerpts that show Janet using Kelly and Carl role-play as a means of accomplishing different parenting tasks and suggest that this phenomenon can be conceptualized as a new kind of frames lamination; specifically, I demonstrate how Janet, in conjunction with Natalie, reshapes this prior text to create what I call blended frames (see also Gordon 2008).

My introduction of the notion of blended frames builds on a concept drawn from work by Tannen and Wallat (1993) while also extending the notion of laminated frames. In their examination of framing as it occurs in a videotaped pediatric exam/interview, Tannen and Wallat give an example of a "leaky frame" where verbal material from the "examination frame" leaks into the "social encounter frame." In verbally creating the social encounter frame, the pediatrician uses a teasing register and directs her utterances to the child; for instance, while examining the child's stomach, she creates the social encounter frame by saying "No peanut butter and jelly in there?" The examination frame, created verbally when the pediatrician describes her findings for the benefit of medical students who will later view the video, is characterized by a clipped style and medical jargon. At one point, however, while examining the child's stomach, the pediatrician asks the child in a teasing register, "Is your spleen palpable over there?" Tannen and Wallat suggest that when the pediatrician referred to "spleen palpable" in a teasing voice, the examination frame accidentally leaked into the social encounter frame. This idea that frames can be mixed together inspires my understanding of what I have referred to as *blended frames*; however, in contrast to leaks, which seem to be accidental, blending appears to be an intentional discourse strategy. In addition, the pediatrician's strategic use of language to entertain the child while examining her can also be conceptualized as a kind of blending in which an adult verbally creates one frame, and physically constructs another (see Gordon 2008).

To date, relatively few studies have focused on pretend play as a resource parents draw on to parent, that is, to direct their children about what to do or how to behave. Those that consider this phenomenon have provided rich descriptions and documented cross-cultural differences, however, most do not explore it as interrelated to the larger notions of intertextuality and framing. For instance, Haight and Miller (1993) observe and analyze the videotapes of naturally occurring play sessions between nine full-time mothers and their children. They find that pretend play, or make-believe, is used by both mothers and children "to express and regulate feelings, support an argument, enliven daily routines, teach, and influence each other's behavior" (Haight & Miller 1993:72). The authors observed one mother using pretend play to deny her daughter a pacifier; specifically, the mother does so by animating a puppet-like mitten using a high-pitched voice. They remark that another mother regularly used play to enliven daily routines: This mother, they note, managed to entertain her child by engaging in pretending while preparing meals, running errands, and cleaning house. This description is reminiscent of Janet's behaviors and also recalls the general playfulness of the Neeley-Mason family. It is also similar to work by M. H. Goodwin (2007:94), who finds that in the discourse of one family, "parents and children interspersed whatever activity they were undertaking with playful moments of exploration of possible ways the world could be understood." Goodwin thus suggests that play of various types—such as pretend play and sound and word play—can be a crucial component of interactions in which parents facilitate children's knowledge exploration.

Cross-cultural studies of play suggest that uses of play by parents are variable not only by individual and family but also by culture. Haight and her colleagues (Haight et al. 1994; Haight 1999; Haight et al. 1999) examine American and Chinese caregiver–child dyads to explore pretend play as a socializing practice that is culturally situated in middle-class Chinese, European American, and African American families. The authors find that although caregivers in all three groups participate extensively in play with their children, there are variations in play. For example, Haight et al. (1994) observed that the European American parents tended to introduce pretend play to encourage the child to try something new or do something frequently resisted, like wearing a bicycle helmet, or to redirect the child from forbidden or irritating behaviors, like throwing temper tantrums. In contrast, the Chinese caregivers more frequently initiated pretend play in the contexts of teaching proper conduct (Haight et al. 1999). In another comparative study, Göncü et al. (1999) find similarity, observing that in both urban middle-class American and Turkish families, mothers pretend that a spoonful of food is an airplane arriving at the hangar (the child's mouth) to encourage the child to eat.

Sirota (2002) delves into some of the complexity of the interface between work and play in the context of two middle-class American families' discourse. Considering naturally occurring videotaped interactions of these families, her analysis demonstrates how play and housework "shade almost imperceptibly into one another" (Sirota 2002:1), how both parents and children are involved, and how play activities are used by participants to accomplish consequential action. She focuses on two sequences, showing how in both cases, family members weave play into task activities through use of pitch, gesture, laughter, and intertextual repetition. Sirota also argues that bringing play into everyday life can be seen as a moral act in that play has come to be viewed as integral to children's development.

These studies provide a background to my analysis of how work and play frames are interrelated and discursively constructed. I conceptualize the work–play interrelationship as an example of frames laminating—blended frames—thus situating this configuration in a larger theory of intertextuality and framing. In so doing, I link my findings to research on conceptual blending, a theory of meaning-making similar in certain ways to frames theory as developed by Goffman and extended by sociolinguists.[2] Although conceptual blending primarily locates meaning in speakers' mental representations (Coulson & Oakley 2000), and I consider blended frames and the meanings associated with them primarily as they are emergent in social interaction and constructed through particular linguistic features, there are similarities between the way I conceptualize frames blending as part of a larger theory of framing and how cognitive linguists have described certain instances of conceptual blending and the theory in general. Importantly, both framing and conceptual blending view meaning-making as a constructive and emergent process. Although conceptual blending uses the notion of frame, it is primarily as a mental (rather than social) construct. However, activities and interactions are described and analyzed using this framework. Consider, for instance, Coulson and Fauconnier's (1999:145) description of what they call "trash-can basketball":

Imagine two college students are up late studying for an exam. Suddenly, one crumples up a piece of paper and heaves it at the wastepaper basket. As the two begin to shoot the "ball" at the "basket," the game of trashcan basketball is born. Because it involves the integration of knowledge structures from different domains, trashcan basketball can be seen as the product of conceptual blending. In conceptual blending, frames from established domains (known as *inputs*) are combined to yield a hybrid frame (a *blend* or *blended model*) that contains partial structures from each of its inputs, as well as unique representational structure of its own. For example, in trashcan basketball, the input domains are trash disposal and (conventional) basketball, and the resultant blend incorporates a bit of both domains to yield a novel concept.

In the examples I consider, Janet uses Kelly/Carl pretend play as a means to do parenting work, with the "input domains" being pretend play (based on storybook material as well as conventional or family-specific play scripts) and (conventional) ways of doing parenting in the Neeley-Mason family. Through Janet's uses of pretend play to do parenting and Natalie's active participation in these interactions, the interlocutors create novel exchanges.

Although theorizing in cognitive linguistics on blending extends beyond the kinds of examples presented in this chapter in that it views blending as "a very general set" of sense-making processes (Coulson 2001:123), I believe my analysis is compatible with the notion of conceptual blending: my examples serve as clear illustrations of a specific type. Furthermore, my analysis also complements work in cognitive linguistics, which focuses primarily on short, sentence-length snippets of data and constructed examples, by looking at naturally occurring conversational data and performing a fine-grained interactional sociolinguistic analysis. The need for this kind of work has been noticed by cognitive linguists; for instance, Coulson and Oakley (2000:192) note that blending theory "is an excellent candidate for extension beyond *post hoc* analysis, particularly in the realms of anthropology and ethnography."

"Come on Kelly, Let's Get in Our Car Seat"

The first excerpt I consider that illustrates how a play frame and a task frame are linguistically blended shows Janet reshaping bits of prior text drawn from the book *I'll Share with You* as a means to get Natalie buckled into her car seat. Janet had picked up Natalie from her preschool classroom just prior to lunchtime. They walked out to the car, and Natalie climbed into her car seat. Janet tries to get her buckled in by encouraging her to put her arms through the straps of the car seat as Natalie introduces pretend play in which Janet plays the role of Carl and she plays the role of Kelly. Importantly, although Janet agrees to engage in pretend play with Natalie, she uses the play to encourage her daughter to get properly situated in her car seat. Janet thus does not follow the plot of the book itself.

(1a) 1   Janet: Put your hand through, ((*straps of car seat*))
      2   Natalie: (Mom) I'm- I'm gonna be <u>Kelly</u>,
      3   and you be <u>Carl</u>.
      4   Janet: Oh okay.
      5   Natalie: Okay.
      6   Janet: Okay let's put our other hand through.
      7   Natalie: (Mom,)
      8   would (you) like to be <u>Carl</u> and I'll be <u>Kelly</u>.
      9   Janet: Sure.
     10   Natalie: Be <u>Carl</u>,
     11   and I'll be <u>Kelly</u>.
     12 ⇨ Janet: Come on Kelly,
     13 ⇨   let's get in our car seat so we can go home.
     14 ⇨   I'm hungry for lunch,
     15 ⇨   how about you <u>Kelly</u>?
     16   Natalie: Yeah!

Janet first directs Natalie to put her hand through the straps of her car seat in her own voice and in a nonplay frame (line 1). Natalie responds by suggesting that they engage in role-play (lines 2–3, *Mom I'm- I'm gonna be Kelly, and you be Carl*) and by putting her hand through the strap (which becomes evident when Janet asks her to put her other hand through the strap in line 6). Janet, though she verbally agrees with Natalie's suggestion that they play (line 4, *Oh okay*), delays play and instead focuses on getting Natalie buckled into her car seat (line 6, *Okay let's put our other hand through* [the strap of the car seat]). Natalie then restates her wish to play (lines 7–8), and when Janet accepts again in her own voice (line 9, *Sure*), Natalie instructs *Be Carl, and I'll be Kelly* (lines 10–11). After this reinsistence on play, Janet uses the play frame to encourage Natalie to finish getting buckled in her car seat: She addresses Natalie as "Kelly" to send the metamessage that she is enacting the Carl role (i.e., pretending) while suggesting *let's get in our car seat so we can go home* (lines 12–13). In this utterance, Janet adopts an inclusive perspective parents often take up by using *let's* to issue a control act (Blum-Kulka 1997). So Janet is at once playing Carl (addressing Natalie as "Kelly") and "doing parenting" (issuing a directive pertaining to Natalie's behavior). Note that the address term "Kelly" signals a play frame and Janet has accepted and is playing the role of Carl; throughout the week of recording, Janet never alters her voice quality to indicate that she is enacting the Carl role (though she does so for other roles). Natalie complies with "Carl's" request, and the car seat is not mentioned again. Instead, Janet gets into the driver's seat and they drive home, with the interaction turning to a discussion about what happened during the school day, the uncharacteristically warm weather, and what Janet and Natalie will have for lunch, all in the roles of Kelly and Carl (seventy-three lines of transcript total, some of which are included in the next excerpt, 1b). Note that discussion about what to have for lunch while in-role also entertains Natalie while in the car and serves to prepare her for lunchtime at home, perhaps working to ease the transition from preschool to home. Transitions, as Kendall (2006) shows, can be difficult times of the day in families, including in this one; her research suggests that through increased attention to framing and footing, parents may be able to circumvent the tantrums of young children. This is one reason I believe Janet's use of frames blending can be conceived of as strategic.

"Hey Kelly, That's Not Using Manners"

The next excerpt shows Janet using a pretend play frame originally introduced by Natalie to teach or remind Natalie about the proper use of manners, thus blending frames. As it begins, Janet and Natalie are in the car, driving home, engaged in Kelly/Carl role-play. Janet is using the play frame to tell Natalie that she enjoyed observing her preschool class that day when Natalie realizes she does not have a pair of gloves she likes to play with. These gloves, which Janet does not like Natalie to play with but relents to placate her, were received at a doctor's appointment (they are apparently similar to the kind of gloves Natalie's preschool teachers wear while changing a child's diapers, and are made of latex or rubber). In a phone conversation with Jill in which she explains how Natalie insists on playing with the medical gloves, Janet says that they are "purple gloves that we stole from the doctor's the other day"; she also describes them as "those ridiculous medical gloves." In the excerpt, Janet uses the Carl role not only to direct Natalie to use her manners but also to preempt (and circumvent) a possible later conflict at lunchtime regarding the gloves.

(1b)	1	Janet:	<u>Kelly</u>,
	2	Natalie:	What.
	3	Janet:	um . I liked <*yawning*> being in your class today.>
	4	Natalie:	When did you stay in my class.
	5	Janet:	This morning.
	6		It was nice to see the kids in your class,
	7		and see what everybody was playing with.
	8	Natalie:	Where's my (purple) gloves.
	9	Janet:	Oh what happened.
	10	Natalie:	Give- give them back to me.
	11 ⇨	Janet:	Hey <u>Kelly</u>,
	12 ⇨		that's not using manners.
	13	Natalie:	Please?
	14	Janet:	Well we have to wash our hands when we get home.
	15	Natalie:	Please?
	16	Janet:	I'll give them to you now,
	17		but when we get home we have to wash hands,
	18		okay?
	19	Natalie:	Then can I put them back on?
	20 ⇨	Janet:	Well I don't want you eating lunch with them <u>Kelly</u>.
	21		((*short pause*))
	22		You can put them on for story time.

23		How's that.
24		You can wear them now,
25		till we get home.
26	Natalie:	Can I wear them- *<whiney>* the other one.
27		My other one.>
28	Janet:	Oh.
29		Say "can you get that for me please."
30		Let's remember our manners.
31 ⇨		Can you remember your manners <u>Kelly</u>.
32	Natalie:	No.
33 ⇨	Janet:	<u>Ke:lly</u>,
34	Natalie:	What.
35 ⇨	Janet:	well <u>Mommy</u> wouldn't like that,
36 ⇨		if we didn't remember our manners.
37	Natalie:	Um . <u>Carl</u>,
38		wh- why you driving.
39	Janet:	Well,
40		because.

Janet invokes the play frame through addressing Natalie as "Kelly" as she reminds her about her manners (lines 11–12, 31, 33). She reinforces her footing as pretend-play character Carl (sibling of Kelly) by pointing out that *Mommy*—another character in the book—*wouldn't like that, if we didn't remember our manners* (lines 35–36). In these ways, she accomplishes parenting work—making sure her child speaks politely—while also continuing to engage in pretend play.

Janet's utterance in line 20, *Well I don't want you eating lunch with them Kelly*, is also worthy of attention: It uses the same play frame to preempt a possible conflict situation at lunchtime, should Natalie want to wear the medical gloves then. (Across the week of recording, there are numerous altercations and tantrums involving these gloves, and lunchtime is a frequent time for tantrums in general.) Here again, Janet addresses Natalie as "Kelly" while doing parenting work.

Also present in this segment are utterances where Janet does not address Natalie as "Kelly" but where she puts further conditions on the gloves, for example, pointing out that Natalie will have to wash her hands before lunchtime (lines 14, 16–18) and indicating that she can wear the gloves during story time before the afternoon nap (line 22), which Janet later allows Natalie to do. For these utterances, it is ambiguous as to whether Janet is speaking in the role of Carl or in her own voice as Mommy. Eventually, in line 37, Natalie changes the topic but remains in the play frame, asking "Carl" why he is driving (she thus observes a conflict between the play frame and the activity in which "Carl" is engaged), which is followed by a discussion of a prior hospital visit of Natalie's grandmother.

"Okay Kelly, We'll Have a Nice Talk as Soon as You Bring the Books Back In"

Later the same day, Janet uses the characters of Kelly and Carl to ease Natalie toward naptime. She instructs Natalie to select books for naptime, Natalie offers Kelly and Carl role-play as an alternative activity, and Janet subsequently speaks as Carl to direct Natalie to select books for naptime, thereby blending frames. At the beginning of the excerpt, Natalie has just found a nightgown for naptime. (She insisted on napping in a nightgown.)

(2a)	1		Janet:	Okay,
	2			go get some books for us.
	3		Natalie:	(I wanna- I wanna- I wanna-)
	4		Janet:	Yeah,
	5		Natalie:	(to be) <u>Carl</u>,
	6			I want to have a talk <u>Carl</u>.
	7			[Carl,]
	8	⇨	Janet:	[Okay] <u>Kelly</u>,
	9	⇨		we'll have a nice talk as soon as you →
	10	⇨		bring the books back in.
	11			((short pause, Natalie goes to get books))
	12			Oh! ((to self))
	13			Okay. ((to self))
	14		Natalie:	Hello <u>Carl</u>. ((from other room))
	15			<u>Carl,</u> ((coming into room))
	16			I have my favorite big book,
	17			<u>Carl</u>.
	18	⇨	Janet:	What did you find <u>Kelly</u>.
	19		Natalie:	I found- I [found] Victoria.

20 ⇨	Janet:	[Oh.]
21 ⇨		Well I'm sure we'll want more than one book.
22 ⇨		Right?
23 ⇨		Why do you only have one book for us.

In excerpt 2a, Natalie introduces Kelly and Carl pretend play by addressing Janet as "Carl" (line 6) rather than going to select books to read before naptime as Janet requested. In response, Janet uses the role-play frame and her role as Carl to encourage Natalie to select the books (lines 8–10, *Okay Kelly, we'll have a nice talk as soon as you bring the books back in*). Furthermore, when Natalie returns with only one book, Janet continues to address her as "Kelly" (line 18), and sends her to select more books (lines 20–23). She thus parents Natalie while playing the role of Carl.

As the exchange continues (in thirty-six lines not shown), Natalie returns with two more books, then asks if she can play with her gloves (the medical gloves), and Janet, apparently recalling that she agreed that Natalie could play with the gloves, reluctantly goes to find them. Then, Janet reintroduces the Kelly and Carl role-play to remind Natalie about proper naptime behavior, shown in excerpt 2b.

(2b)	60	Natalie:	Hi,
	61		[did you bring me] my gloves?
	62 ⇨	Janet:	[Kelly,]
	63	Natalie:	What.
	64 ⇨	Janet:	let's have a talk Kelly.
	65	Natalie:	Okay.
	66		((*short pause*))
	67		I'm ready for the talk.
	68	Janet:	This is a serious talk about naptime.
	69	Natalie:	Okay.
	70	Janet:	Now,
	71		yesterday . you played and talked and did not sleep,
	72		TODAY we need to do a little better.
	73	Natalie:	Okay.
	74	Janet:	Now,
	75		even if you don't want to sleep,
	76		I need you to lay quiet.

77		You can look at your books,
78		but Mommy has got to sleep.
79		[Okay,]
80	Natalie:	[If I] don't want to sleep I can play with my toys →
81		or look at my books.
82	Janet:	Right.
83		QUIETLY.
84	Natalie:	Okay.

Janet introduces talk about naptime behavior by addressing Natalie as "Kelly." This signals a pretend play frame and clearly works to capture Natalie's attention (the proposal that they "talk" likely interests Natalie in particular, because talking seems to be one of her favorite activities). Janet subsequently uses the play frame to do parenting work: She discusses the rules of naptime, for instance Natalie must lay quietly (line 76). Note that as the conversation continues, the metamessage of play seems to gradually fade, and eventually Janet refers to herself as "Mommy" and talks about her own need to sleep in line 78.

Another Voice: Miss Mandy

Carl is not the only role used by Janet to blend work and play frames. In excerpt 3, occurring Friday at home, Janet adopts a different identity to get Natalie to cooperatively select books to read and climb into the bed to nap—the identity of Natalie's preschool teacher, Miss Mandy. Although the "Miss Mandy" role is based on a real person, not a character from a literary text, there are similarities in the way Miss Mandy and other nonliterary characters are enacted to do parenting work and the way Carl is enacted to do so (see Gordon 2008 for other examples). Janet had picked up Natalie from preschool. In the car on the way home, Natalie said she wanted to wear the medical gloves and pretend to change Janet's and her dolls' diapers. Janet laughed at this suggestion but said they could do that at naptime. On arriving home, Janet and Natalie sat down with something to drink. Natalie sang songs, and then suggested to Janet, "After I be Miss Mandy, YOU be Miss Mandy, okay?" Janet agreed she would. While Janet tried to eat her lunch, Natalie repeatedly requested that she pretend to be Miss Mandy.

After saying she was busy eating her lunch didn't quiet Natalie, Janet said she could only pretend to be Miss Mandy if Natalie showed her how to do it. For a few minutes, Natalie pretended to change a doll's diaper, but then started whining. When Natalie suggests she play the role of Mommy and Janet play the role of Natalie, Janet accepts, and they engage in this pretend play throughout lunch (see Gordon 2002). When it is time to go upstairs for naptime, Natalie begins to throw a tantrum because she cannot find the medical gloves she wanted to wear to pretend to be Miss Mandy. Janet convinces her that they can use leather gloves instead, and Janet pretends to be Miss Mandy and pretends to change Natalie's diaper. Then Natalie asks for the gloves, and the following interaction ensues upstairs in Janet and Steve's bedroom. What I have described in the transcript as the "Miss Mandy voice" is high-pitched and airy (I do not know how accurately it represents the real Miss Mandy's voice).

(3)	1		Janet:	*<Miss Mandy voice>* Here you are dear,
	2			you can have one of my gloves.
	3	⇨		Would you like to put on your nightgown now? >
	4		Natalie:	Yeah.
	5	⇨	Janet:	*<Miss Mandy voice>* I have an idea Natalie,>
	6		Natalie:	What.
	7	⇨	Janet:	*<Miss Mandy voice>* Why don't you pick →
	8	⇨		some books for us,
	9	⇨		and we'll take them back to the classroom →
	10	⇨		and read them together.
	11			((*short pause*))
	12	⇨		How does that sound.>
	13		Natalie:	I want to take them back to the classroom →
	14			and read them.
	15		Janet:	*<Miss Mandy voice>* That's right,
	16			because we're going to have naptime,
	17			on our little cot.
	18			Okay!
	19	⇨		Go pick some books now!>
	20		Natalie:	Where's our co:t.

21		Janet:	<*Miss Mandy voice*> Oh it's in the other room.>
22		Natalie:	Which room.
23	⇨	Janet:	<*Miss Mandy voice*> Well get the books→
24	⇨		and I'll show you.>
25		Natalie:	Read the book Miss Mandy,
26			while I'm in the- when you go to bed.
27	⇨	Janet:	<*Miss Mandy voice*> Well you have to →
28	⇨		pick the books first dear!>
29		Natalie:	I want these books.
30	⇨	Janet:	<*Miss Mandy voice*> Bring them to me!>
31			((*short pause*))
32		Natalie:	I want all these books,
33			see?

Janet uses the Miss Mandy character to encourage Natalie to get ready for naptime: to put on her nightgown (line 3), to select books to read (lines 7–10, 19, 23–24, 27–28) and to bring the books to her (line 30). Thus, Janet blends frames of parenting work (getting Natalie ready for naptime) with play: She pretends to be Miss Mandy and introduces play elements into the interaction, like the presence of a "cot" for naptime and a "classroom," while also issuing parenting-related directives.

At other times during the recording week, Janet uses other pretend-play characters to accomplish parenting. For instance, while assuming a Fairy Godmother identity, Janet tells Natalie to mind her manners at lunch and encourages her to get ready for naptime. (It is not clear whether the Fairy Godmother figure is drawn from a specific storybook or children's film.) Steve blends frames in a similar way—for instance, while pretending to be a doctor, he tries to get Natalie to drink her juice at breakfast— though his use of blending as a strategy is comparatively infrequent. Although not all of these cases involve reshaping literary prior text, all involve reshaping some shared prior language experience(s), such as what the participants know about doctor–patient interaction from watching TV, reading books, and actual hospital visits they may have experienced together.

Blending Frames in Everyday Talk

In these examples, Janet uses language to at once create play and parent Natalie. I have suggested that blended frames are created as certain features send a metamessage of play (e.g., referring to Natalie as "Kelly"), whereas others signal a task frame (e.g., task-related directives). However, how the interlocutors actually perceive the definition of these social situations is somewhat ambiguous. As Goffman (1974:8) points out, "the view that one person has of what is going on is likely to be quite different from that of another. There is a sense in which what is play for the golfer is work for the caddy." This quotation, which could apply to virtually any framed activity, is particularly applicable to the excerpts of talk considered thus far in this chapter. It is unclear, for instance, whether Janet actually conceives role-play as play; that is, it is not obvious whether she becomes *engrossed* (Goffman 1974:345) in the play or views it as just another variety of parenting work. Elsewhere in the recordings, Janet describes engaging in role-play with Natalie in general as both fun and frustrating (see Gordon 2006, 2008). Janet may feel at times like a caddy, at times like a golfer, and at times somewhere in between, even when she is not using the play to do parenting work. For Natalie, it seems that she views most of these situations as simply play, although there are cases where she is clearly using play as a tactic for delay or distraction.

When Janet uses play to accomplish parenting work, she performs a type of *fabrication*, which constitutes an "intentional effort of one or more individuals to manage activity so that a party of one or more others will be induced to have a false belief about what is going on" (Goffman 1974:84). Although I do not believe Janet is trying to deceive her daughter into having a "false" understanding of what is occurring, she does use language in a way that seems to intentionally lead to Natalie to have a different view of the situation; this difference of interpretation between interlocutors is a feature of fabrication. Similar to how the college students in Coulson and Fauconnier's (1999) conceptual blending analysis of a game of trashcan basketball come (on their own) to understand a wad of paper as a basketball, Janet shapes task-oriented directives into play utterances, thus attempting to get Natalie to view tasks as play. As a parenting strategy, blending thus does seem to invite a child to view a task as part of play. However, it is unclear how exactly Natalie interprets what is occurring in these exchanges, that is, if she understands nonplay tasks (like selecting books to read at naptime) as play, or if she senses that nonplay is creeping into play frames through her mother's in-role task-oriented directives. At times, Natalie actually uses the play frame to assert her own agenda, rejecting, for instance, a play plot that involves accomplishing a task related to preparing for naptime or using a pretend character role to try to get something she wants (see Gordon 2008). This suggests that Natalie may not be fully immersed in the fabrication. Blending is a useful metaphor for capturing how these situations can be defined. Blended frames might be classified as a kind of "marginal play" (Shore 1996) for both participants; in marginal play, we are "unsure of our footing, unclear as to whether we are located within a game world or in the 'real' world beyond the play" (Shore 1996:107). These situations thus further demonstrate the complex framings available in everyday family interaction.

REFRAMING: CREATING FRAMES THROUGH
RESHAPING BITS OF STORYBOOK TEXT

I turn to considering a phenomenon related to frames blending—reframing—or the process by which participants sequentially shift frames in conversation. My analysis builds on the growing body of research on frame manipulation in everyday talk, in particular on Tannen's (2006) discussion of reframing and rekeying. Tannen analyzes three verbal conflicts in three families: the Neeley-Masons, the Patterson/Foleys, and the Shepherd/Sylvans (her study focuses on the discourse of Clara Shepherd and Neil Sylvan). Tannen conceptualizes the repetition of elements of an argument as the argument unfolds and is reframed across conversations as a kind of what Tovares (2005) calls "intertextuality in action." By "reframing," Tannen refers to a change in what the discussion is about—for instance, an argument about whether Neil will take a package back to the post office for Clara is reframed as an argument about who does more housework. In addition, as the argument plays out and is reframed, there is at times a "change in the tone or tenor of the interaction" (Tannen 2006:601). Tannen, following Goffman (1974), refers to this phenomenon as "rekeying." For example, when the topic of an argument is later treated with laughter, a rekeying has occurred: What was a serious conflict is transformed into something humorous. In the examples I examine, similar kinds of reframing and rekeying occur, in the sense that what is going on in the social situation and the tone of the interaction change. Crucially, I illustrate how the participants reshape and integrate prior text from two children's storybooks in their reframing and rekeying of interaction. Thus, I illustrate how prior text is a resource not only for laminating frames (signaling at least two frames at once) but also for transforming them moment by moment, that is, shifting them as conversation unfolds.

"That Hole Means Rabbit": Recontextualizing a Line from *Pooh Goes Visiting*

Janet and Natalie reshape shared bits of literary prior text to construct an evolving "mosaic of quotations" (Kristeva 1980 [1967]:66) that frames and reframes interaction. I begin demonstrating how this takes place by presenting the beginning of the extended interaction in which reshaping occurs. The interaction takes place one afternoon (Tuesday, the family's last day of recording). It begins while Janet and Natalie are at a playground near their house, and it continues as they walk home from the playground and arrive back home. In excerpt 4a, Natalie indirectly intertextually references a storybook while Janet pushes her on a swing.

(4a) 13   Natalie: I see a hole right there.
      14   Janet: Yeah.
      15 ⇨ Natalie: I guess that hole means Rabbit.
      16   Janet: <*laughs*>
      17   Natalie: I guess.
      18   Janet: <*laughs*>
      19 ⇨ Natalie: I see a hole (means) Rabbit.
      20 ⇨ Janet: You think that hole means Rabbit?
      21   Natalie: Yep!
      22   Janet: <*laughs*>
      23   Natalie: Like Pooh Bear.
      24   Janet: Just like Pooh Bear.
      25   Natalie: Yep!

The arrowed lines in this excerpt are reshaped versions of material from a Winnie the Pooh book called *Pooh Goes Visiting*, by A. A. Milne, which Janet read aloud to Natalie three days before at bedtime.

The reading of this book on that particular occasion was somewhat unusual in that Janet had three friends over for an informal dinner party, and the women were all in Natalie's room during the bedtime ritual, talking quietly among themselves. (Janet had decided the only way to get Natalie to go to bed was to have everyone present in her room; although these friends did not actually participate in the bedtime ritual, this is another example of how this family includes others in family behavior.) The beginning of Janet's reading is shown in excerpt 5 (her friends' background talk is not shown), and note that this book seems to be much loved and this is undoubtedly not the first reading of it.

(5) 1   Janet: Our last story is *Pooh Goes Visiting.*
     2   <*reading*> Winnie the Pooh was walking→
     3   through the forest when he came to a large hole,
     4 ⇨   "That hole means Rabbit," he said.
     5   Pooh pushed his way through the hole,
     6   and at last he got in.>

The line of dialogue shown in line 4, "That hole means Rabbit" is the original version of Natalie's utterance about Rabbit at the playground (*I guess that hole means Rabbit*, excerpt 4a, line 15). Thus, Natalie uses indirect means to intertextually reference this book (in other words, she never explicitly names it). Janet, for her part, evidences that she recognizes Natalie's prior text—they both agree that seeing a hole and interpreting it as "meaning Rabbit" is "like Pooh Bear" (excerpt 4a, lines 23 and 24). The co-interlocutors thus jointly participate in pretending based on the text of a book with which they have shared familiarity. As these interlocutors mutually remember and reshape a text from their shared experience—in this case, bits of a book likely read many times at bedtime or naptime—they create solidarity. Neither mother nor child explicitly names the text they cite, yet their talk folds seamlessly, with Janet laughing (possibly at Natalie's precociousness); they may experience what Tannen (1986:70–71) calls "the aesthetic pleasure of indirectness," resulting in a shared sense of rapport. This sense of rapport further develops, I suggest, as material from the second storybook is integrated into the conversation.

Kelly and Carl: Characters from *I'll Share with You*

The second book interwoven into this interaction also enters without being explicitly named. First, as the playground interaction continues, Natalie asks her mother to push her more on the swing, and Janet agrees (these six lines are not shown). Then Natalie introduces pretend play in which she will play the role of Kelly and Janet will play the role of Carl.

(4b)   32   Natalie: I'm <u>Kelly</u> and you're <u>Carl</u>.
      33   Janet: Oh boy!
      34   <*clears throat*>
      35   <u>Kelly and Carl are brother and</u> . ((*trails off*))

The first sentence of the story *I'll Share with You* reads, "Kelly and Carl are sister and brother." Thus when Janet says "Kelly and Carl are brother and" and trails off in the interaction with Natalie (excerpt 4b, line 35), she recontextualizes that sentence (though she has reversed the words *brother* and *sister*). In so doing, Janet transforms the material from the book, reframing it into a kind of play—a fill-in-the blank renarration.

Although the purpose of this chapter is not to suggest what triggers intertextual repetition, it is notable that Natalie brings up Kelly and Carl while her mother pushes her on a swing at the playground; on pages 3 and 4 of *I'll Share with You,* there is a drawing of Mommy pushing Kelly on a swing. Thus, Natalie's talk about Kelly and Carl, like her talk about the rabbit hole, seems to be inspired by her physical environment.

Integrating Linguistic Material from Two Storybooks: A Role-Play Discussion

The fill-in-the blank renarration frame Janet linguistically introduces is not, as becomes apparent as the interaction continues, the type of play that Natalie seemed to have in mind when she assigned the pretend roles Kelly and Carl. Rather, Natalie apparently wants to reshape the prior text to create a frame of pretend role-play, as seen in excerpt 4c. She thus reframes the ongoing talk.

(4c)   35   Janet: <u>Kelly and Carl are brother and</u> . ((*trails off*))
      36   Natalie: I'm <u>Kelly</u> and you're <u>Carl</u>.
      37   Janet: <*chuckles*> Okay.

38	Natalie:	Okay.
39		((*short pause*))
40		There's a <u>hole</u> right there <u>Carl</u>,
41		just right there.
42	Janet:	I see it <u>Kelly</u>.
43		What do you think it <u>means</u>?
44	Natalie:	I think it <u>means Rabbit</u>.
45	Janet:	*<laughs>*
46	Natalie:	*<laughs>*
47	Janet:	*<laughs>*
48	Natalie:	I see a <u>hole</u> right there.
49	Janet:	What do you think it <u>means</u> <u>Carl</u>.
50		[I mean] <u>KELLY</u>.
51	Natalie:	[I think—]
52		I think it <u>means Rabbit</u>.
53	Janet:	<u>Rabbit</u>!?
54	Natalie:	*<laughing>* <u>Rabbit</u>!>
55	Janet:	Is your name <u>Winnie the Pooh</u>?
56	Natalie:	*<laughs>*
57		Nope!
58	Janet:	*<chuckles>*
59		<u>Kelly</u>,
60	Natalie:	What.
61	Janet:	what do you suppose <u>that hole means</u>.
62	Natalie:	<u>That hole means Rabbit</u>!
63	Janet:	*<chuckling>* Ah!>
64		((*short pause*))

In this excerpt, Natalie introduces play in which the participants, as Kelly and Carl, discuss the hole that they see in the ground. The ensuing talk intermingles aspects of the two storybooks—character names from one book, and lines or script features from another (both underscored)—in a creative and fun way, as evidenced by the presence of laughter. This reframes the prior text into another version of Bateson's "this is play"; it creates a frame of pretend play in which two characters discuss a hole they see. This is thus also as an instance of embedded frames: Storybook prior text is reframed into a "discussion of a rabbit hole" frame embedded within a role-play frame. The excerpt additionally illustrates one way in which aspects of two storybooks can be playfully woven together, a phenomenon that has been observed to occur in the play of preschool children (e.g., Rowe 1998).

Transformation into a Knowledge Display Frame

The next transformation of the prior text is particularly interesting in that the play frame is suspended, as Natalie seems to speak in her own voice and shape the already reshaped prior text from *Pooh Goes Visiting* as a means of displaying knowledge to (or sharing knowledge with) her mother. Thus, as the interaction between mother and child continues as shown in excerpt 4d, the intertextual reshaping continues and reframing occurs. The conversation is also rekeyed—Natalie seems serious in her declaration, and Janet responds seriously as well. There is no laughter in these lines.

(4d) 65 ⇨ Natalie: Whenever I see a green light,
    66 ⇨   it <u>means</u> go.
    67   Janet: Oh that's true,
    68   isn't it.
    69   ((*short pause*))

In lines 65–66 Natalie uses the basic pattern provided by her previous reshaping of storybook prior text (*I see a hole right there/I guess that hole means Rabbit*, excerpt 4a, lines 13, 15) to display her recognition of the meaning of a green traffic light. She also shares this knowledge with her mother, who confirms her observation.

Although the basic syntactic frame of *I see X/X means Y* serves as prior text in this interaction, it is worth noting that the term *mean* is subtly transformed across the reshapings. That is, *mean* does not mean exactly the same thing in excerpts 4a and 4c as it does in 4d. In 4a and 4c, in which a hole "means" Rabbit, the utterance can be glossed as something like *that hole indicates the location of Rabbit's home*; in 4d, in which a green traffic light means go, the utterance can be glossed as *a green light signals that a pedestrian (or car) is allowed to go*. Though this shift in meaning is perhaps not even perceived by the participants, it is part of how the prior text is reshaped.

Creating a Game within Role-Play

The next time the linguistic material from the storybook prior texts resurfaces, it is for the purpose of play—the interaction is reframed again by the participants into pretend role-play. Following the talk about the green light, in twenty-seven lines (not shown here) Natalie and Janet chat about Natalie's jacket and ballet class. Subsequently, the Kelly and Carl play talk about Rabbit's hole resumes. This time Natalie (as Kelly) asks Janet (as Carl) what the hole means; this is a reversal from excerpt 4c in which Janet (as Carl) asked Natalie (as Kelly) what the hole meant. In addition, within this pretend-play frame discussion, a teasing name-substitution game frame emerges, where the name "Rabbit" is replaced by other characters from books from the Winnie the Pooh series. As in excerpt 4c, this can be conceived of as an example of frames embedding: The rim of the frame can be described as "this is pretend play" within which a "discussion of the rabbit hole" occurs. However, the discussion itself becomes reframed as a game as the conversation unfolds (beginning with Janet's utterance in line 113).

(4e) 96 Natalie: <u>Carl</u>,
       97 Janet: [Yes <u>Kelly</u>.]
       98 Natalie: [what do] you think <u>that hole means</u>.
       99 Janet: Hm . I think <u>that hole</u> must <u>mean Rabbit</u>!
      100 Natalie: <*laughs*>
      101 Janet: <*chuckles*>
      102 Natalie: <*laughs*>
      103   <*laughing*> What do you think <u>that hole means</u>.>
      104 Janet: I think it MUST <u>mean Rabbit</u>!
      105 Natalie: <*laughs*>
      106 Janet: [<*laughs*>]
      107 Natalie: [<*laughs*>]
      108 Janet: <*laughs*>
      109 Natalie: <*laughs*>
      110   ((*short pause*))
      111   What do you think <u>that hole means</u>.
      112 Janet: <u>Kelly</u>,
      113   I think it <u>means Piglet</u>.
      114   ((*short pause*))
      115   <*laughs*>
      116 Natalie: What do you think <u>that hole means</u>.
      117 Janet: I think it <u>means Piglet</u>.

118   Natalie: *\<laughing\> No!\>*
119   Janet: No!?
120   Natalie: *\<laughing\> No!\>*
121   Janet: It doesn't <u>mean</u> Piglet?
122   Natalie: *\<laughing\> No!\>*
123   Janet: Oh,
124   what does it <u>mean</u>,
125   <u>Eeyore</u>?
126   Natalie: <u>Rabbit</u>!
127   Janet: Oh <u>Rabbit</u>!
128   [It must <u>mean Rabbit</u>.]
129   Natalie: [(?? ???)]
130   Janet: It must <u>mean Rabbit</u>.
131   Natalie: Yep!
((followed by prolonged laughter))

As Natalie and Janet enact the Kelly and Carl roles, respectively, Janet introduces a new frame wherein a rabbit's hole is playfully and humorously interpreted as meaning "Piglet" and "Eeyore"—a little pig and a donkey who are Winnie the Pooh's friends (and who, not surprisingly, do not live in rabbit holes). Although at first Natalie does not verbally respond to this frame's introduction (note the pause in line 114, indicating no verbal reaction from Natalie), when Janet repeats herself and reasserts that the hole indicates Piglet (line 117), Natalie laughingly contradicts her mother, thus actively participating in the game. This game surfaces briefly again forty-two lines later in the conversation when Natalie asks Janet, "What do you think that hole means Carl," and Janet responds, "I think that hole must mean Tigger" (Tigger is Winnie the Pooh's bouncy, tiger-like friend).

Directing Natalie's Behavior

Later in the interaction, written prior text is used as a resource in creating a particular kind of parenting frame, here a frame in which Janet directs Natalie's behavior, thus constructing a type of blended frame. After mother and child talk about some workers they see on the roof of a nearby house, Janet says they have to go home soon but Natalie can do one more thing before they go. They play (in the woodchips) for approximately twelve minutes before Janet tries to get

Natalie to leave the playground. Janet suggests that they "race" home and she counts "one, two three, GO!" but Natalie refuses to play this game. Then the Kelly/Carl role-play and the discussion of the rabbit hole reemerge when Janet uses the talk as a way of gaining Natalie's cooperation to walk home from the playground.

(4f) 688 Janet: Want to hold hands?
      689 Natalie: No.
      690 Janet: Come on.
      691 Natalie: I don't want to hold hands.
      692 Janet: All right,
      693   come on.
      694   Hey <u>Kelly</u>,
      695 Natalie: [What.]
      696 Janet: [what] do you think <u>that hole</u> over there <u>means</u>.
      697 Natalie: <u>That hole means Rabbit</u>.
      698 Janet: <*chuckles*>
      699 Natalie: (Where's <u>that hole</u>.)
      700 Janet: What do you suppose <u>that means</u>.
      701   ((*short pause*))
      702 Natalie: (Okay,) ((*Natalie seems to stumble while walking*))
      703   (okay here we go.)
      704   (Whoa.)
      705   <u>That hole means Rabbit!</u>
      706 Janet: <*chuckles*>
      707   Come on.

In this excerpt, Janet is reshaping prior text as a means of securing Natalie's cooperation to leave the playground. This is thus an example of a kind of frames blending, as Janet is not only getting Natalie to cooperate (by distracting her), she is also playing with her. Reframing here thus results in blended frames.

Teaching

On Janet and Natalie's arrival back at their house, the prior text from *Pooh Goes Visiting* is reshaped to create a "knowledge sharing" frame; this time Janet is the one doing the sharing. Janet and Natalie stop in their yard to look at the plants growing in the garden. The pattern of seeing something in the world and interpreting it as "meaning" something—as in *I see a hole right there. I guess that hole means Rabbit* (Natalie, excerpt 4a, lines 13, 15)—resurfaces here as Janet explains to Natalie that flower buds indicate a coming change of seasons.

(4g)	721	Janet:	Let's see what's going on in our garden.
	722		((*short pause*))
	723		Let's see if we see any buds.
	724	Natalie:	What!
	725 ⇨	Janet:	I said let's see if we see any buds.
	726		Oh look,
	727		let me show you.
	728		Look!
	729	Natalie:	What.
	730 ⇨	Janet:	Do you see those red things?
	731	Natalie:	What.
	732 ⇨	Janet:	That <u>means</u> spring is coming.
	733		That's gonna be leaves.
	734		And look,
	735		there's a little flower.
	736	Natalie:	Where.
	737 ⇨	Janet:	See that [little blue flower?]
	738	Natalie:	[Where's the flower.]
	739	Janet:	Right over here [against the wall.]
	740	Natalie:	[Where's the flower.]
	741	Janet:	Look baby.
	742 ⇨	Natalie:	Flower.
	743 ⇨	Janet:	See it?
	744	Natalie:	Yeah.
	745 ⇨	Janet:	That <u>means</u> spring is coming.
	746		Oh boy!

Here, "what is going on in interaction" could be defined as knowledge sharing or, perhaps more accurately, given the mother–child relationship, as teaching. The prior text is again intertextually reshaped to accomplish action. The meaning of *mean* in this excerpt is once more slightly different from its prior uses. However, my interpretation that

this talk is related to the storybook prior text is reinforced by the fact
that the talk about "that hole" resurfaces one more time, beginning
with Natalie's next utterance:

(4h) 747 Natalie: What do you think this <u>hole means</u> in here.
      748 Janet: I think <u>that</u> must <u>mean PIGLET.</u>
      749   ((*short pause*))
      750   <*chuckles*>
      751 Natalie: I think <u>that hole means Rabbit.</u>
      752 Janet: Oh maybe you're right.
      753 Natalie: What's this kind of tree.

In 4h, Janet again tries to introduce the name substitution game frame,
where the hole can mean any one of Winnie the Pooh's friends—in this
case, Piglet. Note that this time the game is not embedded within
a role-play frame (Janet and Natalie are not playing Carl and Kelly).
Although this game can be viewed as a way for Janet to engage in
teasing with Natalie, here only Janet laughs at her substitution, and then
Natalie reintroduces the phrase *I think that hole means Rabbit*, a more
accurate rendition of the prior text of the book.

Following what occurs in excerpt 4h, Janet and Natalie look at a
few more things in the garden, and then go into the house to prepare
dinner. However, elsewhere during the week, the names Kelly and Carl
repeatedly resurface; this was evidenced by excerpts analyzed in the first
half of this chapter.

Integrating and Transforming Storybook Prior Text
to Frame and Reframe

Prior text serves as a resource for creating numerous frames of interaction; in this section, I demonstrated how bits of prior text from two
children's books are integrated and reshaped across one extended
mother–child interaction to frame and reframe the definition of the
social situation. The idea of seeing a hole and interpreting that "that
hole means Rabbit" emerges as play when Natalie pretends a hole she
sees means Winnie the Pooh's friend Rabbit lives there; these bits of
prior text are reshaped and integrated with character names from
another book (*I'll Share with You*) to become a pretend-play question-
and-answer discussion between "Kelly" and "Carl" of the meaning of

the hole; material from *Pooh Goes Visiting* is reshaped by Natalie again to display her knowledge of the meaning of green traffic lights; it is subsequently reshaped to become a game of character name substitution played by the pretend characters Kelly and Carl; Janet uses it to accomplish a parenting task by blending "leaving the playground" with the frame of the Kelly-Carl pretend-play discussion of the rabbit hole; it is also reshaped by Janet to teach her daughter to identify developing buds as a sign of springtime. Finally the talk about the hole once again resurfaces as the character name substitution game, this time played by Natalie and Janet and not "Kelly" and "Carl."

Although I have described in chronological order how this prior text is used to frame and reframe interaction across this extended conversation, I want to emphasize more than the sequential order of the reframings the variety of frames created through reshaping these quite small bits of prior text—frames of play, knowledge sharing, parenting—and the process of transformation, which involved recontextualizations, word substitutions, and uses of contextualization cues such as laughter. Prior text is transformed and interwoven in creative ways to shift frames; it is also rekeyed (e.g., from serious to humorous). Prior research suggests that children draw on literary language in a variety of ways in everyday interaction (Wolf & Heath 1992; Rowe 1998); I have shown how this actually occurs in the context of parent–child discourse. In so doing, my analysis has illuminated how integrating and reshaping bits of literary prior texts enables the participants to create frames, reframe interaction, and sometimes embed frames (as when the rabbit hole discussion was embedded in Kelly and Carl role-play) and blend frames (as when role-play was used as a means of encouraging Natalie to leave the playground).

Rowe's (1998) findings that children use books to fuel play, that they sometimes integrate aspects of more than one book together, and that they reenact book plots with varying degrees of faithfulness ring true in what occurs in interaction between Janet and Natalie. Although their conversation is between an adult and a child rather than between children, books fuel conversation, both play and nonplay; bits of two storybooks are integrated together in novel ways; and the interlocutors maintain various degrees of "faithfulness" to the text (e.g., "that hole means Rabbit" is more faithful to the book than "that hole means Piglet"). In demonstrating how the prior text is reshaped, I have also shown how reshaping serves as a resource for reframing and rekeying talk.

STORYBOOK PRIOR TEXT, BLENDING FRAMES, AND
MAKING MEANINGS

In sum, my analysis of blended frames and reframing furthers my investigation into Goffman's idea that many types of frames lamination are possible in interaction while also emphasizing the important role of intertextuality in framing. First, I identified blended frames and showed how they are linguistically created, in particular through reshaping prior text from a children's storybook. Like overlapping frames, blended frames accomplish two activities at once. However, whereas overlapping frames refer simultaneously to a prior context of enunciation and a present one through repetition, an utterance signaling blended frames contains elements that send metamessages indicating two (seemingly conflicting) definitions of the present situation: a play definition and a nonplay (parenting or task-related) definition. In the same utterance or in utterances in close proximity, some features say "this is play" (e.g., using character names from a book as address terms) while others accomplish a parenting task (e.g., directives), thus blending frames.

My exploration of how one mother and her young child reshape and integrate linguistic material from two storybooks in one extended interaction contributes to our understanding of how framing occurs moment by moment in everyday talk while also extending recent application of the notions of reframing and rekeying (Tannen 2006). Further, it builds on the idea that intertextuality is something that serves as a resource for undertaking "action" (Tovares 2005). I illustrated how linguistic material is used to "do" various activities in mother–child talk, for instance, to play, comment on another person's manners, and share knowledge. In reframing prior text to undertake action, laminated frames are created as well, as when a reframing of storybook prior text was blended with the task of getting Natalie to leave the playground, or when a rabbit-hole discussion was embedded in role-play. Thus, reframing and laminating frames are not separate phenomena; they are interrelated. Furthermore, it is important to note that intertextually repeating storybook prior text—in the form of character names, or lines of text—is not only a means of reframing and a resource for creating blended frames and embedded frames, it is also a way of creating overlapping frames, although I have not highlighted that process here. Following theorizing by Bakhtin, I suggest that as these speakers repeat, they necessarily take an evaluative stance of some kind toward what they repeat. However, in the excerpts considered in this chapter, the evaluative component (e.g., mocking or showing admiration for the book writer's words) is not prominent, whereas creating (re)definitions of situations is.

In my analysis, I also suggested that my notion of frames blending and the idea of conceptual blending as described in cognitive linguistics are related: trashcan basketball, as discussed by Coulson and Fauconnier (1999) and Coulson (2001), is not so different from Janet's blending of tasks and play. However, trashcan basketball is identified as a somewhat "exotic" case in conceptual blending theory, as conceptual blending is a much more general process by which all meanings are made; the theory is able to explain, for instance, how meanings emerge in political advertisements and bumper stickers (Coulson & Oakley 2000) and even how people experience pain and understand cause and effect (Fauconnier & Turner 2000). I believe that the analysis of frames blending presented here serves as a concrete example not only of frames lamination (in the Goffmanian sense) but also of how "our robust powers of blending are useful throughout our everyday lives" (Fauconnier & Turner 2002:52). It also begins to answer Coulson and Oakley's (2000) call for qualitative and ethnographic examinations of blending in actual social encounters.

Finally, the excerpts I have analyzed in this chapter additionally suggest that storybooks can serve as productive sources of prior text for interactions between parents and children, as resources for reframing and blending frames. This is different from chapters 2–4, which focused on spoken prior text. In reshaping the line of text from *Pooh Goes Visiting* and the names of "Kelly" and "Carl" from *I'll Share with You* in different interactions, Janet and Natalie create intertextual links with these written texts, as two links on a chain. However, they also indirectly point to a number of shared prior interactions—in this case, the family's ritual reading of books at bedtime and naptime, and prior discussions about and play involving material from these books—thus referencing a web of interrelated texts. These words not only echo specific written prior texts but reflect bits of the family's history of talk as well. Consequently, in more than one sense reshaping literary prior text serves as a way of binding parent and child together. As they repeat and recontextualize, this mother and child evoke shared memories—of book content, ritualized book reading experiences, and conversations about or involving books—as they blend frames and reframe interaction. In this way, using literary prior text in the way Janet and Natalie do depends crucially on their shared prior experiences of not only reading together but talking and reshaping language together as well.

SIX

Conclusion

Intertextuality, Framing, and the Study
of Family Discourse

A THEORY OF INTERTEXTUALITY AND FRAMING

In capturing the idea that all texts are linked to other texts, the notion of intertextuality emphasizes that creating and interpreting meaning are processes that extend beyond individual texts. In what can be regarded as an early study of intertextuality, Tannen (2007 [1989]) identifies repetition, both within and across interactions, as a fundamental meaning-making strategy. My analysis builds on this insight and delves into how intertextuality is used in the creation of meanings by bringing together intertextuality with framing, a widely utilized theory that explains how meaning is created moment by moment in discourse. By bringing together intertextuality and framing in a new way in my analysis of family interaction, I demonstrate ways that intertextuality plays a fundamental role in the processes of both family-making and meaning-making.

I have illustrated how through intertextually repeating, family members accomplish framing in discourse: They create frames, reframe interaction, and laminate frames in various ways, creating overlapping, embedded, and blended meanings; they also metaphorically frame the family as a distinctive group. Intertextual repetition accordingly enables family members to jointly recall prior interactions and recontextualize and respond to these interactions, signal multiple metamessages at once, create increasingly specific definitions of a social situation, combine family work with play, accomplish action, create routines and rituals, construct a shared culture, and extend family boundaries. Thus, intertextual repetition is a resource for creating frames and a means of doing what Goffman refers to as "laminating" frames; in short, intertextuality is a fundamental component of making and layering the subtle meanings composed in everyday talk.

Meaning-making, as a basic human process, has been considered in a variety of fields. Work in cognitive linguistics has proposed conceptual blending as a theory of how meaning is created, as discussed in chapter 5 (e.g., Fauconnier & Turner 2000). Cultural anthropologists have highlighted the importance of cultural models (e.g., Shore 1996) as well as rituals (e.g., Tambiah 1985; Shore 2003) in making meaning. Psychologists too have cited the meaning-making power of rituals (e.g., Fiese 2006; Fiese et al. 2002); researchers in psychology have also proposed narrative as a primary means of creating meaning (e.g., Bruner 1987; Harvey et al. 2000), an idea that has also been explored in linguistics, among other fields. In interactional sociolinguistics and discourse analysis, a primary theory for understanding and explaining the meaning-making process is framing (e.g., Tannen 1993a).

In this larger interdisciplinary body of work exploring meaning-making, certain terms appear and reappear, among them *frame, schema, script, storyline,* and *plot.* These notions—though used differently across disciplines—all at their essence relate to what Tannen (1993c:15) has referred to as "structures of expectation." Expectations are largely shaped by prior experience and by human beings' abilities to recognize patterns in individual interactions and in their wider cultural contexts. Recurrence and repetition are central notions in defining rituals, including everyday rituals (e.g., Troll 1988; Gillis 1996; Shore 1996, 2003; K. M. Jackson 2005). Conversation is also made up of patterns: Following Goffman (1967:21), many sociolinguists and discourse analysts view interaction in general through the lens of ritual in the sense that there are certain "rules of conduct" co-conversationalists follow, creating patterns of turns, moves, frames, and so on. Narrative discourse is structured in patterned ways (e.g., Labov and Waletzky 1967; Labov 1997). In short, meaning-making—whether it is analyzed through the lens of framing, conceptual blending, or another theory—crucially depends on prior experience and our abilities to remember, reshape, and create and recognize patterns. Meaning-making is thus inextricably interconnected with intertextuality.

The analyses I presented have argued for and delved into this interconnectedness in a concrete way: I focused on instances of intertextual repetition in recorded conversations and demonstrated how, through intertextually repeating specific bits of prior texts, most often words but also paralinguistic features, syntactic structures, speech acts, and interactive routines, participants construct frames in various configurations. In this way, I suggested, they create various meanings across interactions and multiple meanings at once; I have also demonstrated how family members use intertextual repetition to construct themselves as a social group by creating family-specific frames and meanings. Thus I have aimed to show not only how intertextual repetition serves as a resource for framing but also how intertextuality and framing as theories are best viewed as intertwined, in particular in the context of discourse between interlocutors who share a long history of talk.

I have conceptualized intertextual repetition as an example of what Becker calls "reshaping" and reshaping as a means of what Gumperz refers to as "contextualization." In other words, I have proposed that intertextually repeating bits of prior discourse is a powerful contextualization cue, a way of sending particular metamessages that interlocutors (and the analyst) can glean and interpret to discern frames. As with other contextualization cues, such as laughter and uses of intonation and pitch, for intertextual repetition to function successfully as a discourse strategy, shared background knowledge is essential. In the case of intertextual repetition, "shared background knowledge" refers to not only general cultural knowledge but also specific shared prior interactive experiences that interlocutors (and the analyst) are able to recall and relate to a new context. This differs from other ways of understanding the creation of intertextuality; for instance, other research demonstrates how intertextuality is created through genre features (Briggs & Bauman 1992; Fairclough 1992); through shared narrative theme, evaluation, point, and style (Schiffrin 2000); through quoting (Matoesian 1999); through the replaying of recorded interactions (Matoesian 2000); and even through undertaking particular actions (Tovares 2005; Al Zidjaly 2006; Scollon 2007). However, viewing intertextuality as created through the intertextual repetition of shared prior text is compatible with these studies; all fit into the idea that texts are not isolated but interrelated and composed of bits of other (prior) texts and into the theme that intertextuality is fundamental in the creation and negotiation of meanings.

Of course, intertextuality and framing, even when taken together, cannot elucidate the intended or interpreted meanings of every utterance in interaction. In fact, some of the uncertainty in determining exactly what is going on at a particular conversational moment can be attributed to intertextuality; as Fairclough (1992:272) remarks, intertextuality "is the source of much of the ambivalence in texts," because different meanings may emerge from making different intertextual connections. Other uncertainties depend on the fact that there is no one-to-one correspondence between a particular contextualization cue and a particular meaning; as Gumperz notes in a discussion with Carlo L. Prevignano and Aldo di Luzio (2003:17), "Ambiguities always exist." However, my analysis demonstrated that by integrating intertextuality and framing, we gain a much richer—and, I would suggest, more precise—understanding of how family members create meanings and construct themselves as a family through talk than we would by applying these theories separately.

INTERTEXTUALITY AND/AS METHODOLOGY

One way that approaches to discourse analysis vary is by the breadth of the contexts in which utterances are considered. This ranges from those that tend to keep context focused narrowly within a single transcript of conversation, or even within adjacent turns (e.g., ethnomethodology-based conversation analysis in its strictest sense) to those that extend beyond what is actually linguistically produced, considering for example participants' social identities and cultural backgrounds (e.g., interactional sociolinguistic studies such as this one, studies in the ethnography of communication, and other anthropologically oriented approaches).[1] Nonetheless, it is a common practice for discourse analysts across approaches to collect and examine relatively bounded, isolated interactions. This can be viewed as problematic, as this study has shown. I am not the only researcher to argue this, of course. As Asif Agha (2005:1) points out, "the data of social life plucked from their isolable moments invariably point to lived moments that lie beyond them," while Gunther Kress (2000:134) comments, "the boundaries of the text . . . are not the boundaries of meaning-making."

The theory of intertextuality attempts to deal with this issue by viewing all texts and interactions as made up of bits and pieces of, and interconnected with, those prior. As Anna Solin (2004:268) remarks, in the past twenty years or so, linguists have come to embrace the ideas of intertextuality and dialogism. Indeed, many analyses of single speech events have incorporated insights from intertextuality. For instance, Matoesian (1999) examines what he calls "reported speech" in trial discourse, thereby analyzing the interactive power of traces of source texts that were not actually recorded or analyzed; Fairclough (1992) discusses what he calls "constitutive intertextuality" (or interdiscursivity) by considering the heterogeneity of genre features in single print texts; and Schiffrin (2000) segments a larger spoken life history interview into relatively bounded units and draws intertextual connections between them to explore the linguistic portrayal of a family relationship. Such studies offer important insights into the various ways that intertextuality can be usefully conceptualized and explored in linguistic analyses of relatively isolated interactions. However, other research finds larger electronic corpora (e.g., online search-engine results: Hill 2005) and longitudinal studies (e.g., long-term ethnographic research and recording: Hamilton 1996; Wortham 2005, 2006) suitable for investigating intertextuality in language.

Charles Frake (1977:1) argues, "Methods link data—what we construe to be observations of some particular reality—with theory, our proposals for understanding reality in general." As remarked by Solin (2004:271), "there are no stable analytic procedures for approaching the phenomenon" of intertextuality. Our various methods—of both data collection and analysis—shape how we theorize the concept. For example, Matoesian's (1999) study of reported speech brings out how speakers shape the purported words of others to create particular footings; however, his examination necessarily focuses on unshared prior text. Fairclough's (1995:212) analysis, though revealing the heterogeneity of textual composition, relies not on the examination of actual prior discourses but on the analysts' awareness of genre features, making the process highly dependent on "the analyst's experience of and sensitivity to relevant orders of discourse, as well as the analyst's interpretative and strategic biases." Schiffrin's (2000) study of a life history interview, while providing a careful analysis of linguistic features that work together to portray a significant, ongoing relationship across a life history telling, provokes interesting questions about where intratextuality ends and intertextuality begins—her data could easily be conceptualized as "one text." I describe these studies not with the intent of criticizing their findings but to demonstrate how methodology influences conceptualizations of intertextuality by highlighting some aspects of the notion while clouding others. In addition, the methods of data collection used to compile the data set I draw on—family members self-recording nearly continuously for seven to fourteen days—fundamentally influenced how I went about analysis, my findings, and how I have come to view intertextuality as a theory.

The way I have approached intertextuality in this study—through instances of intertextual repetition—relates to the most basic conceptualization of intertextuality—the idea that all texts and interactions are metaphorical mosaics, literally made up of bits of other prior texts and interactions. In chapters 2 and 3, I studied links between conversations that exist in an ever-developing web of family talk, suggesting through patterns in this web, the family itself is constructed. In chapters 4 and 5, I linked conversations chronologically occurring but separated by varying interludes of time, doing a type of chain analysis, to show how particular meanings are constructed. Viewing intertextuality in this way, as something best studied not within interactions but across interactions, highlights how specific bits of prior text are actually reshaped and transformed—that is, unlike most prior linguistic studies on intertextuality my analysis brings to light the form and contexts of both "original" prior texts and their reshapings. In so doing, my study reveals the fundamental interconnectedness between having access to shared prior text and the mutual creation of meanings, as well as the role of reshaping shared prior text in creating the family as a social group.

However, my analysis of linked family interactions, of course, has its shortcomings. Solin points out some of the weaknesses of chain analysis, based on using it in her own research (2004:290–291):

> The restrictions in chain analysis mainly relate to the construction of chains for the purpose of analysis. The construction of intertextual chains is an interpretive exercise: intertextual chains do not simply present themselves to the analyst. It involves selecting core "moments" from the wealth of textual interaction taking place. It involves cutting off a set of texts from time and space and from practices of text production and consumption. Thus, the analysis of intertextuality in the form of chains cannot represent the complexities of intertextual relations as continuously occurring interactive networks.

Moreover, chain analysis does not allow the analysis of all the intertextual relations that individual texts on the chain have. Most texts on the particle chain have a wealth of relations to texts from various domains, but chain analysis only considers the way in which texts relate to other texts on the chain.

Following this perspective, in identifying excerpts to analyze as paired, or as existing in a string or chain, or in the broader web of a family's talk, I necessarily undertook an interpretive and selective task. I selected moments that showed linguistic evidence of linking through the repetition of key words, phrases, and other linguistic features. In doing so, I depended on listening to the recordings and reading through the transcripts repeatedly, my own (imperfect) memory of these experiences, the (imperfect, though much appreciated) memories of other researchers working on the larger project, and the search function of Microsoft Word. Then, I "cut off" excerpts of conversation and recontextualized them, presenting them as adjacent pairs or sets of excerpts, although in some cases the exchanges actually occurred days apart. Even though I analyzed a very rich data set, I was limited by the data set as well. I was restricted to seven to fourteen days of conversation among individuals who had been talking with each other for years and would continue to do so; thus, I likely missed many examples of intertextual repetition because I did not have access to the relevant prior text. I was also limited by the participants' (sometimes imperfect) commitment to recording; although this study is quite lengthy compared to many family discourse studies, there were some gaps in the data (which led me to focus on the families who taped the most consistently). Furthermore, by relying on recorded data, I was unable to consider features such as participants' use of gaze, posture, gesture, and so on. This obviously limited my understanding of intertextuality to the verbal channel; it also excluded analysis of nonverbal signs as contextualization cues, which may have helped clarify the framing process.

One way of dealing with the uncertainty inherent in analyzing and making plausible interpretations of recorded data is by accompanying them with data of other types. The analyses presented in this book primarily drew on recordings and transcripts; however, in making interpretations I also drew on information based on my experiences observing and talking with members of the families prior to listening to the audiotapes; I carefully read the field notes of other research project members regarding the participants I did not observe; I employed information I gained from follow-up conversations and email message exchanges with the participants conducted by myself and other project members; in addition, in one case, I accessed written texts that surfaced as prior text in interaction (the children's storybooks in chapter 5). Such procedures not only enriched the analysis but also served as a means of helping to validate interpretations made.[2]

In addition, methods themselves led to the creation of intertextuality. In fact, in his study of the talk of one family, Varenne (1992) considers the process of linking collected data and transcripts of the data with information gained from follow-up interviewing and findings of prior research—in other words, doing analysis, making interpretations, and researching and writing up findings—as an intertextual exercise. I was struck by this impression, in particular because I recontextualize not only the public, published words of other researchers but also the private voices of family members engaging in everyday talk. By repeating the words of others throughout this analysis, I have in some sense fundamentally altered them. Family members likely do not think about "ba-ba" as a term that creates intertextuality, nor do they view "rocks and rubs" as a ritual that constructs child-centered frames. Neither is "tinkles" a word I ever thought I would encounter (let alone analyze for an extended period of time) in academic research. In juxtaposing and interconnecting academic words and family words, academic perspectives and personal talk, this analysis has transformed both. I hope that in doing so, by creating this type of intertextuality, I have provided a means of conceptualizing in systematic terms patterns of everyday talk while still allowing the creative, emotion-laden, and private nature of the talk shine through.

FAMILY AS AN INTERACTIVE CONSTRUCTION

I suggest that one reason family members engaging in everyday talk intertextually repeat one another relates to the idea that the family is not just a biological, legal, financial, or societal construct but also a discursive one. Family members remember and draw on shared prior interactions of various types to create shared meanings and affirm a shared past, that is, to (re)create a sense of familyness. There is no "the family" but many families, each with its own unique history of talk.

Why repeat the words of other family members on some occasions but not others, some words and phrases but not others? In these data, intertextual repetition sometimes seemed to be prompted by a visual cue, as when Natalie apparently saw a hole in the ground while at the playground with her mother and recalled a rabbit hole in a book her mother had read to her several nights before at bedtime; the two interactions were linguistically linked through the participants' mutual reshapings of a line from the storybook. In other cases, a recurring topic of talk or theme in interaction between family members triggered intertextual repetition of particular words; for instance, how Janet and Steve talked about recording for the study in two separate conversations and the word "superior" surfaces each time as they jokingly jockey for position. Thus recurrent alignments between participants also seem to be related to the occurrence of intertextual repetition. Another example of this was Janet and Steve's creation of recurrent, playful alignments through a specific interactional routine: the mutual exchange of terms of endearment. Everyday family rituals (e.g., "rocks and rubs") and events (e.g., "shenanigans" at naptime) also provoked repetition as family members enacted and discussed these throughout their recording periods. Regardless of the particular prompt for participants to intertextually repeat, clearly noticing something in the ongoing discourse or in one's environment and memory of a prior something related plays a vital role. So does the ongoing quest and enjoyment of jointly remembering, crafting new meanings from old words, and (re)creating the family.

Although much research in sociolinguistics and linguistic anthropology views the family through a social constructionist lens, as I have here, the design of this study highlighted the constructed nature of the family in a particularly useful way. This study showed not only how members of a nuclear family used language in patterned, ritualized ways to construct themselves as a social group, but also how language is used in patterned ways to incorporate people who are not technically members of the family (i.e., not related by blood, adoption, marriage, commitment ceremony, etc.). This was possible because unlike many prior studies that have examined family discourse by audio- or video-recording dinner table conversations involving family members only, the design of this study required family members to record themselves over a relatively lengthy period of time in the various contexts in which they found themselves; members were thus captured talking not only with each other but also with people outside the nuclear family, including extended family members, co-workers, and friends. Family communication research that looks only at the discourse of those whom the analyst views as family members and only at conversations occurring during dinnertime loses the possibility of considering the symbolic and interactional family membership of others. In a time when "the family" does not have one standard meaning (except perhaps in myths and in our imaginations), and in the context of the relatively short-lived and thus continually self-inventing American family (Shore 2003), this type of analysis seems particularly important. As families continue to emerge and exist in various forms—as blended families, as three-generation households, as same-sex parent families—and as working parents enlist extended family and friends to help in child care, it is important to continue to widen our methodological and analytical nets if we want to capture what might actually constitute family in everyday talk.

In addition, it is important to consider family interaction as it occurs across a variety of contexts beyond the dinner table, as a number of recent studies have noted. Although a few of the conversational excerpts I analyze occurred at family mealtime, most did not. They occurred while in the car, putting the child to bed, playing outside, sitting in front of the television or computer, while one parent was feeding the child and the other was otherwise occupied, and so on. Indeed, members of these families often do not eat at the same time (even if everyone is at home and in the same room); as Kendall (2006:411) notes, "to understand family discourse at mealtime in these families, it is necessary to redefine 'family dinner' to include meals in which all family members are present but not everyone is eating, and to consider the wider context in which these interactions occur." There are concerns that family dinner is a ritual that is rapidly-declining in some families (Mestdag & Vandeweyer 2005); it is certainly the case that in these working families with small children the ritual took less traditional shapes. Even in families for which family dinner is an ongoing ritual, considering family interaction across a variety of contexts enables analysis of how talk structures and plays into everyday family activities beyond the dinner table; it also provides the opportunity to investigate how relatively well-studied aspects of language use—such as parental control acts and family narratives—vary across family situations.

The fieldwork episode that I described at the beginning of this book involving a nearly three-year-old child and talk about eating grapes caught my attention because it brought into relief how my outsider status—more specifically, my lack of access to family prior text—prevented me from fully understanding the child's seemingly simple utterance, "You just pop them in." In describing this experience and in analyzing linked interactions of greater symbolic significance in the discourse of these families, I hope to have demonstrated why it is so important to think about intertextuality and framing as fundamentally interconnected. By analyzing everyday interactions structured by the recurrence of everyday words and through the (re)creation of frames through this integrated perspective, I hope to have highlighted vital threads and patterns that help us understand the fabric of everyday family discourse while also providing insight into intertextuality and framing as theory.

Postscript

"Old Habits Never Die, They Just Mutate"

More than eight years have gone by since Janet and Steve, Kathy and Sam, and Clara and Neil carried recorders with them to collect the data used for this study. The children (and the parents) are all older now, and the families have changed in various ways.

The third family used as a comparison for my analysis of familylect terms has transformed dramatically: Clara and Neil have separated.

The Patterson/Foley family has changed, too. Kathy gave birth to a girl shortly after recording; about three years and eight months later, she gave birth to another girl, so Kira is twice a big sister. Kathy completed her degree, and Sam finished his doctoral coursework. Now Kathy is a full-time stay-at-home mom with the couple's three girls, and Sam continues to work full-time.

The family whose discourse is the focus of my research, the Neeley-Mason family, has undergone a number of changes as well. After recording, Janet gave birth to a son; the family reported by email that they used a number of the same words and phrases with him that they did with Natalie ("tinkles," "shenanigans," "meltdown," "brush choppers," and "rocks and rubs"). Janet finished her degree a few years later and started her own therapy practice. Steve was able to quit his restaurant jobs when he took a job at a bank; for a couple of years, he also baked and decorated specialty cakes, which he sold. Although Janet and Steve are currently taking a break from acting because the children's theater where they had performed closed, they hope to get back to it in the future. Happily, Jill and Tim got married, with Steve officiating and Janet serving as maid of honor; the couple subsequently had a baby. Research team members were sad to find out that Janet's mother passed away.

The Neeley-Mason family's composition thus has changed—a lost grandmother, a new brother, and "cousin" for Natalie—and it seems that the family's language has changed, too. When I emailed the Neeley-Masons in January 2005, five years after the family's recording week, inquiring into the phrase "rocks and rubs," Steve responded: "We still read [Natalie] books before bedtime and 'rocks & rubs' has given way to 'minutes' where we just lay in bed with her for a few minutes before saying goodnight. Old habits never die, they just mutate."

Many or perhaps even most of the language habits examined in this book have likely transformed in various ways since the families' recording periods, as family conversations have continued to unfold day after day and as topics like "tinkles" have faded from everyday talk as the children have grown older. Over eight years after recording, Janet reported in an email message that the family continues to use the words "shenanigans," "meltdown," and "brush choppers"; "buppie," "tinkles," and "rocks and rubs" have faded out of use. However, all of these language habits live on in other ways: in family members' minds, as intimate memories; in the minds of members of the research team, myself included, as compelling examples of language in use, of the dynamics of everyday talk, and of human creativity; and, in books like this one, as part of the academic conversation on family.

Appendix

Transcription Conventions

These transcription conventions were developed by Shari Kendall and Deborah Tannen for use in the research study "Mothers and Fathers at Work and at Home: Creating Parental Identities through Talk," at Georgetown University.

((words))	Double parentheses enclose transcriber's comments in italicized font.
<u>word</u>	Underlining is used to indicate repeated words that are analytically important.
⇨	This symbol precedes lines of particular analytical importance.
(words)	Single parentheses enclose uncertain transcription.
new line	Each new line represents an intonation unit.
→	This arrow, used only at the end of a line of transcript, indicates that the intonation unit continues onto the next line.
—	A dash indicates a truncated intonation unit.
-	A hyphen indicates a truncated word.
?	A question mark indicates a relatively strong rising intonation.
.	A period indicates a falling, final intonation.

,	A comma indicates a continuing intonation.
. .	One or two dots surrounded by spaces indicate a short silence.
:	A colon indicates an elongated vowel.
CAPS	Capitals indicate emphatic stress.
<*laughs*>	Angle brackets enclose descriptions of vocal noises, for instance, *laughs, coughs.*
<*manner*> words	Angle brackets enclose descriptions of the manner in which an utterance is spoken, for example, *high-pitched, laughing, sarcastic*
[words]	Square brackets enclose simultaneous talk.

Notes

1. All names of study participants are pseudonyms.

2. The Work and Family Project was co-directed by Deborah Tannen and Shari Kendall and was funded by the Alfred P. Sloan Foundation in a grant to Tannen and Kendall and in a follow-up grant to Tannen, Kendall, and me. I was involved first as a research team member and later as a postdoctoral fellow and co-principal investigator. Other research team members included Alexandra Johnston, Philip LeVine, Sigrid Norris, and Alla Tovares.

3. The first four dual-income families who were willing and able to record at home and work over the designated time period were accepted for participation in the study. In keeping with the Sloan Foundation's interests, the families were required to be dual-income and roughly middle-class; all four of the participating families happened to be white. I examine the discourse of the three families with one young child; the fourth family had older children (the youngest in high school). Participants were located through various means. Tannen accepted a number of invitations to give lectures and interviews in the Washington, DC, area and mentioned our interest in recruiting families for the project. She also contacted the director of a women's center in northern Virginia, looking for volunteer families. Finally, flyers were posted at various locations in and around Washington, including video stores, cafés, and food stores.

4. For examples, see Tannen (2007 [1989]), Johnstone (1994a, 1994b), Couper-Kuhlen (1996), Brown (2000), Meinhof and Smith (2000), Wong

(2000), Hellermann (2003), Bauman (2004), Cekaite and Aronsson (2004), Schiffrin (2006), and Tovares (2007).

5. Note that in the spirit of Bakhtin, I specifically focus on the *evaluative* stances speakers adopt in reshaping prior text and the alignments that result from these. However, speakers and listeners also create other kinds of stances in interaction through various means; for a nuanced discussion of the negotiation of some different kinds of stances in the context of family discourse, see C. Goodwin (2007).

6. See also Günthner (1997, 1999) and Holt and Clift's (2007) edited volume.

7. This is a very rich and growing area of research. For instance, Tannen (2007 [1989]) examines repetition on various levels of discourse in both conversational and literary discourse, while contributors to Johnstone's edited volumes (1994a, 1994b) consider repetition in contexts as varied as joke-telling in conversation (Norrick 1994), therapist–client interaction (Ferrara 1994), and second language acquisition tutoring (Tomlin 1994). Schiffrin (2006) takes a broad view of repetition, investigating repairs, reformulations, and narrative retellings in her exploration of face-to-face interactions and public discourse.

8. My understanding of ambiguity and polysemy of repetition is related to Tannen's (1994) analysis of the ambiguity and polysemy of various linguistic strategies in terms of power and solidarity. Tannen argues that any utterance can potentially be used to create power (or hierarchy) or solidarity (or connection/intimacy), therefore utterances are ambiguous in this regard. Any utterance can also be polysemous—it can reflect power and solidarity at the same time. For instance, Tannen considers the case of the linguistic strategy of simultaneous talk: Talking while someone else is talking, often viewed as a move for power or dominance, is routinely used among members of some groups as a way of showing solidarity and active listenership. Producing simultaneous talk can be a move for power—as when one speaker tries to "steal" the conversational floor from another. However, it can also be viewed as a move of solidarity, as a means of showing interest in what the other participant is saying. Or it could be both at once. Although, for the most part I do not explicitly focus on the push and pull between the interactional dimensions of power and solidarity, I draw on Tannen's framework in the sense that I conceptualize repetition as a strategy that is potentially ambiguous and polysemous in terms of the range of meanings it can create in any given use.

9. For discussions on how the term *frame* has been variously used (as well as related concepts like script and schema) in fields as diverse as artificial intelligence, cognitive linguistics, and sociolinguistics, see Tannen and Wallat (1993), Coulson (2001:17–20), and Bednarek (2005).

10. For linguistic studies that use and develop frames theory as a way of exploring interaction, see Tannen (1993a, 1993c), and Ribeiro (1993, 1994); for those that do so in analyzing family discourse, see Gordon (2002, 2008) and

Kendall (2006). For studies that draw on frames theory—or elements of it—as a means of investigating identity construction in the context of family, see Schiffrin (1996, 2000, 2002), Kendall (1999, 2003, 2004, 2007), Gordon (2004, 2006), and Tannen, Kendall, and Gordon's (2007) edited volume. Note that a number of the studies examining linguistic identity construction use the notions of framing or footing in conjunction with the concept of "positioning" (Davies and Harré 1990) or the notions of "act" and "stance" (Ochs 1992, 1993). It seems to be commonly understood that the idea of "positioning" and Ochs's discussion of "indexing" identities are related to the notion of footing, although researchers have used these terms in different ways. In this book, I occasionally use the verb *position* to mean "take up" or "assign" a footing. Although I do not explore differences between footing and positioning here, recent research uses these terms contrastively but in tandem. Ribeiro (2006:74), for instance, argues that changes in positioning constitute prominent alterations in participant stance, whereas changes in footing are more subtle and represent "micro interactional shifts." Similarly, Kendall (2007:127) views positions as closely related to larger discourses, cultural ideologies, and role identities but finds footing and framing to be most useful for investigating how social indexicals are utilized on a micro-level, moment-by-moment basis in interaction. Schiffrin (2006:210) suggests that while positioning relates to the creation of relationships and identities, footing "deconstructs the speaker's relationship to what is said."

11. Influential studies of family discourse that focus on interaction at the dinner table include Blum-Kulka's (1997) cross-cultural study *Dinner Talk*, which examines the discourse of Jewish American, Israeli, and American Israeli families, and a body of research by Elinor Ochs and her colleagues in the United States (e.g., Ochs & Taylor 1992a, 1992b, 1995; Ochs, Smith, & Taylor 1996; Ochs et al. 1992; Taylor 1994) and in Italy (e.g., Ochs, Pontecorvo, & Fasulo 1990; Pontecorvo & Fasulo 1997).

12. For publications from these projects, see *Text & Talk*'s (2006, 26, no. 4/5) special issue *Family Discourse, Framing Family*, edited by Deborah Tannen (the Work and Family Project) and Marjorie Harness Goodwin (CELF); *Discourse & Society*'s (2007, 18, no. 1) special issue *Morality as Family Practice*, edited by Elinor Ochs and Tamar Kremer-Sadlik (CELF); and Tannen, Kendall, and Gordon's (2007) edited volume *Family Talk*, which considers data from the Work and Family Project.

13. The recorders used were Sony TCD-D100s, which are approximately 4.5 × 3.5 × 1 inches.

14. Research team members who shadowed participants were Shari Kendall, Alexandra Johnston, Philip LeVine, Sigrid Norris, and me. As a research team member, I shadowed Janet Neeley-Mason and Clara Shepherd, logged the entirety of the content of their tapes, and transcribed many of their interactions. I transcribed as many interactions as I could from the remaining

participants' tapes and listened to those that interested me but were originally transcribed by other research team members. The transcripts are stored in searchable Microsoft Word files and were coded with key words to identify salient events, such as arguments and apologies.

15. Tannen (2004) examines this family's talk, illustrating how the dogs are framed as family members.

16. See Gordon (2004) for a discussion of how this family uses language to construct the political aspect of their shared family identity.

17. Meetings involved the project co-principal investigators (Tannen and Kendall), research team members (Alexandra Johnston, Philip LeVine, Sigrid Norris, Alla Tovares, and me), and sometimes other Georgetown University graduate students who had assisted with transcribing.

18. The concept of playback derives from early sociolinguistic work by William Labov (Labov & Fanshel 1977; see also Fanshel & Moss 1971). It is commonly used in interactional sociolinguistic studies (see e.g., Gumperz 1982; Tannen 2005 [1984]). In the context of interactional sociolinguistics, playback usually refers playing a recording back to interlocutors who participated in the interaction, or playing it to others with the same cultural/ linguistic background as the original interlocutors, and gathering reactions in an open-ended way. I did not usually literally play back the tapes, but I did check back with family members regarding my interpretations of specific interactions, usually by email.

CHAPTER 2

1. Ochs and Schieffelin's work highlights (among other things) that although in American white middle-class families using baby talk with young children is typical, ways of interacting with babies and children vary greatly across social and cultural groups.

2. Note that when I inquired about the term "choppers" via e-mail five years after the family finished recording, Steve confirmed that "brush choppers" is a phrase the family continues to use for brushing Natalie's teeth. The family also reported using the phrase with Natalie's younger brother.

3. See Kendall (2006) for a similar discussion of child-centered footings in a "sociable frame" in the discourse of this family; Kendall examines these footings as part of her study of how family dinnertime homecomings are linguistically negotiated.

4. Note that "shenanigans" is also used on one occasion to refer to the behaviors of a nonfamily member: Once, Janet uses the term to playfully describe the behavior of a member of the children's theater troupe to which she and Steve belong. This conversation involves Janet, Steve, the actor whose "shenanigans" are up for discussion, and other troupe members.

5. The term "meltdown" is also used on one occasion in conversation between Janet and Steve to refer to someone outside the family. While watching the television drama *Felicity*, they characterize a father as having a "meltdown" when his daughter discovers the secrets that he was fired from his job and had been taking sleeping pills.

6. In sociolinguistics, linguistic anthropology, and discourse analysis, the term "ritual" has been used in various manners: to describe speech events in which what is said is patterned and not literally true, such as the case of "ritual insults" (Labov 1972a); to examine "sequential acts which are socially significant" in service encounters (Kuiper & Flindall 2000:184); and to explore language use in events like funerals (Cook & Walter 2005) and other religious activities (Philips 1983).

7. See Gordon (2008) for a frame analysis of how parents in all three families use play as a means of accomplishing parenting tasks.

CHAPTER 3

1. Steve provided this information via email.

2. Austin (1962) and Searle (1969) provide seminal insights into how interlocutors use language to do things in the world. I identify different speech acts here in terms of how they function in interaction in a general way.

3. This is an interesting parallel to one excerpt of conversation analyzed in Gordon (2003). In both cases, the parental team emphasizes the importance of talking to and interacting appropriately with someone outside the family, a fundamental component of language socialization.

4. Marinova (2004) analyzes Natalie's shifting participation status throughout the telling.

CHAPTER 4

1. Note that "passive" refers to the fact that the speaker readily shapes the words to the current task; the words do not "resist." Words that resist the task of the current speaker are called "active double-voiced words." See Morson and Emerson (1990) and Todorov (1984 [1981]) for discussions.

2. When I presented this example publicly for several different audiences, it was pointed out to me more than once that Kathy's utterance sounded familiar and may itself be a repetition of prior text drawn from an unidentified source in the public domain. This may be another layer of meaning present in this interaction.

3. To my knowledge, members of the research team never referred to participating family members as "subjects" or "research subjects"; Steve and Janet seem to have come up with these terms themselves.

4. See Tannen (1994) for a discussion of the interrelationship of power and solidarity in interaction, and Tannen (1990) for a discussion of symmetry as a strategy for solidarity building, in particular among women.

5. This comment is an interesting one: Although Jill and Tim are symbolic family members, as was demonstrated in the last chapter, Janet's comment suggests that they in some respect are "outsiders"—family members shouldn't "misbehave" in front of company.

6. Tannen (2001:20–23, 2006) also analyzes this extended argument.

7. "Pull-Ups" is a registered brand of Kimberly-Clark Worldwide. However, the name brand has come to be used more generally to talk about toilet-training diapers.

CHAPTER 5

1. See Gordon (2008) for other examples of blending frames and reframing in interactions involving all three families with small children that participated in this study.

2. I was actually not aware of cognitive linguistic research on conceptual blending when I initially considered what blending might mean; however, I discovered that the commonalities extend beyond the use of particular terms (e.g., frame, schema, script) and particular examples to more general understandings about meaning-making processes.

CHAPTER 6

1. See Schiffrin (1994) for an in-depth discussion of various approaches to analyzing discourse, including their backgrounds and sample analyses.

2. See Corsaro (1982) and Tannen (2005 [1984]) for discussions of how analytical interpretations of recorded interaction can be confirmed.

References

Agar, Michael. 1994. *Language shock: Understanding the culture of conversation.* New York: Quill.

Agha, Asif. 2005. Introduction: Semiosis across encounters. *Journal of Linguistic Anthropology* 15(1), 1–5.

Al Zidjaly, Najma. 2006. Disability and anticipatory discourse: The interconnectedness of local and global aspects of talk. *Communication & Medicine* 3(2), 101–112.

Aronsson, Karin. 2006. Commentary 1. Doing family: An interactive accomplishment. *Text & Talk* 26(4/5), 619–626.

Austin, J. L. 1962. *How to do things with words.* Cambridge, MA: Harvard University Press.

Bakhtin, M. M. 1981. *The dialogic imagination: Four essays*, trans. Caryl Emerson and Michael Holquist, ed. Michael Holquist. Austin: University of Texas Press.

Bakhtin, M. M. 1984. *Problems of Dostoevsky's poetics*, trans. and ed. Caryl Emerson, with an introduction by Wayne C. Booth. Minneapolis: University of Minnesota Press.

Bakhtin, M. M. 1986. The problem of speech genres. *Speech genres and other late essays*, trans. Vern W. McGee, ed. Caryl Emerson and Michael Holquist, 60–102. Austin: University of Texas Press.

Bateson, Gregory. 1972. *Steps to an ecology of mind.* New York: Ballantine.

Bauman, Richard. 2004. *A world of others' words: Cross-cultural perspectives on intertextuality.* Malden, MA: Blackwell.

Becker, A. L. 1994. Repetition and otherness: An essay. *Repetition in discourse: Interdisciplinary perspectives*, vol. 2, ed. Barbara Johnstone, 162–175. Norwood, NJ: Ablex.

Becker, A. L. 1995. *Beyond translation: Essays towards a modern philology*. Ann Arbor: University of Michigan Press.

Bednarek, Monika A. 2005. Frames revisited—the coherence-inducing function of frames. *Journal of Pragmatics* 37(5), 685–705.

Bergen, Karla Mason, Elizabeth A. Suter, and Karen L. Daas. 2006. "About as solid as a fish net": Symbolic construction of a legitimate parental identity for nonbiological lesbian mothers. *Journal of Family Communication* 6(3), 201–220.

Bergman, Anni, and Ilene Sackler Lefcourt. 1994. Self-other action play: A window into the representational world of the infant. *Children at play: Clinical and developmental approaches to meaning and representation*, ed. Arietta Slade and Dennie Palmer Wolf, 133–147. New York: Oxford University Press.

Blum-Kulka, Shoshana. 1990. "You don't touch lettuce with your fingers": Parental politeness in family discourse. *Journal of Pragmatics* 14(2), 259–288.

Blum-Kulka, Shoshana. 1997. *Dinner talk: Cultural patterns of sociability and socialization in family discourse*. Mahwah, NJ: Erlbaum.

Blum-Kulka, Shoshana, and Catherine E. Snow. 1992. Developing autonomy for tellers, tales and telling in family narrative-events. *Journal of Narrative and Life History* 2(3), 187–217.

Boxer, Diana. 2002. Nagging: The familial conflict arena. *Journal of Pragmatics* 34(1), 49–61.

Briggs, Charles L., and Richard Bauman. 1992. Genre, intertextuality, and social power. *Journal of Linguistic Anthropology* 2(2), 131–172.

Brown, Penelope. 2000. Conversational structure and language acquisition: The role of repetition in Tzeltal. *Journal of Linguistic Anthropology* 8(2), 197–221.

Bruner, Jerome. 1987. Life as narrative. *Social Research* 54(1), 11–32.

Buttny, Richard. 1997. Reported speech in talking race on campus. *Human Communication Research* 23(4), 477–506.

Buttny, Richard. 1998. Putting prior talk into context: Reported speech and the reporting context. *Research on Language and Social Interaction* 31(1), 45–58.

Byers, Lori. 1997. Telling the stories of our lives: Relational maintenance as illustrated through family communication. Doctoral dissertation, Ohio University.

Campbell, John Edward. 2003. Always use a modem: Analyzing frames of erotic play, performance, and power in cyberspace. *Electronic Journal of Communication/La Revue Electronique de Communication* 13(1). Retrieved on August 10, 2008, from www.cios.org/www/ejc/v13n1.htm.

Cekaite, Asta, and Karin Aronsson. 2004. Repetition and joking in children's second language conversations: Playful recyclings in an immersion classroom. *Discourse Studies* 6(3), 373–392.

Cook, Guy, and Tony Walter. 2005. Rewritten rites: Language and social relations in traditional and contemporary funerals. *Discourse & Society* 16(3), 365–391.

Cook-Gumperz, Jenny. 1992. Gendered contexts. *The contextualization of language*, ed. Peter Auer and Aldo di Luzio, 177–198. Amsterdam: John Benjamins.

Corsaro, William A. 1982. Something old and something new: The importance of prior ethnography in the collection and analysis of audiovisual data. *Sociological Methods & Research* 11(2), 145–166.

Corsaro, William A. 1983. Script recognition, articulation, and expansion in children's role play. *Discourse Processes* 6(1), 1–19.

Coulson, Seanna. 2001. *Semantic leaps: Frame-shifting and conceptual blending in meaning construction*. Cambridge: Cambridge University Press.

Coulson, Seanna, and Gilles Fauconnier. 1999. Fake guns and stone lions: Conceptual blending and privative adjectives. *Cognition and function in language*, ed. Barbara Fox, Dan Jurafsky, and Laura A. Michaelis, 143–158. Stanford, CA: CSLI.

Coulson, Seanna, and Todd Oakley. 2000. Blending basics. *Cognitive Linguistics* 11(3/4), 175–196.

Couper-Kuhlen, Elizabeth. 1996. The prosody of repetition: On quoting and mimicry. *Prosody in conversation*, ed. Elizabeth Couper-Kuhlen and Margret Selting, 367–405. Cambridge: Cambridge University Press.

Davies, Bronwyn, and Rom Harré. 1990. Positioning: The discursive production of selves. *Journal for the Theory of Social Behavior* 20(1), 43–63.

de Léon, Lourdes. 2007. Paralellism, metalinguistic play, and the interactive emergence of Zinacantec Mayan siblings' culture. *Research on Language and Social Interaction* 40(4), 405–436.

Dickson, Paul. 2007. *Family words: A dictionary of the secret language of families*. Oak Park, IL: Marion Street Press.

Eder, Donna. 1988. Building cohesion through collaborative narration. *Social Psychology Quarterly* 51(3), 225–235.

Erickson, Frederick. 1990. The social construction of discourse coherence in a family dinner table conversation. *Conversational organization and its development*, ed. Bruce Dorval, 207–238. Norwood, NJ: Ablex.

Ervin-Tripp, Susan, Mary Catherine O'Connor, and Jarrett Rosenberg. 1984. Language and power in the family. *Language and power*, ed. Cheris Kramarae, Muriel Schulz, and William O'Barr, 116–135. New York: Sage.

Ervin-Tripp, Susan, and Amy Strage. 1985. Parent-child discourse. *Handbook of discourse analysis*, Vol. 3, ed. Teun A. van Dijk, 67–78. New York: Academic Press.

Everts, Elisa. 2003. Identifying a particular family humor style: A sociolinguistic discourse analysis. *Humor* 16(4), 369–412.

Fairclough, Norman. 1992. Intertextuality in critical discourse analysis. *Linguistics and Education* 4(3–4), 269–293.

Fairclough, Norman. 1995. *Critical discourse analysis: The critical study of language*. London: Longman.

Fairclough, Norman. 2000. Discourse, social theory, and social research: The discourse of welfare reform. *Journal of Sociolinguistics* 4(2), 163–195.

Falk, Jane. 1979. The duet as a conversational process. Doctoral dissertation, Princeton University.

Fanshel, David, and Freda Moss. 1971. *Playback: A marriage in jeopardy examined*. New York: Columbia University Press.

Fauconnier, Gilles, and Mark Turner. 2000. Compression and global insight. *Cognitive Linguistics* 11(3–4), 283–304.

Fauconnier, Gilles, and Mark Turner. 2002. *The way we think: Conceptual blending and the mind's hidden complexities*. New York: Basic Books.

Fein, Greta G. 1981. Pretend play in childhood: An integrative review. *Child Development* 52(4), 1095–1118.

Ferrara, Kathleen. 1994. Repetition as rejoinder in therapeutic discourse: Echoing and mirroring. *Repetition in discourse: Interdisciplinary perspectives*, vol. 2, ed. Barbara Johnstone, 66–95. Norwood, NJ: Ablex.

Fiese, Barbara H. 2006. *Family routines and rituals*. New Haven, CT: Yale University Press.

Fiese, Barbara H., Thomas J. Tomcho, Michael Douglas, Kimberly Josephs, Scott Poltrock, and Tim Baker. 2002. A review of 50 years of research on naturally occurring family routines and rituals: Cause for celebration? *Journal of Family Psychology* 16(4), 381–390.

Fivush, Robyn, Jennifer Bohanek, Rachel Robertson, and Marshall Duke. 2004. Family narratives and the development of children's emotional well-being. *Family stories and the lifecourse: Across time and generations*, ed. Michael W. Pratt and Barbara H. Fiese, 55–76. New York: Routledge.

Frake, Charles O. 1977. Plying frames can be dangerous. *Quarterly Newsletter of the Institute for Comparative Human Development (Rockefeller University)* 1(3), 1–7.

Friedrich, Paul. 1989. Language, ideology, and political economy. *American Anthropologist* 91(2), 295–312.

Garvey, Catherine. 1976. Some properties of social play. *Play: Its role in development and evolution*, ed. Jerome S. Bruner, Alison Jolly, and Kathy Sylva, 570–584. New York: Basic Books.

Geertz, Clifford. 1973. *The interpretation of cultures*. New York: Basic Books.

Gillis, John R. 1996. *A world of their own making: Myth, ritual, and the quest for American family values*. New York: Basic Books.

Goffman, Erving. 1959. *The presentation of self in everyday life.* New York: Doubleday.

Goffman, Erving. 1963. *Behavior in public places: Notes on the social organization of gatherings.* New York: Free Press.

Goffman, Erving. 1967. *Interaction ritual: Essays on face-to-face behavior.* New York: Pantheon.

Goffman, Erving. 1974. *Frame analysis.* New York: Harper & Row.

Goffman, Erving. 1981. Footing. *Forms of talk,* 124–159. Philadelphia: University of Pennsylvania Press.

Göncü, Artin, Ute Tuermer, Jyoti Jain, and Danielle Johnson. 1999. Children's play as cultural activity. *Children's engagement with the world: Sociocultural perspectives,* ed. Artin Göncü, 148–170. Cambridge: Cambridge University Press.

Goodwin, Charles. 2006. Retrospective and prospective orientation in the construction of argumentative moves. *Text & Talk* 26(4/5), 443–461.

Goodwin, Charles. 2007. Participation, stance and affect in the organization of activities. *Discourse & Society* 18(1), 53–73.

Goodwin, Marjorie Harness. 1990. *He-said-she-said: Talk as social organization among black children.* Bloomington: Indiana University Press.

Goodwin, Marjorie Harness. 2006. Participation, affect, and trajectory in family directive/response sequences. *Text & Talk* 26(4/5), 515–543.

Goodwin, Marjorie Harness. 2007. Occasioned knowledge exploration in family interaction. *Discourse & Society* 18(1), 93–110.

Goodwin, Marjorie Harness, and Charles Goodwin. 1987. Children's arguing. *Language, gender, and sex in comparative perspective,* ed. Susan U. Philips, Susan Steele, and Christine Tanz, 200–248. Cambridge: Cambridge University Press.

Gordon, Cynthia. 2002. "I'm Mommy and you're Natalie": Role-reversal and embedded frames in mother-child discourse. *Language in Society* 31(5), 679–720.

Gordon, Cynthia. 2003. Aligning as a team: Forms of conjoined participation in (stepfamily) interaction. *Research on Language and Social Interaction* 36(4), 395–431.

Gordon, Cynthia. 2004. "Al Gore's our guy": Linguistically constructing a family political identity. *Discourse & Society* 15(5), 607–631. (Reprinted with minor alterations in *Family talk: Discourse and identity in four American Families,* ed. Deborah Tannen, Shari Kendall, and Cynthia Gordon, 233–262. New York: Oxford University Press, 2007.)

Gordon, Cynthia. 2006. Reshaping prior text, reshaping identities. *Text & Talk* 26(4/5), 545–571.

Gordon, Cynthia. 2007a. "I just feel horribly embarrassed when she does that": Constituting a mother's identity. *Family talk: Discourse and identity in four*

American families, ed. Deborah Tannen, Shari Kendall, and Cynthia Gordon, 71–101. New York: Oxford University Press.

Gordon, Cynthia. 2007b. Repetition and identity experimentation: One child's use of repetition as a resource for "trying on" maternal identities. *Selves and identities in narrative and discourse*, ed. Michael Bamberg, Anna De Fina, and Deborah Schiffrin, 133–157. Philadelphia: John Benjamins.

Gordon, Cynthia. 2008. A(p)parent play: Blending frames and reframing in family talk. *Language in Society* 37(3), 319–349.

Gordon, Cynthia, Deborah Tannen, and Aliza Sacknovitz. 2007. A working father: One father's talk about family at work. *Family talk: Discourse and identity in four American families*, 195–230, ed. Deborah Tannen, Shari Kendall, and Cynthia Gordon. New York: Oxford University Press.

Gubrium, Jaber F., and James A. Holstein. 1990. *What is family?* Mountain View, CA: Mayfield.

Gumperz, John J. 1982. *Discourse strategies*. Cambridge: Cambridge University Press.

Gumperz, John J. 1992. Contextualization revisited. *The contextualization of language*, ed. Peter Auer and Aldo di Luzio, 39–53. Philadelphia: John Benjamins.

Günthner, Susanne. 1997. The contextualization of affect in reported dialogues. *The language of emotions: Conceptualization, expression, and theoretical foundation*, ed. Susanne Niemeier and René Dirven, 245–275. Philadelphia: John Benjamins.

Günthner, Susanne. 1999. Polyphony and the "layering of voices" in reported dialogues: An analysis of the use of prosodic devices in everyday reported speech. *Journal of Pragmatics* 31(5), 685–708.

Haight, Wendy L. 1999. The pragmatics of caregiver-child pretending at home: Understanding culturally specific socialization practices. *Children's engagement with the world: sociocultural perspectives*, ed. Artin Göncü, 128–147. Cambridge: Cambridge University Press.

Haight, Wendy, Tracy Masiello, K. Laurie Dickson, Elizabeth Huckeby, and James Black. 1994. The everyday contexts and social functions of spontaneous mother-child pretend play in the home. *Merrill-Palmer Quarterly* 40(4), 509–522.

Haight, Wendy L., and Peggy J. Miller. 1993. *Pretending at home: Early development in a sociocultural context*. Albany: State University of New York Press.

Haight, Wendy L., Xiao-lei Wang, Heidi Han-tih Fung, Kimberly Williams, and Judith Mintz. 1999. Universal, developmental, and variable aspects of young children's play: A cross-cultural comparison of pretending at home. *Child Development* 70(6), 1477–1488.

Hamilton, Heidi E. 1996. Intratextuality, intertextuality, and the construction of identity as patient in Alzheimer's disease. *Text* 16(1), 61–90.

Harvey, Mary R., Elliot G. Mishler, Karestan Koenen, and Patricia A. Harney. 2000. In the aftermath of abuse: Making and remaking meaning in narratives of trauma and recovery. *Narrative Inquiry* 10(2), 291–311.

Hellermann, John. 2003. The interactive work of prosody in the IRF exchange: Teacher repetition in feedback moves. *Language in Society* 32(1), 79–104.

Hill, Jane H. 2005. Intertextuality as source and evidence for indirect indexical meanings. *Journal of Linguistic Anthropology* 15(1), 113–124.

Holstein, James A., and Jaber F. Gubrium. 1995. Deprivatization and the construction of domestic life. *Journal of Marriage and the Family* 57(4), 894–908.

Holstein, James A., and Jaber F. Gubrium. 1999. What is family? Further thoughts on a social constructionist approach. *Marriage and Family Review* 28(3/4), 3–20.

Holt, Elizabeth. 2000. Reporting and reacting: Concurrent responses to reported speech. *Research on Language and Social Interaction* 33(4), 425–454.

Holt, Elizabeth, and Rebecca Clift. 2007. *Reporting talk.* Cambridge: Cambridge University Press.

Hoyle, Susan. 1993. Participation frameworks in sportscasting play: Imaginary and literal footings. *Framing in discourse,* ed. Deborah Tannen, 114–145. New York: Oxford University Press.

Jackson, Kathy Merlock. 2005. Preface and acknowledgments. *Rituals and patterns in children's lives,* ed. Kathy Merlock Jackson, ix–x. Madison: University of Wisconsin Press.

Jackson, Maggie. 2002. *What's happening to home? Balancing work, life, and refuge in the information age.* Notre Dame, IN: Sorin.

Johnstone, Barbara, ed. 1994a. *Repetition in discourse: Interdisciplinary perspectives,* vol. 1. Norwood, NJ: Ablex.

Johnstone, Barbara, ed. 1994b. *Repetition in discourse: Interdisciplinary perspectives,* vol. 2. Norwood, NJ: Ablex.

Johnstone, Barbara, et al. 1994. Repetition in discourse: A dialogue. *Repetition in discourse: Interdisciplinary perspectives,* vol. 1, ed. Barbara Johnstone, 1–20. Norwood, NJ: Ablex.

Junefelt, Karin, and Tiia Tulviste. 1997. Regulation and praise in American, Estonian, and Swedish mother-child interaction. *Mind, Culture, and Activity* 4(1), 24–33.

Kangasharju, Helena. 1996. Aligning as a team in multiparty conversation. *Journal of Pragmatics* 26(3), 291–319.

Kangasharju, Helena. 2002. Alignment in disagreement: forming oppositional alliances in committee meetings. *Journal of Pragmatics* 34(10), 1447–1471.

Kendall, Shari. 1999. The interpenetration of (gendered) spheres: An interactional sociolinguistic analysis of a mother at work and at home. Doctoral dissertation, Georgetown University.

Kendall, Shari. 2003. Creating gendered demeanors of authority at work and at home. *The handbook of language and gender*, ed. Janet Holmes and Miriam Meyerhoff, 600–623. Malden, MA: Blackwell.

Kendall, Shari. 2004. Framing authority: Gender, face, and mitigation at a radio network. *Discourse & Society* 15(1), 55–79.

Kendall, Shari. 2006. "Honey, I'm home!": Framing in family dinnertime homecomings. *Text & Talk* 26(4/5), 411–441.

Kendall, Shari. 2007. Father as breadwinner, mother as worker: Gendered positions in feminist and traditional discourses of work and family. *Family talk*, ed. Deborah Tannen, Shari Kendall and Cynthia Gordon, 123–163. New York: Oxford University Press.

Kress, Gunther. 2000. Text as the punctuation of semiosis: Pulling at some of the threads. *Intertextuality and the media: From genre to everyday life*, ed. Ulrike H. Meinhof and Jonathan Smith, 132–154. Manchester, UK: Manchester University Press.

Kristeva, Julia. 1980 [1967]. Word, dialogue and novel. *Desire in language: A semiotic approach to literature and art*, trans. Thomas Gora, Alice Jardine, and Leon S. Roudiez, ed. Leon S. Roudiez, 64–91. New York: Columbia University Press.

Kuiper, Koenraad, and Marie Flindall. 2000. Social rituals, formulaic speech and small talk at the supermarket checkout. *Small talk*, ed. Justine Coupland, 183–207. Harlow, UK: Longman.

Kyratzis, Amy. 1999. Narrative identity: Preschoolers' self-construction through narrative in same-sex friendship group dramatic play. *Narrative Inquiry* 9(2), 427–455.

Labov, William. 1972a. *Language in the inner city: Studies in the black English vernacular*. Philadelphia: University of Pennsylvania Press.

Labov, William. 1972b. Some principles of linguistic methodology. *Language in Society* 1(1), 97–120.

Labov, William. 1997. Some further steps in narrative analysis. *Journal of Narrative and Life History* 7(1–4), 395–415.

Labov, William, and David Fanshel. 1977. *Therapeutic discourse: Psychotherapy as conversation*. New York: Academic Press.

Labov, William, and Joshua Waletzky. 1967. Narrative analysis: Oral versions of personal experience. *Essays on the verbal and visual arts: Proceedings of the 1966 Annual Spring Meeting of the American Ethnological Society*, ed. June Helm, 12–44. Seattle: University of Washington Press.

Langellier, Kristin M., and Eric E. Peterson. 1993. Narrative and social control. *Critical perspectives*, ed. Dennis K. Mumby, 49–76. Newbury Park, CA: Sage.

Lerner, Gene H. 1993. Collectivities in action: Establishing the relevance of conjoined participation in conversation. *Text* 13(2), 213–245.

Luckmann, Benita. 1970. The small life-worlds of modern man. *Social Research* 37(4), 580–596.

Mandelbaum, Jenny. 1987. Couples sharing stories. *Communication Quarterly* 35(2), 144–170.

Marinova, Diana. 2004. Telling a meal-time story—to whom and why. Paper presented at The Annual Conference of the American Association of Applied Linguistics, Portland, Oregon, May.

Marinova, Diana. 2007. Finding the right balance between connection and control: A father's identity construction in conversations with his college-age daughter. *Family talk: Discourse and identity in four American families*, ed. Deborah Tannen, Shari Kendall, and Cynthia Gordon, 103–120. New York: Oxford University Press.

Matoesian, Greg. 1999. Intertextuality, affect, and ideology in legal discourse. *Text* 19(1), 73–109.

Matoesian, Greg. 2000. Intertextual authority in reported speech: Production media in the Kennedy Smith rape trial. *Journal of Pragmatics* 32(7), 879–914.

Meinhof, Ulrike H., and Jonathan Smith, eds. 2000. *Intertextuality and the media: From genre to everyday life.* Manchester: Manchester University Press.

Mestdag, Inge, and Jessie Vandeweyer. 2005. Where has family time gone? In search of joint family activites and the role of the family mean in 1966 and 1999. *Journal of Family History* 30(3), 304–323.

Morson, Gary Saul. 1989. Parody, history, and metaparody. *Rethinking Bakhtin*, ed. Gary Saul Morson and Caryl Emerson, 63–86. Evanston, IL: Northwestern University Press.

Morson, Gary Saul, and Caryl Emerson. 1990. *Mikhail Bakhtin: Creation of a prosaics.* Stanford, CA: Stanford University Press.

Norrick, Neal R. 1994. Repetition as a conversational joking strategy. *Repetition in discourse: Interdisciplinary perspectives*, vol. 2, ed. Barbara Johnstone, 15–28. Norwood, NJ: Ablex.

Nydegger, Corrine N., and Linda S. Mitteness. 1988. Etiquette and ritual in family conversation. *American Behavioral Scientist* 31(6), 702–716.

Ochs, Elinor. 1992. Indexing gender. *Rethinking context: Language as an interactive phenomenon*, ed. Alessandro Duranti and Charles Goodwin, 335–358. Cambridge: Cambridge University Press.

Ochs, Elinor. 1993. Constructing social identity: A language socialization perspective. *Research on Language and Social Interaction* 26(3), 287–306.

Ochs, Elinor, Clotilde Pontecorvo, and Alessandra Fasulo. 1990. Socializing taste. *Ethnos* 61(1–2), 7–46.

Ochs, Elinor, and Tamar Kremer-Sadlik, eds. 2007. Morality as family practice. Special issue of *Discourse & Society* 18(1).

Ochs, Elinor, and Bambi B. Schieffelin. 1984. Language acquisition and socialization: Three developmental stories and their implications. *Culture theory:*

Essays on mind, self, and emotion, ed. Richard A. Schweder and Robert A. LeVine, 276–320. Cambridge: Cambridge University Press.

Ochs, Elinor, Ruth Smith, and Carolyn Taylor. 1996. Detective stories at dinnertime: Problem-solving through co-narration. *The matrix of language: Contemporary linguistic anthropology*, ed. Donald Brenneis and Ronald H.S. Macaulay, 39–55. Boulder, CO: Westview (originally printed in *Cultural Dynamics* 2[1989], 238–257).

Ochs, Elinor, and Carolyn Taylor. 1992a. Family narrative as political activity. *Discourse & Society* 3(3), 301–340.

Ochs, Elinor, and Carolyn Taylor. 1992b. Mother's role in the everyday reconstruction of "father knows best." *Locating power: Proceedings of the Second Berkeley Women and Language Conference*, ed. Kira Hall, Mary Bucholtz, and Birch Moonwomon, 447–463. Berkeley, CA: Berkeley Women and Language Group.

Ochs, Elinor, and Carolyn Taylor. 1995. The "father knows best" dynamic in family dinner narratives. *Gender articulated*, ed. Kira Hall and Mary Bucholtz, 97–120. New York: Routledge.

Ochs, Elinor, Carolyn Taylor, Dina Rudolph, and Ruth Smith. 1992. Story-telling as a theory-building activity. *Discourse Processes* 15(1), 37–72.

Pash, Diana M. 2008a. Gay family values: Gay co-father families in straight communities. *The changing landscape of work and family in the American middle classes: Reports from the field*, eds. Elizabeth Rudd and Laura Descartes, 159–188. Lanham, MD: Lexington.

Pash, Diana M. 2008b. The lived worlds of gay co-father families: Narratives of family, community, and cultural life. Doctoral dissertation, University of California, Los Angeles.

Paugh, Amy. 2005. Multilingual play: Children's code-switching, role play, and agency in Dominica, West Indies. *Language in Society* 34(1), 63–86.

Philips, Susan Urmston. 1983. *The invisible culture: Communication in classroom and community on the Warm Springs Indian Reservation*. Prospect Heights, IL: Waveland.

Pontecorvo, Clotilde, and Alessandra Fasulo. 1997. Learning to argue in family shared discourse: The reconstruction of past events. *Discourse, tools, and reasoning: Essays on situated cognition*, ed. Lauren B. Resnick, Roger Saljo, Clotilde Pontecorvo, and Barbara Burge, 406–442. Berlin: Springer.

Prevignano, Carlo L., and Aldo di Luzio. 2003. A discussion with John J. Gumperz. *Language and interaction: Discussions with John J. Gumperz*, ed. Susan L. Eerdmans, Carlo L. Prevignano, and Paul J. Thibault, 7–29. Amsterdam: John Benjamins.

Randall, Jessy. 2005. Mongo no like legging: Family expressions deserving wider recognition. *VERBATIM* 30(1), 7–10.

Ribeiro, Branca Telles. 1993. Framing in psychotic discourse. *Framing in discourse*, ed. Deborah Tannen, 77–113. New York: Oxford University Press.

Ribeiro, Branca Telles. 1994. *Coherence in psychotic discourse*. Oxford: Oxford University Press.

Ribeiro, Branca Telles. 2006. Footing, positioning, voice. Are we talking about the same things? *Discourse and identity*, ed. Anna De Fina, Deborah Schiffrin, and Michael Bamberg, 48–82. Cambridge: Cambridge University Press.

Rowe, Deborah Wells. 1998. The literate potentials of book-related dramatic play. *Reading Research Quarterly* 33(1), 10–35.

Sacks, Harvey. 1992. *Lectures on conversation*, vols. 1 and 2, ed. Gail Jefferson, with an introduction by Emanuel A. Schegloff. Cambridge, UK: Blackwell.

Schieffelin, Bambi B., and Elinor Ochs, eds. 1986. *Language socialization across cultures*. Cambridge: Cambridge University Press.

Schiffrin, Deborah. 1987. *Discourse markers*. Cambridge: Cambridge University Press.

Schiffrin, Deborah. 1994. *Approaches to discourse*. Malden, MA: Blackwell.

Schiffrin, Deborah. 1996. Narrative as self-portrait: Sociolinguistic constructions of identity. *Language in Society* 25(2), 167–203.

Schiffrin, Deborah. 2000. Mother/daughter discourse in a Holocaust oral history: "Because then you admit that you're guilty." *Narrative Inquiry* 10(1), 1–44.

Schiffrin, Deborah. 2001a. Language and public memorial: "America's concentration camps." *Discourse & Society* 12(4), 505–534.

Schiffrin, Deborah. 2001b. Language, experience and history: "What happened" in World War II. *Journal of Sociolinguistics* 5(3), 323–351.

Schiffrin, Deborah. 2002. Mother and friends in a Holocaust life story. *Language in Society* 31(3), 309–353.

Schiffrin, Deborah. 2006. *In other words: Variation in reference and narrative*. Cambridge: Cambridge University Press.

Schilling-Estes, Natalie. 2004. Exploring intertextuality in the sociolinguistic interview. *Sociolinguistic variation: Critical reflections*, ed. Carmen Fought, 44–61. New York: Oxford University Press.

Scollon, Ron. 2007. Discourse itineraries: Nine processes of resemiotization. *Advances in discourse studies*, ed. Vijay Bhatia, John Flowerdew, and Rodney H. Jones, 233–244. Abingdon, UK: Routledge.

Searle, John R. 1969. *Speech acts*. Cambridge: Cambridge University Press.

Shore, Bradd. 1996. *Culture in mind: Cognition, culture, and the problem of meaning*. New York: Oxford University Press.

Shore, Bradd. 2003. Family time: Studying myth and ritual in working families. Emory Center for Myth and Ritual in American Life, Working Paper no. 27.

Sillars, Alan L. 1995. Communication and family culture. *Explaining family interactions*, ed. Mary Anne Fitzpatrick and Anita L. Vangelisti, 375–399. Thousand Oaks, CA: Sage.

Sinha, Chris. 2005. Blending out of the background: Play, props and staging in the material world. *Journal of Pragmatics* 37, 1537–1554.

Sirota, Karen Gainer. 2002. Doing things with play: The play of everyday life. University of California, Los Angeles Sloan Center for the Ethnography of Everyday Life (CELF), Working Paper no. 16.

Sirota, Karen Gainer. 2006. Habits of the hearth: Children's bedtime routines as relational work. *Text & Talk* 26(4/5), 493–514.

Solin, Anna. 2001. *Tracing texts: Intertextuality and environmental discourse.* Helsinki, Finland: Department of English, University of Helsinki.

Solin, Anna. 2004. Intertextuality as mediation: On the analysis of intertextual relations in public discourse. *Text* 24(2), 267–296.

Søndergaard, Bent 1991. Switching between seven codes within one family—A linguistic resource. *Journal of Multilingual and Multicultural Development* 12(1&2), 85–92.

Spitulnik, Debra. 1997. The social circulation of discourse and the mediation of communities. *Journal of Linguistic Anthropology* 6(2), 161–187.

Sweetser, Eve. 2000. Blended spaces and performativity. *Cognitive Linguistics* 11(3/4), 305–333.

Tambiah, Stanley Jeyaraja. 1985. *Culture, thought, and social action: An anthropological perspective.* Cambridge, MA: Harvard University Press.

Tannen, Deborah. 1986. *That's not what I meant!: How conversational style makes or breaks relationships.* New York: Ballantine.

Tannen, Deborah. 1990. *You just don't understand: Woman and men in conversation.* New York: Ballantine.

Tannen, Deborah, ed. 1993a. *Framing in discourse.* New York: Oxford University Press.

Tannen, Deborah. 1993b. Introduction. *Framing in discourse,* ed. Deborah Tannen, 3–13. New York: Oxford University Press.

Tannen, Deborah. 1993c. What's in a frame? Surface evidence for underlying expectations. *Framing in discourse,* ed. Deborah Tannen, 14–76. New York: Oxford University Press.

Tannen, Deborah. 1994. *Gender and discourse.* New York: Oxford University Press.

Tannen, Deborah. 2001. *I only say this because I love you: Talking to your parents, partner, sibs, and kids when you're all adults.* New York: Random House.

Tannen, Deborah. 2003. Power maneuvers or connection maneuvers? Ventriloquizing in family interaction. *Linguistics, language, and the real world: Discourse and beyond* (Georgetown University Round Table on Languages and Linguistics, 2001), ed. Deborah Tannen and James E. Alatis, 50–62. Washington, DC: Georgetown University Press.

Tannen, Deborah. 2004. Talking the dog: Framing pets as interactional resources in family discourse. *Research on Language and Social Interaction* 37(4),

399–420. (Reprinted with minor alterations in *Family talk: Discourse and identity in four American families*, ed. Deborah Tannen, Shari Kendall, and Cynthia Gordon, 49–69. New York: Oxford University Press, 2007.)

Tannen, Deborah. 2005 [1984]. *Conversational style: Analyzing talk among friends.* New York: Oxford University Press. (1984 edition, Norwood, NJ: Ablex.)

Tannen, Deborah. 2006. Intertextuality in action: Re-keying family arguments in public and in private. *Text & Talk* 26(4/5), 597–617.

Tannen, Deborah. 2007 [1989]. *Talking voices: Repetition, dialogue, and imagery in conversational discourse.* Cambridge and New York: Cambridge University Press.

Tannen, Deborah, and Marjorie Harness Goodwin, eds. 2006. Family discourse, framing family. Special issue of *Text & Talk* 26(4/5).

Tannen, Deborah, and Cynthia Wallat. 1993. Interactive frames and knowledge schemas in interaction: Examples from a medical examination/interview. *Framing in discourse*, ed. Deborah Tannen, 57–76. New York: Oxford University Press.

Tannen, Deborah, Shari Kendall, and Cynthia Gordon, eds. 2007. *Family talk: Discourse and identity in four American families.* New York: Oxford University Press.

Taylor, Carolyn E. 1994. "You think it was a *fight?*" Co-constructing (the struggle for) meaning, face, and family in everyday narrative activity. *Research on Language and Social Interaction* 28(3), 283–317.

Todorov, Tsvetan. 1984 [1981]. *Mikhail Bakhtin: The dialogical principle*, trans. Wlad Godzich. Minneapolis: University of Minnesota Press.

Tomlin, Russell S. 1994. Repetition in second language acquisition. *Repetition in discourse: Interdisciplinary perspectives*, vol. 1, ed. Barbara Johnstone, 172–194. Norwood, NJ: Ablex.

Tovares, Alla V. 2005. Intertextuality in family interaction: Repetition of public texts in private settings. Doctoral dissertation, Georgetown University.

Tovares, Alla V. 2006. Public medium, private talk: Gossip about a TV show as "quotidian hermeneutics." *Text & Talk* 26(4/6), 463–491.

Tovares, Alla V. 2007. Family members interacting while watching TV. *Family talk: Discourse and identity in four American families*, ed. Deborah Tannen, Shari Kendall, and Cynthia Gordon, 283–309. New York: Oxford University Press.

Troll, Lillian E. 1988. Rituals and reunions. *American Behavioral Scientist* 31(6), 621–631.

Tulviste, Tiia, Luule Mizera, Boel De Geer, and Marja-Terttu Tryggvason. 2002. Regulatory comments as tools of family socialization: A comparison of Estonian, Swedish, and Finnish mealtime interaction. *Language in Society* 31(5), 655–678.

Turner, Mark. 2006. Compression and representation. *Language and Literature* 15(1), 17–27.

Varenne, Hervé, with the collaboration of Clifford Hill and Paul Byers. 1992. *Ambiguous harmony: Family talk in America.* Norwood, NJ: Ablex.

Wilce, James M. 2005. Traditional laments and postmodern regrets: The circulation of discourse in metacultural context. *Journal of Linguistic Anthropology* 15(1), 60–71.

Wolf, Shelby Anne, and Shirley Brice Heath. 1992. Cambridge, MA: Harvard University Press.

Wolfram, Walt, and Natalie Schilling-Estes. 1998. *American English: Dialects and variation.* Malden, MA: Blackwell.

Wolin, Steven J., and Linda A. Bennett. 1984. Family rituals. *Family Process* 23(3), 401–420.

Wong, Jean. 2000. Repetition in conversation: A look at "first and second sayings." *Research on Language and Social Interaction* 33(4), 407–424.

Wortham, Stanton E. F. 2005. Socialization beyond the speech event. *Journal of Linguistic Anthropology* 15(1), 95–112.

Wortham, Stanton E. F. 2006. *Learning identity: The joint emergence of social identification and academic learning.* Cambridge: Cambridge University Press.

Index

accent, 22, 26, 40, 65–66, 67,
71, 72
Agar, Michael, 22, 26, 27
Agha, Asif, 14, 192
Al Zidjaly, Najma, 191
Alfred P. Sloan Foundation, 6 n. 2,
6 n. 3, 18
alignment. *See* footing
ambiguity, 10, 10 n. 8, 103, 117, 121,
156, 168–169, 174–175, 192,
195–196
apologies, 31, 47, 63–64, 126,
128, 137
Aronsson, Karin, 7 n. 4, 28
assessment
of child behavior, 77, 82,
86–87, 93, 97–98, 100, 102,
112, 176
in constructed dialogue, 8–9
in double-voiced words, 8,
8 n. 5, 117, 140, 154, 156,
187–188
in narrative, 191

baby talk, 28 n. 1, 32–39, 72
Bakhtin, M. M.
culture, 10, 22, 27, 73–75,
112–113
dialogicality and dialogue, 7–8, 22,
25, 73–74, 155–156
double-voiced words, 8–9, 23,
54–55, 116–117, 124, 140, 155,
187–188
passive double-voiced words, 117,
117 n. 1
Bateson, Gregory, 11–12, 179
Bauman, Richard, 7 n. 4, 191
Becker, A. L.
languaging, 8, 75, 155
prior text, 5, 8, 9, 10,
16–17, 74–75, 143, 155,
191
social group formation, 10, 22, 27,
74–75, 112–113
bedtime. *See* ritual, child's
bedtime
Bennett, Linda A., 14